Absolute Beginner's Guide

to

Computer Basics

Fourth Edition

Michael Miller

800 East 96th Street,
Indianapolis, Indiana 46240

Absolute Beginner's Guide to Computer Basics, Fourth Edition

ISBN-10: 0-7897-3673-x / **ISBN-13:** 978-0-7897-3673-4

Library of Congress Cataloging-in-Publication Data

Miller, Michael, 1958-

  Absolute beginner's guide to computer basics / Michael Miller. -- 4th ed.

    p. cm.

  Includes index.

  ISBN 0-7897-3673-X (pbk.) 1. Computers. I. Title.

  QA76.5.M531412 2007

  004--dc22

                   2006103336

Printed in the United States of America

First Printing: February 2007

10 09 08 07   4 3 2 1

Trademarks

Warning and Disclaimer

Bulk Sales

Que Publishing offers excellent discounts on this book when ordered in quantity for bulk purchases or special sales. For more information, please contact

  U.S. Corporate and Government Sales
  1-800-382-3419
  corpsales@pearsontechgroup.com

For sales outside the United States, please contact

  International Sales
  international@pearsoned.com

This Book Is Safari Enabled

 The Safari® Enabled icon on the cover of your favorite technology book means the book is available through Safari Bookshelf. When you buy this book, you get free access to the online edition for 45 days.

Safari Bookshelf is an electronic reference library that lets you easily search thousands of technical books, find code samples, download chapters, and access technical information whenever and wherever you need it.

To gain 45-day Safari Enabled access to this book:

- Go to http://www.quepublishing.com/safarienabled
- Complete the brief registration form
- Enter the coupon code K6DH-NFAE-62BQ-EAEM-HXNT

If you have difficulty registering on Safari Bookshelf or accessing the online edition, please e-mail customer-service@safaribooksonline.com.

Associate Publisher
Greg Wiegand

Acquisitions Editor
Michelle Newcomb

Development Editor
Kevin Howard

Managing Editor
Patrick Kanouse

Project Editor
Seth Kerney

Copy Editor
Geneil Breeze

Indexer
WorldWise Publishing Services, LLC

Proofreader
Kathy Bidwell

Technical Editor
Vince Averello

Publishing Coordinator
Cindy Teeters

Designer
Anne Jones

Contents at a Glance

Table of Contents

About the Author

Michael Miller is a successful and prolific author with a reputation for practical advice and technical accuracy and an unerring empathy for the needs of his readers.

Mr. Miller has written more than 75 best-selling books in the past 18 years. His books for Que include *Absolute Beginner's Guide to eBay, How Windows Vista Works,* and *Googlepedia: The Ultimate Google Resource.* He is known for his casual, easy-to-read writing style and his practical, real-world advice—as well as his ability to explain a wide variety of complex topics to an everyday audience.

You can email Mr. Miller directly at abg@molehillgroup.com. His website is located at www.molehillgroup.com.

Dedication

To Sherry—finally and forever.

Acknowledgments

Thanks to the usual suspects at Que Publishing, including but not limited to Greg Wiegand, Michelle Newcomb, Kevin Howard, Seth Kerney, Jennifer Gallant, Geneil Breeze, and technical editor Vince Averello.

We Want to Hear from You!

As the reader of this book, *you* are our most important critic and commentator. We value your opinion and want to know what we're doing right, what we could do better, what areas you'd like to see us publish in, and any other words of wisdom you're willing to pass our way.

As an associate publisher for Que Publishing, I welcome your comments. You can email or write me directly to let me know what you did or didn't like about this book—as well as what we can do to make our books better.

Please note that I cannot help you with technical problems related to the topic of this book. We do have a User Services group, however, where I will forward specific technical questions related to the book.

When you write, please be sure to include this book's title and author as well as your name, email address, and phone number. I will carefully review your comments and share them with the author and editors who worked on the book.

Email: feedback@quepublishing.com

Mail: Greg Wiegand
         Associate Publisher
         Que Publishing
         800 East 96th Street
         Indianapolis, IN 46240 USA

For more information about this book or another Que Publishing title, visit our website at www.quepublishing.com. Type the ISBN (excluding hyphens) or the title of the book in the Search field to find the page you're looking for.

INTRODUCTION

Because this is the *Absolute Beginner's Guide to Computer Basics*, let's start at the absolute beginning, which is this: Computers aren't supposed to be scary. Intimidating, sometimes. Difficult to use, perhaps. Inherently unreliable, most definitely. (Although they're better than they used to be.)

But scary? Definitely not.

Computers aren't scary because there's nothing they can do to hurt you. (Unless you drop your notebook PC on your foot, that is.) And there's not much you can do to hurt them, either. It's kind of a wary coexistence between man and machine, but the relationship has the potential to be beneficial. To you, anyway.

Many people think that they're scared of computers because they think they're unfamiliar with them. But that isn't really true.

You see, even if you've never actually used a computer before, you've been exposed to computers and all they can do for at least the last 20 years or so. Whenever you make a deposit at your bank, you're working with computers. Whenever you make a purchase at a retail store, you're working with computers. Whenever you watch a television show or read a newspaper article or look at a picture in a magazine, you're working with computers.

That's because computers are used in all those applications. Somebody, somewhere, is working behind the scenes with a computer to manage your bank account and monitor your credit card purchases.

In fact, it's difficult to imagine, here in the twenty-first century, how we ever got by without all those keyboards, mice, and monitors. (Or, for that matter, the Internet.)

However, just because computers have been around for awhile doesn't mean that everyone knows how to use them. It's not unusual to feel a little trepidation the first time you sit down in front of that intimidating monitor and keyboard. Which keys should you press? What do they mean by double-clicking the mouse? And what are all those little pictures onscreen?

As foreign as all this might seem at first, computers really aren't that hard to understand—or to use. You have to learn a few basic concepts, of course (all the pressing and clicking and whatnot), and it helps to understand exactly what part of the system does what. But once you get the hang of things, computers really are easy to use.

Which, of course, is where this book comes in.

Absolute Beginner's Guide to Computer Basics, Fourth Edition, will help you figure out how to use your new computer system. You'll learn how computers work, how to connect all the pieces and parts, and how to start using them. You'll learn about computer hardware and software, about the Windows Vista and Windows XP operating systems, and about the Internet. And after you're comfortable with the basic concepts (which won't take too long, trust me), you'll learn how to actually do stuff.

You'll learn how to do useful stuff, such as writing letters and balancing your checkbook and creating presentations; fun stuff, such as listening to music and watching movies and editing your digital photos; online stuff, such as searching for information and sending email and chatting with friends via instant messages; and essential stuff, such as copying files and troubleshooting problems and protecting against thieves and hackers.

All you have to do is sit yourself down in front of your computer, try not to be scared (there's nothing to be scared of, really), and work your way through the chapters and activities in this book. And remember that computers aren't difficult to use, they don't break easily, and they let you do all sorts of fun and useful things once you get the hang of them. Really!

How This Book Is Organized

This book is organized into six main parts, as follows:

- Part I, **"Getting Started,"** describes all the pieces and parts of both desktop and notebook PCs, and how to connect everything to get your new system up and running.

- Part II, **"Using Windows,"** introduces the backbone of your entire system, the Microsoft Windows operating system. This section covers both the newer Windows Vista and the older Windows XP operating systems; you'll learn how Windows works, and how to use Windows to perform basic tasks, such as copying and deleting files and folders. (You'll also learn fun stuff, such as how to change the picture on your computer desktop.)

- Part III, **"Upgrading and Maintaining Your System,"** contains all the boring (but necessary) information you need to know to keep your new PC in tip-top shape. You'll learn how to add new pieces of hardware to your system, how to set up either a wired or wireless home network, how to perform routine maintenance, how to track down and fix common PC problems, and how to protect your system against viruses, spyware, and other forms of computer attack.

- Part IV, **"Using Computer Software,"** tells you everything you need to know about running the most popular computer programs. You'll learn how to use Microsoft Works, Microsoft Office, Microsoft Word, Microsoft Excel, Microsoft PowerPoint, Microsoft Money, and Quicken.

■ **Part V, "Using the Internet,"** is all about going online. You'll discover how to surf the Web with Internet Explorer, send and receive email, and chat online via instant messaging. You'll also learn how to shop online, buy and sell in eBay auctions, browse the blogosphere, network socially on MySpace, view and download videos online, and create your own personal web page. This is the fun part of the book.

■ **Part VI, "Exploring the Digital Lifestyle,"** is even more fun. You'll learn how to use your PC with your digital camera to edit and manage your digital photos, how to listen to CDs and download music to your iPod or MP3 player, how to watch DVDs on your computer screen, and how to create your own digital home movies on DVD. It's amazing all the things you can do with your PC!

Taken together, the 38 chapters in this book will help you progress from absolute beginner to experienced computer user. Just read what you need, and before long you'll be using your computer like a pro!

Which Version of Windows?

If you read through the table of contents, you'll notice that there are chapters in this book for both Windows Vista and Windows XP. That's because we're currently in a period of transition. Most new PCs sold today come with the newer Windows Vista pre-installed, but most older PCs are still using the previous Windows XP operating system. The good news is that both versions of Windows work in pretty much the same fashion, so both versions can be covered in this book. That said, most of the specific examples and screenshots in this book are of Windows Vista; if you're still using Windows XP, things may look a little different on your PC screen than they do in these pages.

In addition, Windows Vista includes some new applications that simply aren't present in Windows XP. I cover these new Vista applications in this book, of course, but I also try to present alternative applications for Windows XP users.

So, although this fourth edition of *Absolute Beginner's Guide to Computer Basics* focuses on and is updated for Windows Vista, it should still be usable by Windows XP users. After all, everybody wants to do the same things, no matter which version of Windows you're using!

Conventions Used in This Book

I hope that this book is easy enough to figure out on its own, without requiring its own instruction manual. As you read through the pages, however, it helps to know precisely how I've presented specific types of information.

Menu Commands

Most computer programs operate via a series of pull-down menus. You use your mouse to pull down a menu and then select an option from that menu. This sort of operation is indicated like this throughout the book:

> Select File, Save

or

> Click the Start button and select All Programs, Accessories, Notepad.

All you have to do is follow the instructions in order, using your mouse to click each item in turn. When submenus are tacked onto the main menu (as in the All Programs, Accessories, Notepad example), just keep clicking the selections until you come to the last one—which should open the program or activate the command you want!

Shortcut Key Combinations

When you're using your computer keyboard, sometimes you have to press two keys at the same time. These two-key combinations are called *shortcut keys* and are shown as the key names joined with a plus sign (+).

For example, Ctrl+W indicates that you should press the W key while holding down the Ctrl key. It's no more complex than that.

Web Page Addresses

This book contains a lot of web page addresses. (That's because you'll probably be spending a lot of time on the Internet.)

Technically, a web page address is supposed to start with http:// (as in http://www.molehillgroup.com). Because Internet Explorer and other web browsers automatically insert this piece of the address, however, you don't have to type it— and I haven't included it in any of the addresses in this book.

Special Elements

This book also includes a few special elements that provide additional information not included in the basic text. These elements are designed to supplement the text to make your learning faster, easier, and more efficient.

tip

A *tip* is a piece of advice—a little trick, actually—that helps you use your computer more effectively or maneuver around problems or limitations.

note

A *note* is designed to provide information that is generally useful but not specifically necessary for what you're doing at the moment. Some are like extended tips—interesting, but not essential.

caution

A *caution* tells you to beware of a potentially dangerous act or situation. In some cases, ignoring a caution could cause you significant problems—so pay attention to them!

Let Me Know What You Think

I always love to hear from readers. If you want to contact me, feel free to email me at abg@molehillgroup.com. I can't promise that I'll answer every message, but I do promise that I'll read each one!

If you want to learn more about me and any new books I have cooking, check out my Molehill Group website at www.molehillgroup.com. Who knows—you might find some other books there that you would like to read.

PART

i

GETTING STARTED

1

UNDERSTANDING DESKTOP PCS

Chances are you're reading this book because you just bought a new computer, are thinking about buying a new computer, or maybe even had someone give you his old computer. (Nothing wrong with high-tech hand-me-downs!) At this point you might not be totally sure what it is you've gotten yourself into. Just what is this mess of boxes and cables, and what can you—or *should* you—do with it?

This chapter serves as an introduction to the entire concept of personal computers in general—what they do, how they work, that sort of thing—and computer hardware in particular. It's a good place to start if you're not that familiar with computers, or want a brief refresher course in what all those pieces and parts are, and what they do.

Of course, if you want to skip the background and get right to using your computer, that's okay, too. For step-by-step instructions on how to connect and configure your new PC, go directly to Chapter 3, "Setting Up Your New Computer System." And if you're the proud owner of a new laptop PC, things are a little different than with a desktop system; learn what's what in Chapter 2, "Understanding Notebook PCs."

What Your Computer Can—and *Can't*—Do

What good is a personal computer, anyway?

Everybody has one, you know. (Including you, now!) In fact, it's possible you bought your new computer just so that you wouldn't feel left out. But now that you have your very own personal computer, what do you do with it?

Good for Work

A lot of people use their home PCs for work-related purposes. You can bring your work (reports, spreadsheets, you name it) home from the office and finish it on your home PC, at night or on weekends. Or, if you work at home, you can use your computer to pretty much run your small business—you can use it to do everything from typing memos and reports to generating invoices and setting budgets.

In short, anything you can do with a normal office PC, you can probably do on your home PC.

Good for Play

All work and no play makes Jack a dull boy, so there's no reason not to have a little fun with your new PC. Not only can you use your PC to play some really cool games, you can also use it to track your favorite hobby, create interesting crafts projects, print pictures from your latest family vacation, listen to your favorite music, and watch your favorite videos. In fact, with the right software and hardware, you can even use your PC to edit movies you take with your video camcorder.

Good for Managing Your Finances

You don't have to be a professional accountant to use your PC to manage your finances. Software programs, such as Microsoft Money and Quicken, let you create budgets, write checks, and balance your accounts, right from your computer screen.

Or you can go directly to your bank's website and do all your banking online. You can even set up your system to automatically pay bills and do other banking online—no paper checks necessary.

Good for Keeping in Touch

Want to send a letter to a friend? With your new PC (and a word processing program, such as Microsoft Word), it's a cinch. Even better, save a stamp and send that friend an electronic letter—called an *email*—over the Internet. And if that person is online the same time you are, you can chat with him in real time via an instant messaging program. Many families use their PCs for almost all their communications.

Good for Getting Online

Speaking of email, chances are one of the main reasons you got a PC was to get connected to the Internet. The Internet's a great tool; in addition to email and instant messaging, you can buy and sell just about anything online, read the latest news from popular blogs, and browse the World Wide Web—which is chock-full of interesting and informative content and services. Now you won't feel left out when people start talking about "double-you double-you double-you" this and "dot-com" that—because you'll be online, too.

Getting to Know Your Personal Computer System

Now that you know *why* you have that brand-new personal computer sitting on your desk, you might be interested in just *what* it is that you have. It's important to know what each part of your system is, what it does, and how to hook it all together.

Pieces and Parts—Computer Hardware

We'll start by looking at the physical components of your system—the stuff we call computer *hardware*. As you can see in Figure 1.1, there are a lot of different pieces and parts that make up a typical computer system. You should note, however, that no two computer systems are identical, since you can always add new components to your system—or disconnect other pieces you don't have any use for.

note

This book is written for users of relatively new personal computers—in particular, PCs running either the Windows Vista or the Windows XP operating system. If you have an older PC, most of the advice here is still good, although not all the step-by-step instructions will apply.

FIGURE 1.1

A typical personal computer system.

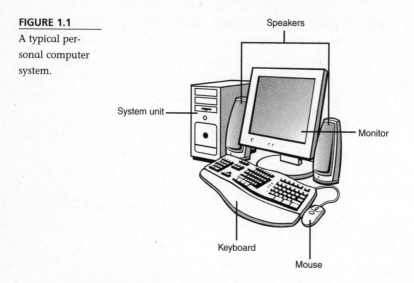

These items are the basic elements you'll find in almost all computer systems. Of course, you can add lots of other items to your personal system, including *printers* (to make printouts of documents and pictures), *scanners* (to convert a printed document or picture to electronic format), *PC cameras* (also known as *webcams*, to send live video of yourself to friends and family), *joysticks* (to play the most challenging games), and external *hard disks* (to back up your precious data). You can also hook up all manner of portable devices to your PC, including *digital cameras*, *camcorders*, and *portable music players* (such as the ubiquitous Apple iPod). You can even add the appropriate devices to connect multiple PCs together in a *network*.

note

Learn more about these pieces and parts in "Computer Hardware Basics," later in this chapter. If you have a notebook PC, those portable pieces and parts are discussed in Chapter 2. If you need help connecting all the pieces and parts, turn to Chapter 3. And if you want to add a new piece of hardware to your basic system, check out Chapter 8, "Adding New Hardware and Devices to Your System."

The Right Tools for the Right Tasks— Computer Software

By themselves, all those little beige and black boxes really aren't that useful. You can connect them and set them in place, but they won't do anything until you have some *software* to make things work.

Computer *hardware* are those things you can touch—your system unit, monitor, and the like. Computer *software*, on the other hand, is something you *can't* touch, because it's nothing more than a bunch of electronic bits and bytes. These bits and bytes, however, combine into computer programs—sometimes called *applications*—that provide specific functionality to your system.

For example, if you want to crunch some numbers, you need a piece of software called a *spreadsheet* program. If you want to write a letter, you need a *word processing* program. If you want to make changes to some pictures you took with your digital camera, you need *graphics editing* software.

In other words, you need separate software for each task you want to do with your computer. Fortunately, most new computer systems come with a lot of this software already installed.

Making Everything Work—with Windows

When you're not using a specific piece of application software, you interface with your computer via a special piece of software called an *operating system*. As the name implies, this program makes your system operate; it's your gateway to the hardware part of your system.

The operating system is also how your application software interfaces with your computer hardware. When you want to print a document from your word processor, that software works with the operating system to send the document to your printer.

note

If you want or need any additional software, you'll have to find and install it yourself—as described in Chapter 13, "Installing New Software."

Most computers today ship with an operating system called Microsoft Windows. This operating system has been around for more than 20 years and is published by Microsoft Corporation.

Windows isn't the only operating system around, however. Computers manufactured by Apple Computing use a different operating system, called the Mac OS. Therefore, computers running Windows and computers by Apple aren't totally compatible with each other. Then there's Linux, which is compatible with most PCs sold today, but used primarily by uber-techie types; it's not an operating system I would recommend for general users.

But let's get back to Windows, of which there have been several different versions over the years. The newest version is called Windows Vista, and if you just purchased a brand-new PC, this is probably the version you're using. If your PC is a little older, you might be running Windows XP, the immediate predecessor to Vista. And if you have a much older PC, or one used in a corporate environment, you could be running yet another version of Windows—Windows 2000, perhaps, or even Windows 98. All versions of Windows do pretty much the same things, although newer versions look prettier, are a bit more stable, and have a few more bells and whistles. Whichever version of Windows you have installed on your PC, you use it to launch specific programs and to perform various system maintenance functions, such as copying files and turning off your computer.

Don't Worry, You Can't Screw It Up—Much

The balance of this chapter goes into a bit more detail about the hardware components of your PC system. Before you proceed, however, there's one other important thing you need to know about computers.

A lot of people are afraid of their computers. They think if they press the wrong key or click the wrong button that they'll break something or will have to call in an expensive repairperson to put things right.

This really isn't true.

note

You can learn more about Windows Vista in Chapter 4, "Getting to Know Windows Vista." If you have an older version of Windows, check out Chapter 5, "Using Windows XP on Older Computers."

The important thing to know is that it's really difficult to break your computer system. Yes, it's possible to break something if you drop it, but in terms of breaking your system through normal use, it just doesn't happen that often.

It *is* possible to make mistakes, of course. You can click the wrong button and accidentally delete a file you didn't want to delete or turn off your system and lose a document you forgot to save. You can even take inadequate security precautions and find your system infected by a computer virus. But in terms of doing serious harm just by clicking your mouse, it's unlikely.

So don't be afraid of the thing. Your computer is a tool, just like a hammer or a blender or a camera. After you learn how to use it, it can be a very useful tool. But it's *your* tool, which means *you* tell *it* what to do—not vice versa. Remember that you're in control and that you're not going to break anything, and you'll have a lot of fun—and maybe even get some real work done!

Computer Hardware Basics

As you just read, computer hardware are those parts of your system you can actually see and touch. This includes your system unit and everything connected to it, including your monitor, keyboard, mouse, and printer.

We'll take a close look at all the various pieces of hardware you can have in a computer system—including those parts you can't always see because they're built in to your system unit. So, if you're curious about microprocessors and memory and modems and monitors, read on—this is the chapter for you!

Your PC's System Unit—The Mother Ship

The most important piece of hardware in your computer system is the *system unit*. This is the big, ugly box that houses your disk drives and many other components. Most system units, like the one in Figure 1.2, stand straight up like a kind of tower—and are, in fact, called either *tower* or *mini-tower* PCs, depending on the size.

FIGURE 1.2

A system unit in a mini-tower configuration.

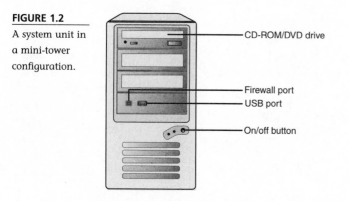

CD-ROM/DVD drive

Firewall port
USB port

On/off button

The back of the system unit typically is covered with all types of connectors. This is because all the other parts of your computer system connect to your system unit, and they all have to have a place to plug in. And, because each component has its own unique type of connector, you end up with the assortment of jacks (called *ports* in the computer world) that you see in Figure 1.3.

And, as you've probably noticed, some PCs put some of these connectors on the front of the case—in addition to the back. This makes it easier to connect portable devices, such as an iPod music player or a digital video camcorder, without having to muck about behind your PC.

All the good stuff in your system unit is inside the case. With most system units, you can remove the case to peek and poke around inside.

To remove your system unit's case, make sure the unit is unplugged, then look for some big screws or thumbscrews on either the side or back of the case. (Even better—read your PC's instruction manual for instructions specific to your unit.) With the screws loosened or removed, you should then be able to either slide off the entire case, or pop open the top or back.

note

Desktop computer systems are composed of all these separate components. Laptop PCs, on the other hand, have all that stuff crammed into a single case. So, you don't have a separate system unit, monitor, keyboard, and mouse—they're part of one compact unit. Learn more about laptop computers in Chapter 2.

FIGURE 1.3

The back of a typical system unit—just look at all those different connectors!

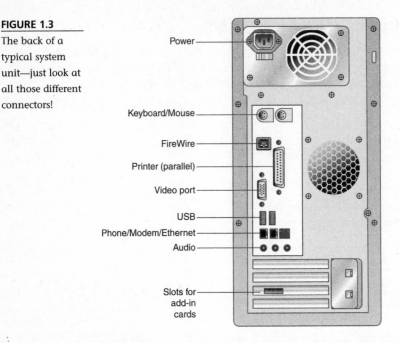

Power

Keyboard/Mouse

FireWire

Printer (parallel)

Video port

USB

Phone/Modem/Ethernet

Audio

Slots for add-in cards

When you open the case on your system unit, as shown in Figure 1.4, you see all sorts of computer chips and circuit boards. The really big board located at the base of the computer (to which everything else is plugged into) is called the *motherboard*, because it's the "mother" for your microprocessor and memory chips, as well as for the other internal components that enable your system to function. This motherboard contains several slots, into which you can plug additional *boards* (also called *cards*) that perform specific functions.

Most PC motherboards contain six or more slots for add-on cards. For example, a video card enables your motherboard to transmit video signals to your monitor. Other available cards enable you to add sound and modem/fax capabilities to your system.

caution

Always turn off and unplug your computer before attempting to remove the system unit's case—and be careful about touching anything inside. If you have any built-up static electricity, you can seriously damage the sensitive chips and electronic components with an innocent touch.

FIGURE 1.4

What your PC looks like on the inside—a big motherboard with lots of add-on boards attached.

Microprocessors: The Main Engine

We're not done looking at the system unit just yet. Buried somewhere on that big motherboard is a specific chip that controls your entire computer system. This chip is called a *microprocessor* or a *central processing unit (CPU)*.

The microprocessor is the brains inside your system. It processes all the instructions necessary for your computer to perform its duties. The more powerful the microprocessor chip, the faster and more efficiently your system runs.

Microprocessors carry out the various instructions that let your computer compute. Every input and output device hooked up to a computer—the keyboard, printer, monitor, and so on—either issues or receives instructions that the microprocessor then processes. Your software programs also issue instructions that must be implemented by the microprocessor. This chip truly is the workhorse of your system; it affects just about everything your computer does.

Different computers have different types of microprocessor chips. Many IBM-compatible computers use chips manufactured by Intel. Some use Intel-compatible chips manufactured by AMD and other firms. But all IBM-compatible computers that run the Windows operating system use Intel-compatible chips.

In addition to having different chip manufacturers (and different chip families from the same manufacturer), you'll also run into microprocessor chips that run at different speeds. CPU speed today is measured in gigahertz (GHz). A CPU with a speed of

1GHz can run at one *billion* clock ticks per second! The bigger the gigahertz number, the faster the chip runs. If you're still shopping for a new PC, look for one with the combination of a powerful microprocessor and a high clock speed for best performance. And the latest dual-core chips are even faster; you get the equivalent of two CPUs in one!

Computer Memory: Temporary Storage

Speaking of memory, before your CPU can process any instructions you give it, your instructions must be stored somewhere, in preparation for access by the microprocessor. These instructions—along with other data processed by your system—are temporarily held in the computer's *random access memory (RAM)*. All computers have some amount of memory, which is created by a number of memory chips. The more memory that's available in a machine, the more instructions and data that can be stored at one time.

Memory is measured in terms of *bytes*. One byte is equal to approximately one character in a word processing document. A unit equaling approximately one thousand bytes (1,024, to be exact) is called a *kilobyte (KB)*, and a unit of approximately one thousand (1,024) kilobytes is called a *megabyte (MB)*. A thousand megabytes is a *gigabyte (GB)*.

Most computers today come with at least 512MB of memory, and it's not uncommon to find machines with 2GB or more. To enable your computer to run as many programs as quickly as possible, you need as much memory installed in your system as it can accept—or that you can afford. (I'd say that 1GB is the bare minimum necessary to run a Windows Vista-based system.) Extra memory can be added to a computer by installing a new memory module, which is as easy as plugging a "stick" directly into a slot on your system's motherboard.

If your computer doesn't possess enough memory, its CPU must constantly retrieve data from permanent storage on its hard disk. This method of data retrieval is slower than retrieving instructions and data from electronic memory. In fact, if your machine doesn't have enough memory, some programs will run very slowly (or you might experience random system crashes), and other programs won't run at all!

Hard Disk Drives: Long-Term Storage

Another important physical component inside your system unit is the *hard disk drive*. The hard disk permanently stores all your important data. Some hard disks today can store up to 750 gigabytes of data—and even bigger hard disks are on the way. (Contrast this to your system's random access memory, which stores only a few gigabytes of data, temporarily.)

A hard disk consists of numerous metallic platters. These platters store data *magnetically*. Special read/write *heads* realign magnetic particles on the platters, much like a recording head records data onto magnetic recording tape.

Before data can be stored on any disk, including your system's hard disk, that disk must first be *formatted*. A disk that has not been formatted cannot accept any data. When you format a hard disk, your computer prepares each track and sector of the disk to accept and store data magnetically.

Of course, when you buy a new PC, your hard disk is already formatted for you. (And, in most cases, your operating system and key programs also are prein-stalled.)

CD-ROM Drives: Storage on a Disc

Not all the storage on your PC is inside the system unit. Most PCs have a front-accessible CD-ROM drive, which lets you play audio CDs, install CD-based software programs, and (if the drive is enabled for recording) copy data from your PC's hard drive to a blank CD-ROM disc. (The initials stand for *compact disc–read-only memory*, by the way.)

CD-ROM discs, such as the one in Figure 1.5, look just like the compact discs you play on your audio system. They're also similar in the way they store data (audio data in the case of regular CDs; computer data in the case of CD-ROMs).

caution

If you try to reformat your hard disk, you'll erase all the programs and data that have been installed—so don't do it!

note

On older PCs, you were likely to find a *removable disk drive* for a *floppy disk* or *diskette*. These big 3 1/2" disks could hold only about 1.44MB of data—compared to USB drives that can hold 1GB or more of data. That's why floppy disks are now obsolete.

Information is encoded at a disc-manufacturing plant, using an industrial-grade laser. This information takes the form of microscopic pits (representing the 1s and 0s of computer binary language) below the disc's surface. Similar to hard and floppy disks, the information is arranged in a series of tracks and sectors, but the tracks are so close together that the disk surface is highly reflective.

Data is read from the CD-ROM via a drive that uses a consumer-grade laser. The laser beam follows the tracks of the disc and reads the pits, translating the data into a form your system can understand.

FIGURE 1.5
Store tons of
data, digitally,
on a shiny
CD-ROM disc.

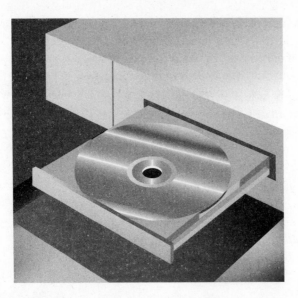

By the way, the *ROM* part of CD-ROM means that you can only read data from the disk; unlike normal hard disks and diskettes, you can't write new data to a standard CD-ROM. However, most PCs include recordable (CD-R) and rewritable (CD-RW) drives that *do* let you write data to CDs—so you can use your CD drive just like a regular disk drive.

DVD Drives: Even More Storage on a Disc

Beyond the CD-ROM is the newer *DVD* medium. DVDs can contain up to 4.7GB of data (for a single-layer disc) or 8.5GB of data (for a double-layer disc). Compared to 650–700MB of storage for a typical CD-ROM, this makes DVDs ideally suited for large applications or games that otherwise would require multiple CDs. Similar to standard CD-ROMs, most DVDs are read-only—although all DVD drives can also read CD-ROMs.

In addition, most DVD drives play full-length DVD movies, which turns your PC into a mini movie machine. And, just as there are recordable CD-ROM drives, you can also find recordable DVD drives, which let you record an entire movie on a single disc.

note

DVD really isn't an acronym for anything in particular. Some manufacturers claim that it stands for *digital versatile disc* or *digital video disc*, but it's really just a bunch of initials with no real meaning.

Some high-end PCs do the standard DVD one step better and utilize one of the new high-definition DVD formats—either *Blu-ray* or *HD DVD*. Both of these formats can store 25GB or more of data, more than enough to hold a high-definition movie. That much storage for PC data may be overkill, however, especially given the initial pricing for these drives. Consider a Blu-ray or HD DVD drive (they're incompatible with each other, by the way) only if you want to watch high-definition movies on your PC screen.

Keyboards: Fingertip Input

Computers receive data by reading it from disk, accepting it electronically over a modem, or receiving input directly from you, the user. You provide your input by way of what's called, in general, an *input device*; the most common input device you use to talk to your computer is the keyboard.

A computer keyboard, similar to the one in Figure 1.6, looks and functions just like a typewriter keyboard, except that computer keyboards have a few more keys. Some of these keys (such as the arrow, PgUp, PgDn, Home, and End keys) enable you to move around within a program or file. Other keys provide access to special program features. When you press a key on your keyboard, it sends an electronic signal to your system unit that tells your machine what you want it to do.

FIGURE 1.6
A standard PC
keyboard.

Most keyboards that come with new PCs hook up via a cable to the back of your system unit. However, some manufacturers make *wireless* keyboards that connect to your system unit via radio signals—thus eliminating one cable from the back of your system.

Mice: Point-and-Click Input Devices

It's a funny name, but a necessary device. A computer *mouse*, like the one shown in Figure 1.7, is a small handheld device. Most mice consist of an oblong case with a roller underneath and two or three buttons on top. When you move the mouse along a desktop, an onscreen pointer (called a *cursor*) moves in response. When you click (press and release) a mouse button, this motion initiates an action in your program.

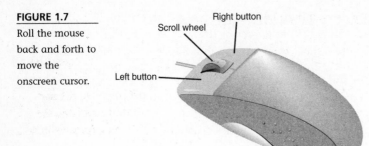

FIGURE 1.7

Roll the mouse back and forth to move the onscreen cursor.

Mice come in all shapes and sizes. Some have wires, and some are wireless. Some are relatively oval in shape, and others are all curvy to better fit in the palm of your hand. Some have the typical roller ball underneath, and others use an optical sensor to determine where and how much you're rolling. Some even have extra buttons that can be programmed for specific functions or a scroll wheel you can use to scroll through long documents or web pages.

Of course, a mouse is just one type of input device you can hook up to your PC. Trackballs, joysticks, game controllers, and pen pads all count as input devices, whether they work in conjunction with a mouse or replace it. You can use one of these alternative devices to replace your original mouse or (in some cases) to supplement it.

Modems: Getting Connected

Many PC systems today still include a *modem*, which enables your computer to connect to telephone lines and transmit data to and from the Internet and commercial online services (such as America Online). The word "modem" stands for "modulator-demodulator," which is how digital data is sent over traditional analog phone lines. The data is "modulated" for transmittal, and "demodulated" upon receipt.

However, as more consumers opt for higher-speed broadband Internet connections (either via cable or DSL), there is less need for the traditional dial-up modem. If you sign up for cable or DSL Internet service, your Internet service provider will provide you with an external *broadband modem* for their service. Most broadband modems connect to your PC either via USB or via an Ethernet connection.

note

If you have a broadband connection, you can connect your cable or DSL modem to your home network to share that connection between multiple PCs. See Chapter 19, "Connecting to the Internet—At Home and on the Road," to learn more.

Sound Cards and Speakers: Making Noise

Every PC comes with some sort of speaker system. While some older PCs had a speaker built into the system unit, systems today come with separate right and left speakers, sometimes accompanied by a subwoofer for better bass. (Figure 1.8 shows a typical right-left-subwoofer speaker system.) You can even get so-called 5.1 surround sound speaker systems, with five satellite speakers (front and rear) and the ".1" subwoofer—great for listening to movie soundtracks or playing explosive-laden videogames.

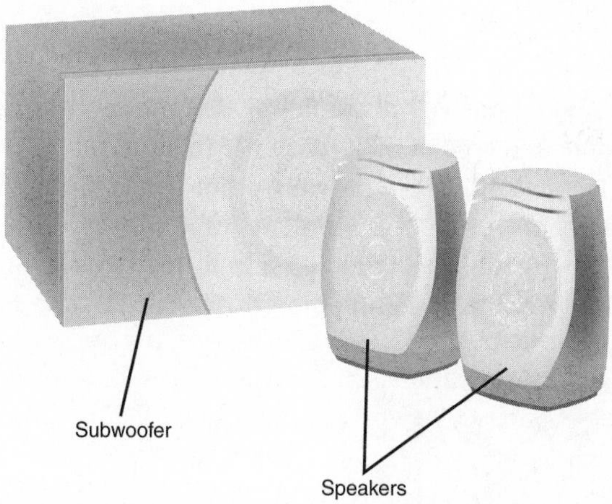

FIGURE 1.8

A typical set of right and left external speakers, complete with subwoofer.

Subwoofer

Speakers

All speaker systems are driven by a sound card that is installed inside your system unit. If you upgrade your speaker system, you also might need to upgrade your sound card accordingly.

Video Cards and Monitors: Getting the Picture

Operating a computer would be difficult if you didn't constantly receive visual feedback showing you what your machine is doing. This vital function is provided by your computer's monitor.

The traditional CRT monitor, similar to the one shown in Figure 1.9, is a lot like a little television set. Your microprocessor electronically transmits words and pictures (*text* and *graphics*, in PC lingo) to your monitor, in some approximation of how these visuals would appear on paper. You view the monitor and respond according to what you see onscreen.

note

Traditional monitors are built around a cathode ray tube, or CRT, similar to the picture tube found in normal television sets.

FIGURE 1.9
A traditional
tube-type video
monitor.

The CRT monitor is going the way of the floppy disk, however, except in very low-
end systems. The preferred type of monitor in use today is the LCD monitor, such as
the one shown in Figure 1.10, which provides a flat-screen display that saves a bit
on desk space. Even better, some LCD monitors come with a widescreen display that
has the same 16:9 (or 16:10) aspect ratio used to display widescreen movies—which
makes them ideal for viewing or editing movies on your PC.

FIGURE 1.10
A space-saving,
flat-screen video
monitor.

You measure the size of a monitor by measuring from corner to corner, diagonally.
The traditional CRT monitor is normally a 14" or 15" model; today's LCD monitors
start at 15" or so and run up to 21" or larger.

Neither CRT or LCD monitors generate the images they display. Instead, screen
images are electronically crafted by a *video card* installed inside your system unit. To
work correctly, both video card and monitor must be matched to display images of
the same resolution.

Resolution refers to the size of the images that can be displayed onscreen and is
measured in pixels. A *pixel* is a single dot on your screen; a full picture is composed
of thousands of pixels. The higher the resolution, the sharper the resolution—which
lets you display more (smaller) elements onscreen.

Resolution is expressed in numbers of pixels, in both the horizontal and vertical directions. Older video cards and monitors could only display 640×480 or 800×600 pixel resolution; you want a card/monitor combination that can display at least 1024×768 resolution—more, if you have a widescreen monitor.

For most users, the video card installed in their new PC works just fine. However, if you do a lot of heavy-duty gaming—especially with some of the newer graphics-intensive games—you may want to consider upgrading your video card to one with more on-board memory, to better reproduce those cutting-edge graphics. And to display all of Windows Vista's cutting-edge graphics, you'll need a card with a separate *graphics processing unit (GPU)*, which takes the graphics processing load off your PC's main CPU. The more graphics processing power, the better your system will look.

> **tip**
>
> The measurement is different for tube-type monitors than it is for flat-screen monitors. This is because a flat-screen monitor displays its images all the way to the edge of the screen, and traditional tube-type monitors don't. For that reason, a 15" flat-screen monitor has the same size picture as a 17" tube-type monitor.

Printers: Making Hard Copies

Your monitor displays images in real time, but they're fleeting. For permanent records of your work, you must add a printer to your system. Printers create hard copy output from your software programs.

You can choose from various types of printers for your system, depending on your exact printing needs. The two main types of printers today are laser and inkjet printers.

Laser printers work much like copying machines, applying toner (powdered ink) to paper by using a small laser. *Inkjet* printers, on the other hand, shoot jets of ink to the paper's surface to create the printed image. Inkjet printers are typically a little lower priced than laser printers, although the price difference is shrinking.

You also can choose from either black-and-white or color printers. Black-and-white printers are faster than color printers and better if you're printing memos, letters, and other single-color documents. Color printers, however, are great if you have kids, and they're essential if you want to print pictures taken with a digital camera.

By the way, there's a type of "combination" printer available that combines a printer with a scanner and a fax machine. If you need all these devices (sometimes called a *multifunction unit,* or *MFU*) and are short on space, these are pretty good deals.

THE ABSOLUTE MINIMUM

Here are the key points to remember from this chapter:

- Your computer system is composed of various pieces of hardware, almost all of which plug into that big beige box called the system unit.

- You interface with your computer hardware via a piece of software called an operating system. The operating system on your new computer is probably some version of Microsoft Windows—either Windows Vista or Windows XP, depending on when it was purchased.

- You use specific software programs to perform specific tasks, such as writing letters and editing digital photos.

- The brains and engine of your system is the system unit, which contains the microprocessor, memory, disk drives, and all the connections for your other system components.

- To make your system run faster, get a faster microprocessor or more memory.

- Data is temporarily stored in your system's memory; you store data permanently on some type of disk drive—typically a hard disk or CD/DVD drive.

2

UNDERSTANDING NOTEBOOK PCs

In Chapter 1, "Understanding Desktop PCs," we discussed the inner workings of a typical desktop PC. But not all PCs are desktop models; portable PCs, sometimes called notebooks or laptops, are becoming increasingly popular, both in the office and in the home.

Although a notebook PC does everything a desktop PC does, how it does those things is a little different. That's because a portable PC combines all the various elements in a desktop PC system (except for a printer) into a single case and then adds a battery so that you can use it on the go.

Notebook PCs: Pros and Cons

If a notebook PC does everything a desktop does but in a smaller, more portable form factor, why hasn't the notebook totally replaced the desktop computer system? As with all things, there are pluses and minuses to switching to a notebook PC.

Why Notebooks Are Great

Notebook PCs are great because they're small. You can take your entire computing life with you—programs, data, you name it. You're no longer tethered to your office desktop, or even to a power outlet. Anywhere you can go, your notebook PC can go with you.

That means that you can both work and play outside the house and outside the office. You can work on a PowerPoint presentation at Starbucks, check email while eating lunch, or even make hotel reservations while you're stopped at a truck stop or resting in an airport lounge. You're always connected, and you're always ready to go.

That also means that you have freedom of movement within your house. Many people buy notebook PCs and never take them out of the house. Instead, they use the notebook in the living room, in the kitchen, in the den, and in the bedroom. Just pick it up and take it to whatever room you want; there's no need to worry about power cords, Ethernet cables, and so on. You can work on a report while sitting on the living room couch, or write email messages from bed.

In addition, one notebook computer can do the job of two (or more) desktops. Instead of having one desktop PC at work and another at home, you can take one notebook between the two locations. A notebook is great when you need to take your work home with you; just close the case and head home.

Why Notebooks Aren't So Great

Perhaps the biggest argument against a notebook PC is that it's probably a little more expensive than a similarly equipped desktop model. That's because all the normal components used in a desktop PC have to be shrunk down to the more compact size of a laptop model. A $500 desktop PC might translate into a $700 or $800 notebook, which is a lot if you're on a budget.

In addition, some people don't like working on a notebook's smaller keyboard and display. Other people don't like the notebook's touchpad pointing device, preferring a traditional mouse instead. Then there's the issue of number crunching; most notebooks don't have a separate numeric keypad, which makes entering numbers a pain. If you're an accountant by trade, you probably don't like the notebook PC form factor.

There are also a few technical limitations. Unlike a desktop PC, a notebook PC isn't expandable. Want to upgrade the video card on your notebook? Tough luck. The configuration you buy is the configuration you have to stick with—save for the memory, which is just about the only thing in a notebook that you can upgrade.

And the configuration you get typically isn't as state-of-the-art as on a comparable desktop PC. In particular, few notebooks come with top-line graphics capabilities, which makes them less than ideal for playing PC games and performing video editing. In fact, many notebooks don't have the graphics horsepower to display the Aero glass interface in Windows Vista. So if performance matters, you may want to stick with a desktop model.

Key Elements of a Notebook PC

A notebook PC, like the one shown in Figure 2.1, looks like a smallish keyboard with a flip-up LCD screen attached. That's what you see, anyway; beneath the keyboard is a full-featured computer, complete with motherboard, central processing unit, memory chips, video and audio processing circuits, hard drive, and battery.

FIGURE 2.1

A typical laptop PC—multiple components in a single package.

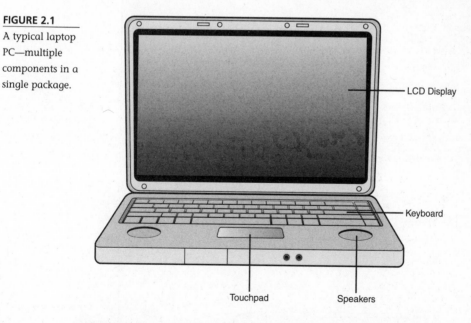

When the screen is folded down, the PC is portable; when the screen is flipped up, the keyboard is exposed. On the keyboard is some sort of built-in pointing device, which is used in place of a standalone mouse. Most notebooks today use a touchpad pointing device; you move your fingers around the touchpad to move the onscreen cursor and then click one of the buttons underneath the touchpad the same way you'd click a mouse.

If you look closely, you'll also see two built-in speakers, typically just above the top edge of the keyboard. Most notebooks also have an earphone jack, which you can use to connect a set of headphones or earbuds, the better to listen to music in a public place. (When you connect a set of headphones or earbuds, the built-in speakers are automatically muted.)

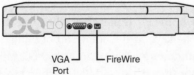

tip

If you have a portable PC, you don't have to use the built-in pointing device. Most portables let you attach an external mouse, which then can be used in addition to the internal device.

Somewhere on the notebook—either on the side or along the back edge—should be a row of connecting ports, like that shown in Figure 2.2. Most notebooks have two or more USB connectors, an Ethernet connector (for connecting to a wired network), a VGA video connector (for connecting to an external display monitor), and perhaps a FireWire connector (for connecting a digital camcorder). Some notebooks also have dedicated ports you can use to connect an external mouse and keyboard, in case you don't like using the built-in keyboard and pointing device.

FIGURE 2.2

Connecting ports on a notebook PC.

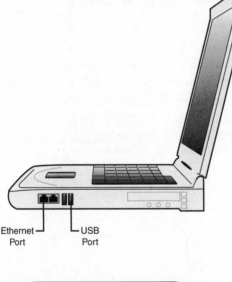

Ethernet Port

USB Port

VGA Port

FireWire

In addition, your notebook probably has a built-in CD or CD/DVD drive, like the one shown in Figure 2.3, typically on the side of the case. Press the little button to open the drive and insert a disc; push the drive back in to begin playing the CD or DVD.

FIGURE 2.3

A side-mounted CD/DVD drive.

CD/DVD Drive

Inside the notebook case are the guts of the computer—everything you have in a desktop PC's system unit but more compact. In fact, most notebooks have *more* inside than does a typical desktop; in particular, most notebook PCs have a built-in WiFi adapter so that the notebook can connect to a wireless home network or public WiFi hotspot.

In addition, virtually all notebook PCs come with some sort of built-in battery. That's because a portable PC is truly portable; in addition to running on normal AC power, a notebook PC can operate unplugged, using battery power. Depending on the PC (and the battery), you might be able to operate a laptop for three or four hours or more before switching batteries or plugging the unit into a wall outlet. That makes a notebook PC great for use on airplanes, in coffeeshops, or anywhere plugging in a power cord is inconvenient.

Different Types of Notebook PCs

Although all notebook PCs have similar components, they're not all created alike. As you can see in Figure 2.4, some notebooks are smaller and lighter than others, whereas some models are more suited for multimedia use—for watching movies and listening to music while you're on the go.

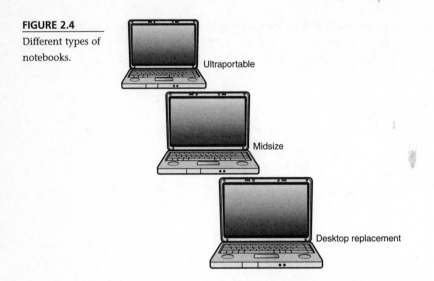

FIGURE 2.4

Different types of
notebooks.

The smallest and most portable type of notebook PC is called an *ultraportable*. These
models typically have a smallish screen (12" or so) with a traditional aspect ratio
and weigh less than 4 pounds. Ultraportables are small and light enough to fit in a
business briefcase and are perfect when all you need to do is check your email and
do a little work when you're on the road. Because the screen is small and the PC
horsepower is low, they get great battery life. On the downside, the screen is small
and the horsepower is low, which means you can't do high-performance work; in
addition, some users find the keyboards a trifle too compact.

In the middle of the pack is the appropriately named *midsize* or traditional notebook. These notebooks are a little bigger and a little heavier than ultraportables but
also offer bigger screens and more comfortable keyboards. These notebooks have
enough horsepower to do most traditional home or office computing tasks and typically have battery life in the 2–3 hour range.

If, on the other hand, you want a notebook that will do everything a desktop PC
does and you won't be using it on batteries much, consider a *desktop replacement*
model. These notebooks are big and heavy and have relatively poor battery life, so
you won't be carrying them around much. They have big screens and lots of computing horsepower, so they can perform the most demanding tasks—including high-
octane game playing and video editing. As the name implies, you can totally
replace your desktop PC with one of these notebooks.

Which type of notebook is best for you? If you travel a lot but don't use your PC
much, consider a lightweight ultraportable. (These are also good for watching DVDs
in the car or on an airplane.) If you use your notebook a lot and need to take your
work with you, a midsize model is a good compromise. And if you want to totally
replace your desktop with a notebook and know you won't be using it on battery
power much, go with a more expensive desktop replacement model.

Special Considerations for Using a Notebook PC

When using a notebook PC, you need to be aware of a few items, different from the way you use a desktop PC.

Conserving Battery Life

First, there's the issue of battery life. Any notebook, even a desktop replacement model, will give you at least an hour of operation before the battery powers down. If you need more battery life than that, here are some things you can try:

- **Dim your screen**—The brighter your screen, the more power your PC uses. Conserve on power usage by dialing down the brightness level of your notebook's screen.

- **Turn it off when you're not using it**—A PC sitting idle is still using power. If you're going to be away from the keyboard for more than a few minutes, turn off the notebook to conserve power—or put the PC into sleep or hibernation mode, which also cuts power use.

- **Don't do anything taxing**—Anytime you write or read a file from your notebook's hard disk, you use power. The same goes with using the CD or DVD drive; every spin of the drive drains the battery. If you use your notebook to watch DVD movies, don't expect the batteries to last as long as if you were just checking email or surfing the Web.

- **Buy a bigger battery**—Many notebook manufacturers sell batteries that have various capacities. You may be able to buy a longer-lasting battery than the one that came in the box.

- **Buy a second battery**—When the first battery is drained, remove it and plug in a fresh one.

- **Buy a smaller notebook**—Ultraportable models use less power and have longer battery life than do midsize notebooks, which in turn are less power-hungry than desktop replacement models. The smaller the screen and the less powerful the CPU, the longer the notebook's battery life.

If worse comes to worst, keep an eye out for an available power outlet. Most coffeeshops and airport lounges have at least one seat next to a power outlet; just carry your notebook's AC adapter with you and be ready to plug in when you can.

Connecting to WiFi Hotspots

One of the joys of using a notebook PC is being able to power up just about anywhere. And, because your notebook probably has built-in wireless connectivity, that also means you can connect to the Internet while you're out and about, thanks to the widespread availability of public WiFi hotspots.

We'll talk more about connecting to hotspots in Chapter 19, "Connecting to the Internet—At Home and on the Road." Just know that you should be able to walk into a Starbucks or similar coffeeshop, or most major hotels, and be able to pick up a wireless Internet signal with no problem. You may have to pay to get connected, but it's great to be able to check your email or make further reservations while you're relaxing over a cup of coffee or in your hotel room.

Securing Your Notebook

One of the great things about a notebook PC is that it's small and easily portable. One of the bad things about a notebook PC is that's it's small and easily portable— which makes it attractive to thieves. Take care to protect your notebook when you're using it in public, which may mean investing in a notebook lock or some similar sort of antitheft device. Of course, just being vigilant helps; never leave your notebook unattended in a coffeeshop or airport terminal.

In addition, be careful about transmitting private data over a public WiFi network. Avoid the temptation to do your online shopping (and transmit your credit card number) from your local coffeeshop; wait until you're safely connected to your home network before you send your private data over the WiFi airwaves.

THE ABSOLUTE MINIMUM

Here are the key points to remember from this chapter:

- A notebook PC contains all the technology of a desktop PC, including the LCD display, crammed into a smaller and lighter case.

- Notebook PCs aren't as upgradable as desktop PCs and often don't include the same state-of-the-art technology.

- You can choose from three general types of notebooks—small and light-weight ultraportables, midsize models that deliver a decent compromise between size and performance, and no-holds-barred desktop replacement models.

- When you use a notebook PC, you must be aware of battery life considerations, as well as issues relating to WiFi connectivity and security.

3

SETTING UP YOUR NEW COMPUTER SYSTEM

Chapter 1, "Understanding Desktop PCs," gave you the essential background information you need to understand how your computer system works. And Chapter 2, "Understanding Notebook PCs," did the same thing for portable computers. With that information in hand, it's now time to connect all the various pieces and parts of your computer system—and get your PC up and running!

Before You Get Started

It's important to prepare the space where you'll be putting your new PC. Obviously, the space has to be big enough to hold all the components—though you don't have to keep all the components together. You can, for example, spread out your left and right speakers, place your subwoofer on the floor, and separate the printer from the system unit. Just don't put anything so far away that the cables don't reach. (And make sure you have a spare power outlet—or even better, a multi-outlet power strip—nearby.)

You also should consider the ergonomics of your setup. You want your keyboard at or slightly below normal desktop height, and you want your monitor at or slightly below eye level. Make sure your chair is adjusted for a straight and firm sitting position with your feet flat on the floor, and then place all the pieces of your system in relation to that.

Wherever you put your system, you should make sure that it's in a well-ventilated location free of excess dust and smoke. (The moving parts in your computer don't like dust and dirt or any other such contaminants that can muck up the way they work.) Because your computer generates heat when it operates, you must leave enough room around the system unit for the heat to dissipate. *Never* place your computer in a confined, poorly ventilated space; your PC can overheat and shut down if it isn't sufficiently ventilated.

For extra protection to your computer, connect the power cable on your system unit to a surge suppressor rather than directly into an electrical outlet. A *surge suppressor*—which looks like a power strip, but with an on/off switch and a circuit breaker button—protects your PC from power-line surges that could damage its delicate internal parts. When a power surge temporarily spikes your line voltage (causes the voltage to momentarily increase above normal levels), a surge suppressor helps to keep the level of the electric current as steady as possible. Most surge suppressors also include circuit breakers to shut down power to your system in the event of a severe power spike.

> **tip**
>
> When you unpack your PC, be sure you keep all the manuals, CD-ROMs, and cables. Put the ones you don't use in a safe place, in case you need to reinstall any software or equipment at a later date.

Connecting the Cables

Now it's time to get connected. Position your system unit so that you easily can access all the connections on the back, and carefully run the cables from each of the other components so that they're hanging loose at the rear of the system unit.

caution

Before you connect *anything* to your system unit, make sure that it's turned off.

Connect in Order

It's important that you connect the cables in a particular order. To make sure that the most critical devices are connected first, follow the instructions in Table 3.1.

Table 3.1   Connecting Your System Components

Order	Connection	Looks Like
1.	Connect your mouse to the mouse connector— or, if you have a USB mouse, connect to an open USB port.	
2.	Connect your keyboard to the keyboard connector—or, if you have a USB keyboard, connect to an open USB port.	
3.	Connect your video monitor to the video connector. Most monitors connect via a standard VGA connector; some LCD monitors have the option of a higher-quality digital connection via a DVI connector—if your computer offers DVI output.	
4.	If your printer uses a USB connection, connect to an open USB port on your PC. If your printer uses a parallel cable, connect to your PC's parallel connector (sometimes labeled "printer" or "LPT1").	
5.	If you're using a dial-up Internet connection, connect a cable from your telephone line to the "line in" connector on your modem or modem board; then connect another cable from the "line out" connector on your modem to your telephone. (You can skip this step if you're using a cable or DSL modem; wait until you have the rest of your system up and running, and then follow the instructions you were given by your Internet service provider to connect the broadband modem.)	

Table 3.1 (continued)

Order	Connection	Looks Like
6.	Connect the phono jack from your speaker system to the "audio out" or "sound out" connector. Run the necessary cables between your right and left speakers and your subwoofer, as directed by the manufacturer.	
7.	Connect any external devices to the appropriate USB, FireWire, parallel, or Ethernet connector. (If you have a wired home network, this is the time to connect the network's Ethernet cable; if you have a wireless network, connect the USB WiFi adapter, instead.)	
8.	Plug the power cable of your video monitor into a power outlet.	
9.	If your system includes powered speakers, plug them into a power outlet.	
10.	Plug any other powered external component into a power outlet.	
11.	Plug the power cable of your system unit into a power outlet.	

Connect by Color

Most PC manufacturers color-code the cables and connectors to make the connection even easier—just plug the blue cable into the blue connector, and so on. If you're not sure what color cable goes to what device, take a look at the standard cable color coding in Table 3.2.

caution

Make sure that every cable is *firmly* connected—both to the system unit and the specific piece of hardware. Loose cables can cause all sorts of weird problems, so be sure they're plugged in really good.

Table 3.2   Connector Color Codes

Connector	Color
VGA (analog) monitor	Blue
Digital monitor (DVI)	White
Video out	Yellow
Mouse	Green
Keyboard	Purple
Serial	Teal or turquoise
Parallel (printer)	Burgundy
USB	Black
FireWire (IEEE 1394)	Gray
Audio line out (right)	Red
Audio line out (left)	White
Audio line out (headphones)	Lime
Speaker out/subwoofer	Orange
Right-to-left speaker	Brown
Audio line in	Light blue
Microphone	Pink
Gameport/MIDI	Gold

Connecting a Notebook PC

One nice thing about notebook PCs is that you don't have nearly as many pieces to connect. Because the monitor, speakers, keyboard, mouse, and WiFi adapter are all built into the notebook unit, the only things you might have to connect are a printer and a power cable. Then you just press the "power" button. Aren't notebooks great?

Turning It On and Setting It Up

Now that you have everything connected, sit back and rest for a minute. Next up is the big step—turning it all on.

It's important that you turn on things in the proper order. Follow these steps:

1. Turn on your video monitor.

2. Turn on your speaker system—but make sure the speaker volume knob is turned down (toward the left).

3. Turn on any other system components that are connected to your system unit—such as your printer, scanner, external modem, and so on. (If your PC is connected to an Ethernet network, make sure that the network router is turned on.)

4. Turn on your system unit.

Note that your system unit is the *last* thing you turn on. That's because when it powers on, it has to sense the other components of your system—which it can do only if the other components are plugged in and turned on.

Powering On for the First Time

The first time you turn on your PC is a unique experience. A brand-new, out-of-the-box system will have to perform some basic configuration operations, which include asking you to input some key information.

This first-time startup operation differs from manufacturer to manufacturer, but typically includes some or all of the following steps:

■ **Windows Product Activation**—You may be asked to input the long and nonsensical product code found on the label attached to the rear of your PC (or on your Windows installation CD, if you received one). Your system then phones into the Microsoft mother ship (via the Internet), registers your system information, and unlocks Windows for you to use. (Note that some manufacturers "pre-activate" Windows at the factory, so you might not have to go through this process.)

For full installation, activation, and registration, your PC will need to be connected to the Internet—typically via a cable or DSL modem connected either to your PC or to a network hub or router.

■ **Windows Registration**—A slightly different process from product activation, registration requires you to input your name and other personal information, along with the Windows product code. This information then is phoned into the Microsoft mother ship (again, via the Internet) to register your copy of Windows with the company, for warranty purposes.

Windows registration is optional; product activation is mandatory.

- **Windows Configuration**—During this process Windows asks a series of questions about your location, the current time and date, and other essential information. You also might be asked to create a username and password.

- **System Configuration**—This is where Windows tries to figure out all the different components that are part of your system, such as your printer, scanner, and so on. Enter the appropriate information when prompted; if asked to insert a component's installation CD, do so.

Many computer manufacturers supplement these configuration operations with setup procedures of their own. It's impossible to describe all the different options that might be presented by all the different manufacturers, so watch the screen carefully and follow all the onscreen instructions.

After you have everything configured, Windows finally starts, and then *you* can start using your system.

Powering On Normally

After everything is installed and configured, starting your computer is a much simpler affair. When you turn on your computer, you'll notice a series of text messages flash across your screen. These messages are there to let you know what's going on as your computer *boots up*.

After a few seconds (during which your system unit beeps and whirrs a little bit), the Windows Welcome screen appears, as shown in Figure 3.1. All registered users are listed on this screen. Click your username or picture, enter your password (if necessary), and then press the Enter key or click the right-arrow button. After you're past the Welcome screen, you're taken directly to the Windows desktop, and your system is ready to run.

note

Some installation procedures require your computer to be restarted. In most cases, this happens automatically; then the installation process resumes where it left off.

note

Technical types call the procedure of starting up a computer *booting* or *booting up* the system. Restarting a system (turning it off and then back on) is called *rebooting*.

FIGURE 3.1

The first thing you see in Windows Vista— the Welcome screen. (Looks slightly different in Windows XP.)

note

If you have only a single user on your PC and that user doesn't have a password assigned, Windows moves past the Welcome screen with no action necessary on your part.

THE ABSOLUTE MINIMUM

Here are the key points to remember when connecting and configuring your new computer:

- Most cables plug into only a specific connector—and on most new systems, they're color-coded for easier hookup.
- Make sure your cables are *firmly* connected; loose cables are the cause of many computer problems.
- Connect all the cables to your system unit *before* you turn on the power.
- Remember to turn on your printer and monitor before you turn on the system unit.
- For full registration and activation, your computer needs to be connected to the Internet.

PART II

USING WINDOWS

4

GETTING TO KNOW WINDOWS VISTA

As you learned back in Chapter 1, "Understanding Desktop PCs," the software and operating system make your hardware work. The operating system for most personal computers is Microsoft Windows, and you need to know how to use Windows to use your PC. Windows pretty much runs your computer for you; if you don't know your way around Windows, you won't be able to do much of anything on your new PC.

Introducing Windows Vista

Windows is a type of software called an *operating system*. An operating system does what its name implies—*operates* your computer *system*, working in the background every time you turn on your PC.

Equally important, Windows is what you see when you first turn on your computer, after everything turns on and boots up. The "desktop" that fills your screen is part of Windows, as are the taskbar at the bottom of the screen and the big menu that pops up when you click the Start button.

If you've recently purchased a new PC, the version of Windows on your PC is probably Windows Vista. Microsoft released different versions of Windows over the years, and Vista is the latest—which is why it comes preinstalled on most new PCs.

If you've used a previous version of Windows— such as Windows XP, Windows 2000, or Windows 98—on another PC, Windows Vista no doubt looks and acts differently from what you're used to. Don't worry; everything that was in the old Windows is still in the new Windows—it's just in a slightly different place.

note

If your PC is a little older, it's probably running Vista's predecessor, Windows XP. Vista operates a bit differently from XP, although they both share many common features and operations. There are enough differences to warrant covering XP separately, so if your PC is running Windows XP, turn to Chapter 5, "Using Windows XP on Older Computers," for more specific instructions.

What's New in Windows Vista

The most visible differences between Windows XP and Windows Vista are in the interface. Vista's interface takes advantage of today's more powerful video cards and offers a slick translucent 3D look. It also enables some impressive three-dimensional program switching, which gives the illusion that you really have separate windows stacked on your virtual desktop.

Beneath the surface, Vista makes better use of the technology built into today's PCs, putting all that extra speed and memory to good work. A Vista-equipped PC starts up faster, loads programs faster, and crashes less frequently. It's also more secure, with built-in anti-spyware and anti-phishing utilities working alongside the established Windows Firewall.

You also get more and better applications with Vista than you did with Windows XP. Vista includes updated versions of Internet Explorer, Windows Media Player, and Windows Movie Maker, as well as new Windows Mail, Windows Calendar, Windows Photo Gallery, and Windows DVD Maker programs. It's safe to say that Vista is better for web browsing and for managing all digital media.

Different Versions of Windows Vista

There are actually several different versions of Windows Vista, each with a slightly different feature set. Which version you have depends on which was installed by your PC's manufacturer. Table 4.1 details the different versions available in the U.S. market.

Table 4.1 Windows Vista Versions

	Home Basic	Home Premium	Ultimate	Business	Enterprise
Target Market					
Home	Yes	Yes	Yes		
Small business			Yes	Yes	
Corporate				Yes	Yes
Interface Features					
Basic User Interface	Yes	Yes	Yes	Yes	Yes
Aero User Interface		Yes	Yes	Yes	Yes
Included Applications					
Internet Explorer 7	Yes	Yes	Yes	Yes	Yes
Windows Calendar	Yes	Yes	Yes	Yes	Yes
Windows DVD Maker		Yes	Yes		
Windows Fax and Scan			Yes	Yes	Yes
Windows Mail	Yes	Yes	Yes	Yes	Yes
Windows Media Center		Yes	Yes		
Windows Media Player 11	Yes	Yes	Yes	Yes	Yes
Windows MeetingSpace	View only	Yes	Yes	Yes	Yes
Windows Movie Maker	Yes	Yes (HD)	Yes (HD)		
Windows Photo Gallery	Yes	Yes	Yes	Yes	Yes
Maintenance Features					
Manual File Backup	Yes	Yes	Yes	Yes	Yes
Scheduled File Backup		Yes	Yes	Yes	Yes
System Image-Based Backup and Recovery			Yes	Yes	Yes

Put simply, the Home Basic edition is preinstalled on low-priced PCs. You'll probably want the Home Premium edition, which has the better-looking Aero interface and a lot more useful applications. If you're in a small business or corporation, you might be using the Business or Enterprise editions. And if you want the version that has everything—essentially a superset of the other versions—you want Windows Vista Ultimate.

Whichever version of Windows Vista you have installed on your PC, you can easily upgrade to another version by using the built-in Windows Anytime Upgrade feature, available from the Windows Control Panel. All you have to do is select the version you want, make sure you're connected to the Internet, and then give Microsoft your credit card number. The upgrade process is automatic, using files already installed on your PC's hard drive.

note

Microsoft is also distributing a stripped-down version of Vista for emerging markets, called Windows Vista Starter Edition. This version is not available in the United States.

Working Your Way Around the Desktop

If you're already familiar with Windows, you can start using Windows Vista without much training. However, if this is your first PC, or if Vista looks a little too different to you, take a few minutes to figure your way around the Vista desktop.

As you can see in Figure 4.1, the Windows Vista desktop includes a number of key elements. Get to know this desktop; you're going to be seeing a lot of it from now on.

The major parts of the Windows desktop include

- **Start button**—Opens the Start menu, which is what you can use to open all your programs and documents.
- **Taskbar**—Displays buttons for your open applications and windows, as well as different toolbars for different tasks.
- **Notification area**—Formerly called the system tray, this part of the taskbar holds the clock, volume control, and icons for other utilities that run in the background of your system.
- **Sidebar and gadgets**—This area on the right side of the desktop holds various utilities, called *gadgets*, that sit on the desktop and perform specific operations.
- **Shortcut icons**—These are links to software programs you can place on your desktop; a "clean" desktop includes just one icon, for the Windows Recycle Bin.
- **Recycle Bin**—This is where you dump any files you want to delete.

FIGURE 4.1

The Windows
Vista desktop—
click the Start
button to get
going.

Shortcut icons

Recycle Bin

Sidebar and gadgets

Start button

Taskbar

Important Windows Operations

To use Windows efficiently, you must master a few simple operations, such as pointing and clicking, dragging and dropping, and right-clicking. You perform all these operations with your mouse.

Pointing and Clicking

The most common mouse operation is *pointing and clicking*. Simply move the mouse so that the cursor is pointing to the object you want to select and then click the left mouse button once. Pointing and clicking is an effective way to select menu items, directories, and files.

Double-Clicking

To launch a program or open a file folder, single-clicking isn't enough. Instead, you need to *double-click* an item to activate an operation. This involves pointing at something onscreen with the cursor and then clicking the left mouse button twice in rapid succession. For example, to open program groups or launch individual programs, simply double-click a specific icon.

Right-Clicking

Here's one of the secret keys to efficient Windows operation. When you select an item and then click the *right* mouse button, you'll often see a pop-up menu. This menu, when available, contains commands that directly relate to the selected object. So, for example, if you right-click a file icon, you'll see commands related to that file—copy, move, delete, and so forth.

Refer to your individual programs to see whether and how they use the right mouse button.

Dragging and Dropping

Dragging is a variation of clicking. To drag an object, point at it with the cursor and then press and hold down the left mouse button. Move the mouse without releasing the mouse button and drag the object to a new location. When you're finished moving the object, release the mouse button to drop it onto the new location.

You can use dragging and dropping to move files from one folder to another or to delete files by dragging them onto the Recycle Bin icon.

Hovering

When you position the cursor over an item without clicking your mouse, you're *hovering* over that item. Many operations require you to hover your cursor and then perform some other action.

Moving and Resizing Windows

Every software program you launch is displayed in a separate onscreen window. When you open more than one program, you get more than one window—and your desktop can quickly get cluttered.

There are many ways to deal with desktop clutter. One way is to move a window to a new position. You do this by positioning your cursor over a blank area at the top of the window frame and then clicking and holding down the left button on your mouse. As long as this button is depressed, you can use your mouse to drag the window around the screen. When you release the mouse button, the window stays where you put it.

You also can change the size of most windows. You do this by positioning the cursor over the

> **tip**
>
> The cursor changes shape—to a double-ended arrow—when it's positioned over the edge of a window.

edge of the window—any edge. If you position the cursor on either side of the window, you can resize the width. If you position the cursor on the top or bottom edge, you can resize the height. Finally, if you position the cursor on a corner, you can resize the width and height at the same time.

After the cursor is positioned over the window's edge, press and hold down the left mouse button; then drag the window border to its new size. Release the mouse button to lock in the newly sized window.

Maximizing, Minimizing, and Closing Windows

Another way to manage a window in Windows is to make it display full-screen. You do this by maximizing the window. All you have to do is click the Maximize button at the upper-right corner of the window, as shown in Figure 4.2.

FIGURE 4.2
Use the
Minimize,
Maximize, and
Close buttons to
manage your
desktop
windows.

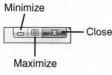

Minimize

Close

Maximize

If the window is already maximized, the Maximize button changes to a Restore Down button. When you click the Restore Down button, the window resumes its previous (premaximized) dimensions.

If you would rather hide the window so that it doesn't clutter your desktop, click the Minimize button. This shoves the window off the desktop, onto the taskbar. The program in the window is still running, however—it's just not on the desktop. To restore a minimized window, all you have to do is click the window's button on the Windows taskbar (at the bottom of the screen).

If what you really want to do is close the window (and close any program running within the window), just click the window's Close button.

Scrolling Through a Window

Many windows contain more information than can be displayed at once. When you have a long

caution

If you try to close a window that contains a document you haven't saved, you'll be prompted to save the changes to the document. Because you probably don't want to lose any of your work, click Yes to save the document and then close the program.

document or web page, only the first part of the document or page is displayed in the window. To view the rest of the document or page, you have to scroll down through the window, using the various parts of the scrollbar (shown in Figure 4.3).

FIGURE 4.3

Use the scrollbar to scroll through long pages.

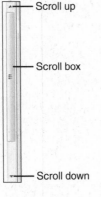

— Scroll up

— Scroll box

— Scroll down

There are several ways to scroll through a window. To scroll up or down a line at a time, click the up or down arrow on the window's scrollbar. To move to a specific place in a long document, use your mouse to grab the scroll box (between the up and down arrows) and drag it to a new position. You can also click on the scrollbar between the scroll box and the end arrow, which scrolls you one screen at a time.

If your mouse has a scroll wheel, you can use it to scroll through a long document. Just roll the wheel back or forward to scroll down or up through a window.

Using Menus

Many windows in Windows use a set of pull-down menus to store all the commands and operations you can perform. The menus are aligned across the top of the window, just below the title bar, in what is called a *menu bar*.

You open (or pull down) a menu by clicking the menu's name. The full menu then appears just below the menu bar, as shown in Figure 4.4. You activate a command or select a menu item by clicking it with your mouse.

Menu bar   Pull-down menu

FIGURE 4.4

Navigating Windows' menu system.

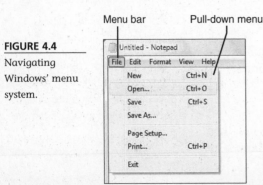

Some menu items have a little black arrow to the right of the label. This indicates that additional choices are available, displayed on a submenu. Click the menu item or the arrow to display the submenu.

Other menu items have three little dots (called an *ellipsis*) to the right of the label. This indicates that additional choices are available, displayed in a dialog box. Click the menu item to display the dialog box.

The nice thing is, after you get the hang of this menu thing in one program, the menus should be similar in all the other programs you use. For example, most of the Office 2007 programs have an Office button that, when clicked, displays a pull-down menu of common file-oriented operations; older programs have a File menu that contains similar operations. Although each program has menus and menu items specific to its own needs, these common menus make it easy to get up and running when you install new software programs on your system.

tip

If an item in a menu, toolbar, or dialog box is dimmed (or grayed), that means it isn't available for the current task.

Using Toolbars and Ribbons

Some Windows programs put the most frequently used operations on one or more *toolbars*, typically located just below the menu bar. (Figure 4.5 shows a typical Windows toolbar.) A toolbar looks like a row of buttons, each with a small picture (called an *icon*) and maybe a bit of text. You activate the associated command or operation by clicking the button with your mouse.

FIGURE 4.5
A typical Windows toolbar.

Toolbar

Other programs substitute a *ribbon* for the toolbar. For example, all the Office 2007 programs have a ribbon that contains buttons for the most-used operations. As you can see in Figure 4.6, each ribbon has different tabs, each containing a different collection of buttons. Click the tab to see the ribbon buttons for that particular type of operation.

tip

If the toolbar is too long to display fully on your screen, you'll see a right arrow at the far-right side of the toolbar. Click this arrow to display the buttons that aren't currently visible.

Tabs

FIGURE 4.6

A new-style ribbon, with tabs for different types of operations.

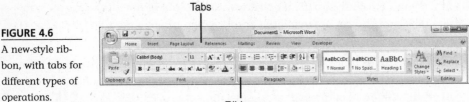

Ribbon

Using Dialog Boxes, Tabs, and Buttons

When Windows or an application requires a complex set of inputs, you are often presented with a *dialog box*. A dialog box is similar to a form in which you can input various parameters and make various choices—and then register those inputs and choices when you click OK. (Figure 4.7 shows the Open dialog box, found in most Windows applications.)

FIGURE 4.7

Use dialog boxes to control various aspects of your Windows applications.

Windows has several different types of dialog boxes, each one customized to the task at hand. However, most dialog boxes share a set of common features, which include the following:

■ **Buttons**—Most buttons either register your inputs or open an auxiliary dialog box. The most common buttons are OK (to register your inputs and close the dialog box), Cancel (to close the dialog box without registering your inputs), and Apply (to register your inputs without closing the dialog box). Click a button once to activate it.

- **Tabs**—These allow a single dialog box to display multiple "pages" of information. Think of each tab, arranged across the top of the dialog box, as a "thumbtab" to the individual page in the dialog box below it. Click the top of a tab to change to that particular page of information.

- **Text boxes**—These are empty boxes where you type in a response. Position your cursor over the empty input box, click your left mouse button, and begin typing.

- **Lists**—These are lists of available choices; lists can either scroll or drop down from what looks like an input box. Select an item from the list with your mouse; you can select multiple items in some lists by holding down the Ctrl key while clicking with your mouse.

- **Check boxes**—These are boxes that let you select (or deselect) various stand-alone options.

- **Sliders**—These are sliding bars that let you select increments between two extremes, similar to a sliding volume control on an audio system.

Using the Start Menu—And Switching Programs

All the software programs and utilities on your computer are accessed via Windows' Start menu. You display the Start menu by using your mouse to click the Start button, located in the lower-left corner of your screen.

As you can see in Figure 4.8, the Windows Vista Start menu consists of two columns of icons. Your most frequently and recently used programs are listed in the left column; basic Windows utilities and folders are listed in the right column. To open a specific program or folder, just click the name of the item.

To view the rest of your programs, click the All Programs arrow. This displays a new submenu called the Programs menu. From here you can access various programs, sorted by type or manufacturer. (When more programs are contained within a master folder, you'll see an arrow to the

note

The operations presented in this chapter are described as how they look and act by default in a typical Windows installation. If you're using someone else's PC, things might not look or act exactly like this. It's normal for two different PCs to look and act a little differently because you can customize so many options for your own personal tastes—as you'll learn in Chapter 6, "Personalizing Windows."

right of the title; click this arrow to expand the menu and display additional choices.)

FIGURE 4.8

Access all the programs on your system from the Start menu.

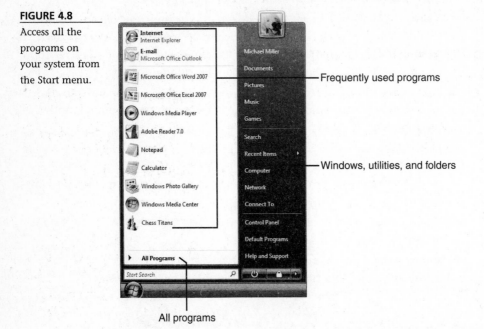

Frequently used programs

Windows, utilities, and folders

All programs

By the way, the All Programs menu works differently in Windows Vista than in Windows XP. In Windows XP, clicking a right arrow caused the menu to cascade to the right; in Vista, clicking a right arrow simply expands the menu in-place, which takes up a lot less screen space.

Launching a Program

Now that you know how to work the Start menu, it's easy to start any particular software program. All you have to do is follow these steps:

1. Click the Start button to display the Start menu.
2. If the program is displayed on the Start menu, click the program's icon.
3. If the program isn't visible on the main Start menu, click the All Programs button, find the program's icon, and then click it.

Another way to find a program to launch is to use the Instant Search box on the Start menu. Just start entering the program's name into the search box, and a list of matching programs appears on the Start menu. When the program you want appears, click it to launch it.

Switching Between Programs

After you've launched a few programs, it's easy to switch from one program to another. Windows Vista offers several different ways to switch between programs, including

- Click any visible part of the application's window, which brings that window to the front.

- Click the application's button in the taskbar, as shown in Figure 4.9. (And here's a tip; if you hover your cursor over a taskbar button, you'll see a "live" thumbnail of the open document or application.)

FIGURE 4.9

Use the taskbar buttons to switch between applications.

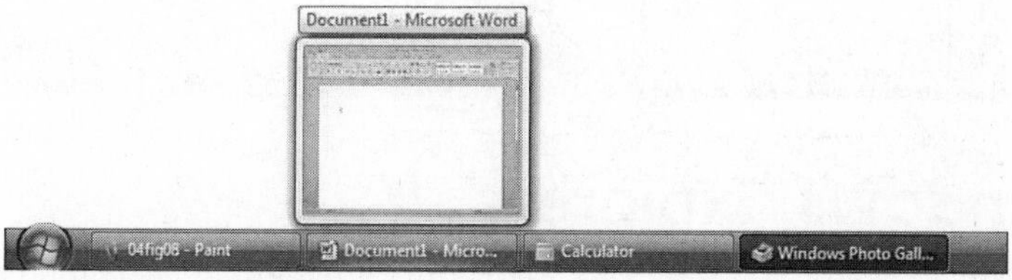

- Hold down the Alt key and then press the Tab key repeatedly until the application window you want is selected. This is called *Windows Flip* and cycles through thumbnails of all open windows, as shown in Figure 4.10. When you're at the window you want, release the Alt key.

FIGURE 4.10

Use Windows Flip to select from thumbnails of all open programs.

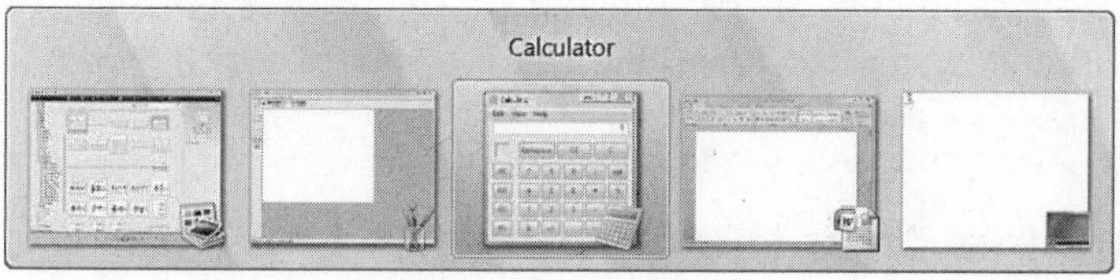

- Hold down the Start button and then press the Tab key to activate the *Flip 3D* feature. This displays a three-dimensional stack of all open windows, as shown in Figure 4.11. Continue pressing the Tab key (or rotate the scroll button on your mouse) to cycle through the windows on the stack.

FIGURE 4.11

Flip 3D lets you flip through a three-dimensional stack of open windows.

Using Windows Explorers

In Windows Vista, all the items stored on your computer—including programs, documents, and configuration settings—are accessible from special windows, called *Explorers*. You use Explorers to find, copy, delete, launch, and even configure programs and documents.

There are many different Explorers in Windows Vista. For example, when you click the Music icon on the Start menu, you open the Music Explorer, which then displays all the songs you have stored on your system, as shown in Figure 4.12. Likewise, clicking the Photos icon opens the Photos Explorer, which displays all the digital photographs on your system.

Browsing for Files with the Documents Explorer

Perhaps the most-used Explorer is the Documents Explorer, which is where you'll find practically all of the documents, photos, music, and other files stored on your computer's hard disk.

Click the Documents icon on the Start menu, and you see a window full of folders, such as the one shown in Figure 4.13. Double-click a folder icon to view the contents of that folder—which could be individual files or additional folders (sometimes called *subfolders*). To launch a program or open a document, double-click that item's icon. To perform other tasks (copying, deleting, and so forth), right-click the icon and select an option from the pop-up menu.

FIGURE 4.12
View all the
music stored on
your system
with the Music
Explorer.

FIGURE 4.13
Browsing
through the
folders and files
stored on your
system with the
Documents
Explorer.

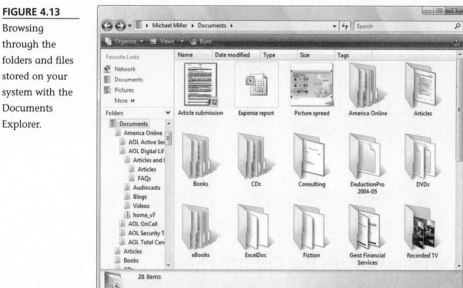

Managing PC Resources with the Computer Explorer

The Computer Explorer lets you access each major component of your system and perform basic maintenance functions. For example, you can use the Computer Explorer to "open" the contents of your hard disk and then copy, move, and delete individual files. To open the Computer Explorer, simply click the Computer icon on the Start menu.

As you can see in Figure 4.14, the Computer Explorer contains icons for each of the major components of your system—your hard disk drive, external drives, CD-ROM or DVD drive, and so on. To view the contents of a specific drive, simply double-click the icon for that drive. You'll see a list of folders and files located on that drive; to view the contents of any folder, just double-click the icon for that folder.

note

In Windows XP, the Computer Explorer was called My Computer.

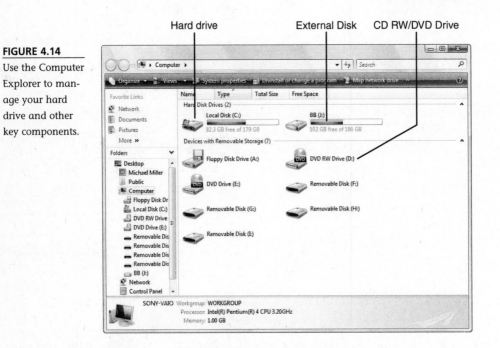

FIGURE 4.14
Use the Computer Explorer to manage your hard drive and other key components.

Managing Windows with the Control Panel

There's one more Windows Explorer, similar to the Computer Explorer, that you need to know about. This Explorer, called the *Control Panel*, is used to manage most of Windows' configuration settings. To open the Control Panel, click the Control Panel icon on the Start menu.

When the Control Panel opens, as shown in Figure 4.15, you can select a particular category you want to configure. Each item you select opens a window with a different set of options; just keep clicking until you find the specific item you want to configure.

FIGURE 4.15

The Windows Vista Control Panel—configuration tasks are organized by category.

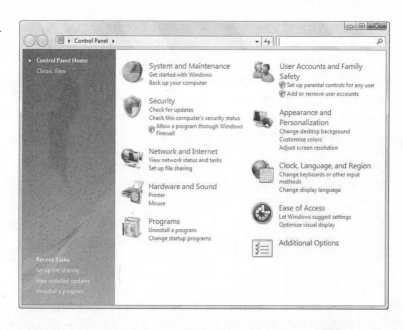

All the Other Things in Windows

Windows is more than just a pretty desktop and some configuration utilities. Windows also includes many accessory programs and system tools you can use to perform other basic system operations.

Windows includes a number of single-function accessory programs, all accessible from the Start menu. These programs include a calculator, some games, two basic word processors (Notepad and WordPad), a drawing program (Paint), a player for audio and video files (Windows Media Player), a photo management/editing program (Windows Photo Gallery), a digital video editing program (Windows Movie Maker), a DVD burning program (Windows DVD Maker), and more. You access all of these accessories from the Start menu and by selecting All Programs. Some programs are right on the All Programs menu; others are a level down on the Accessories menu.

note

To learn more about configuring various Windows settings, see Chapter 6.

In addition to the Windows accessories, Windows Vista also gives you three important Internet utilities. These include a web browser (Internet Explorer 7), an email program (Windows Mail), and a web-based calendar/scheduler program (Windows Calendar). All three of these programs are on the All Programs menu.

Finally, Windows Vista includes a handful of technical tools you can use to keep your system running smoothly. You can access all these tools by clicking the Start button and selecting All Programs, Accessories, System Tools.

Getting Help in Windows

When you can't figure out how to perform a particular task, it's time to ask for help. In Windows Vista, this is done through the Help and Support Center.

To launch the Help and Support Center, click the Start button and then select Help and Support. The Help and Support Center, shown in Figure 4.16, lets you search for specific answers to your problems, browse the table of contents, connect to another computer for remote assistance, go online for additional help, and troubleshoot any problems you may be having. Click the type of help you want and follow the onscreen instructions from there.

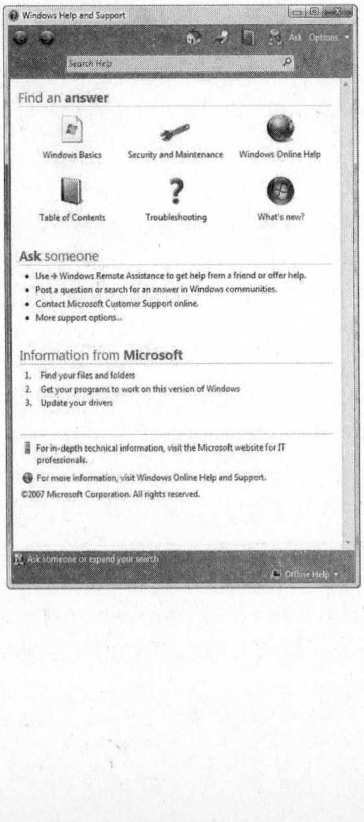

note

To learn about the practical uses of these and other system tools, turn to Chapter 10, "Performing Routine Maintenance."

FIGURE 4.16
Windows Vista's Help and Support center—the place to go for answers.

Shutting Down Windows—And Your Computer

You've probably already noticed that Windows starts automatically every time you turn on your computer. Although you will see lines of text flashing onscreen during the initial startup, Windows loads automatically and goes on to display the Windows desktop.

Powering Down

When you want to turn off your computer, you do it through Windows. In fact, you don't want to turn off your computer any other way—you *always* want to turn off things through the official Windows procedure.

To shut down Windows and turn off your PC, follow these steps:

1. Click the Start button to display the Start menu.

2. Click the right arrow next to the Power button at the lower-right corner of the menu; then select Shut Down.

3. Manually turn off your monitor, printer, and other peripherals.

> **caution**
>
> Do *not* turn off your computer without shutting down Windows. You could lose data and settings that are temporarily stored in your system's memory.

Putting Windows to Sleep

Notice that you don't just click the Power button to shut down your system. If you click the Power button, Windows doesn't shut down; instead, it enters a special *Sleep* mode. When you enter Sleep mode, Windows saves all your open documents, applications, and data to both your PC's hard drive and memory; shuts down your PC's hard drive and monitor; and then enters a special power-saving mode. It doesn't turn off your computer—it simply puts it to sleep.

The advantage of using Sleep mode is that it makes it faster to turn your computer back on—or, more accurately, to wake it up. When you've put Windows into Sleep mode, pressing your computer's On button powers up your equipment, wakes up Windows from Sleep mode, and quickly retrieves all open documents and applications from system memory. It's a lot faster than rebooting from a power-off condition—which is why Sleep is the default operation when you click Vista's Power button.

The Absolute Minimum

This chapter gave you a lot of background about Windows Vista—your new PC's operating system. Here are the key points to remember:

- You use Windows to manage your computer system and run your software programs.

- Most functions in Windows are activated by clicking or double-clicking an icon or a button.

- All the programs and accessories on your system are accessed via the Start menu, which you display by clicking the Start button.

- Use the various Windows Explorers to view and manage the contents of your computer system.

- Use the Control Panel to manage Windows' configuration settings.

- When you can't figure out how to do something, click the Start button and select Help and Support.

5

USING WINDOWS XP ON OLDER COMPUTERS

If you just purchased a new PC, your operating system is probably Windows Vista, as we discussed in Chapter 4, "Getting to Know Windows Vista." But if you have an older PC, you're probably running an older version of Windows—most likely, Windows XP. How does Windows XP differ from Windows Vista? And how does it work? This chapter answers those questions.

Before Vista: Previous Versions of Windows

Windows Vista isn't the first version of Windows. In fact, Windows has been around for more than 20 years, so Vista isn't really reinventing any wheels.

The first version of Windows, imaginatively dubbed Windows 1.0, was released way back in 1985. It was an improvement over the old MS-DOS operating system, which was completely character- and command-based. Windows put a graphical user interface (GUI) on top of the DOS command-line engine and let users navigate through the onscreen windows with a mouse.

That said, Windows 1.0 wasn't all that great. Yes, it was a tad easier on the eyes than the then-reigning DOS operating system, but it wasn't much easier to use—and there weren't many programs available for it. In fact, for several years, Microsoft Word and Excel were the only two applications that took full advantage of the Windows interface.

Fortunately, Windows got better. Microsoft upgraded Windows on a fairly consistent basis over the past two decades, bringing out a new version of Windows every few years or so. Sometimes the new version was a minor update; sometimes it was a complete overhaul. For example, Windows 95 (released, unsurprisingly, in 1995) was a total rewrite of the previous 3.X version of Windows. Windows 98 (which followed in 1998) was a less-significant upgrade, and Windows 98 Second Edition (in 1999) was really no more than a minor bug fix.

Windows XP, released in 2001, was one of the most significant upgrades. It introduced a smooth new interface, full of rounded corners, and was significantly easier to use and more reliable than previous versions. There's a reason why Microsoft waited five years to upgrade XP; this version of Windows worked pretty well.

Windows XP worked so well, in fact, that a significant number of computers are still running it. That's why you're reading this chapter, after all—because your computer has Windows XP installed.

Getting to Know Windows XP

As you can see in Figure 5.1, the Windows XP desktop looks a lot like the Windows Vista desktop but without the see-through windows and the Sidebar. Everything else is where you'd expect it to be—the Start button, the taskbar, the system tray (what Vista calls the *notification area*), the shortcut icons, and the Recycle Bin.

note

Because Windows XP lacks the state-of-the-art graphics engine found in Windows Vista, many of Vista's graphics-intensive features don't exist in XP. For example, the Windows Sidebar (and accompanying Sidebar gadgets) is a Vista-only feature, not available in Windows XP.

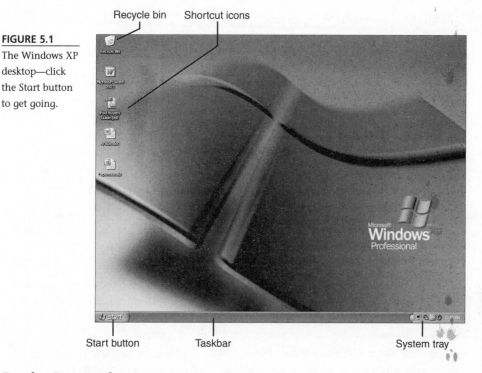

FIGURE 5.1
The Windows XP
desktop—click
the Start button
to get going.

Basic Operations

Basic operations in Windows XP are the same as in Windows Vista. You still have to learn how to point and click, double-click, right-click, drag and drop, and hover. Working with individual windows is also similar; you use the scrollbar to scroll through a long document and the maximize and minimize buttons to display or hide windows.

Within individual applications, Windows XP is a bit more reliant on menus than Windows Vista is. XP applications don't have ribbons, and they don't hide a lot of operations behind a single, somewhat vague Organize menu. Instead, you have the normal application menu bar, as shown in Figure 5.2, with operations neatly organized on pull-down menus; many applications also have one or more toolbars. For example, in most Windows XP applications, all file-related operations—such as opening and saving a file—are found on the File menu.

FIGURE 5.2
A standard
Windows XP
application
menu bar.

Document1 - Microsoft Word

File Edit View Insert Format Tools Table Window Help   Type a question for help

The Start Menu

Opening an application is still done via the Start menu, which appears when you click the Start button. (Note that in Windows XP the Start button actually has the word "start" on it.) Unlike Vista's expanding and contracting All Programs menu, the All Programs menu in Windows XP cascades outward when you click a right-arrow next to an individual folder name, as shown in Figure 5.3. Some users like it one way, some the other.

Switching Between Programs

Because Windows XP doesn't have Vista's fancy three-dimensional graphics, it also lacks the Windows Flip and Flip 3D methods of switching between programs. Instead, you can do any of the following:

> **note**
>
> Throughout this book, I'll make an effort to describe operations for both Windows Vista and Windows XP users. In some instances, however, there will only be space to describe the Vista-specific operations; when you encounter these types of instructions, you'll need to translate them for your Windows XP system.

- Click any visible part of the application's window—including its title bar.

- Click the application's button in the taskbar. (Unlike in Windows Vista, document thumbnails are not displayed above the taskbar buttons.)

- Hold down the Alt key and then press the Tab key repeatedly until the application window you want is selected. This cycles through all open windows; when you're at the window you want, release the Alt key. (Unlike in Windows Vista, this does not display thumbnails of open windows.)

Shutting Down Windows XP

Shutting down Windows XP is actually a little less confusing than shutting down Windows Vista. If you recall, when you click Vista's "power" button, you don't actually turn off the power; instead, you put the computer into a special sleep mode. Not so in Windows XP—when you click the "power" button, you shut off the computer. Simplicity itself.

To shut down Windows and turn off your PC, follow these steps:

1. Click the Start button to display the Start menu.
2. Click the Turn Off Computer button.
3. When the Turn Off Computer dialog box appears, click the Turn Off button.
4. Manually turn off your monitor, printer, and other peripherals.

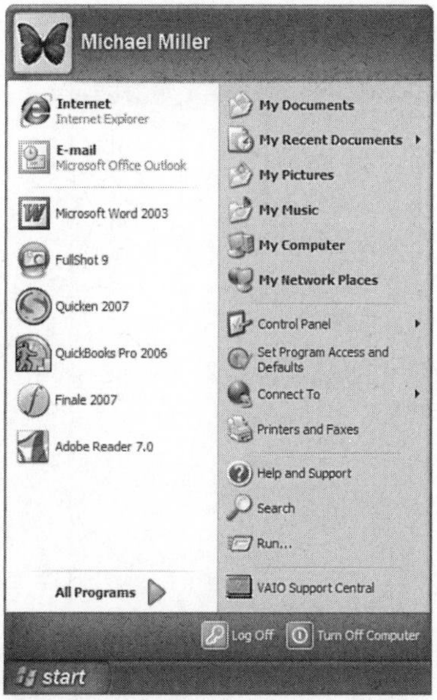

FIGURE 5.3

FIGURE 5.3
Windows XP's
cascading All
Programs menu.

Working with the My Documents Folder

Where Windows Vista uses a similar series of
Explorers to display files, folders, and configuration
data, Windows XP simply displays the contents of
folders within a window. It's pretty much the same
thing, except that each folder has its own distinct
name.

By default, all your documents are stored within
the My Documents folder. You open this folder by
clicking the My Documents icon on the Start menu.

As you can see in Figure 5.4, the My Documents
folder not only contains files and subfolders but
also displays a panel on the left-hand side, called
the Tasks panel. Vista doesn't have a similar panel,
and that's too bad, because the Tasks panel is one
of the most practical parts of Windows XP. All the
common tasks related to the open folder are displayed in this panel. All you have to do is select a
folder or file and then click the appropriate task in the Tasks Panel. It makes copying, moving, and deleting files much easier.

note

Windows XP puts the
word "my" in front of most
of the similar folders found in
Windows Vista. For example, what
Vista calls Documents, XP calls My
Documents; what Vista calls
Computer, XP calls My Computer.

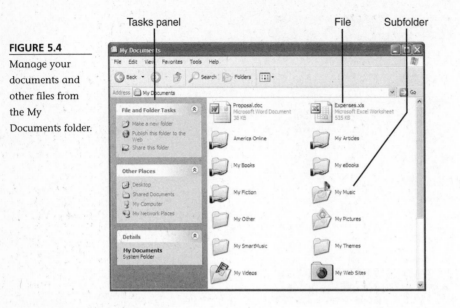

FIGURE 5.4

Manage your documents and other files from the My Documents folder.

Other Folders

The My Documents folder is just one of several similar folders within Windows XP. You'll also find the My Music folder, which contains all your digital music files; the My Pictures folder, which contains all your digital photographs; the My Network Places folder, which contains files and folders stored on other PCs in your computer network; and the My Computer folder, which lets you access all the disk drives on your main computer. And, of course, Windows XP also has its own Control Panel, which you use to configure various aspects of your system.

Windows XP Applications

Windows XP contains many—but not all—of the same built-in applications as Windows Vista. You get Windows Media Player, Windows Movie Maker, and Internet Explorer, as well as Notepad, WordPad, and Paint. Instead of Windows Mail, there's Outlook Express, which works pretty much the same way. What you miss in XP are Vista's new applications, including Windows Photo Gallery, Windows Calendar, and Windows DVD Maker.

Know that depending on when Windows XP was installed on your PC, and how often it's been updated, you may not have the latest version of some of these programs. In particular, new versions of Internet Explorer (7) and Windows Media Player (11) are available for Windows XP. These new versions upgrade the programs so that they look and work pretty much like their Windows Vista cousins. If you haven't yet upgraded to these new versions, go to Microsoft's website (www.microsoft.com) and do so now. There is no charge to download these upgraded versions.

Upgrading from Windows XP to Windows Vista

Now for the $64 question: Should you upgrade your computer from Windows XP to Windows Vista?

It all depends. Assuming that everything is working fine on your existing system, it might not be worth the bother. Yes, Vista comes with a few more built-in applications and is a tad bit more secure; that aside, the benefits of upgrading are few. Why mess with a system that's working?

That said, some users always like to have the latest and the greatest, and Vista does offer a few more bells and whistles than you find with XP. If this sounds like you, the operative question is not *should* you upgrade to Vista, but *can* you upgrade?

You see, not all older PCs have the horsepower to run Vista, which is a more demanding operating system than the older Windows XP. To run Vista, your PC must meet or exceed the following system requirements:

- **Microprocessor**—For the Vista Home Basic edition, a 32-bit or 64-bit microprocessor running at a minimum of 800MHz. For all other editions, you'll need at least a 1GHz microprocessor.
- **Memory**—To run the Vista Home Basic edition, you need at least 512MB RAM. For all other editions, go with a minimum of 1GB of memory.
- **Hard disk**—To run the Vista Home Basic edition, you need at least a 20GB hard drive with 15GB of free space. For all other editions, Microsoft recommends a minimum 40GB hard drive—much bigger is definitely better.
- **Removable storage**—The Vista Home Basic edition needs your PC to have a CD-ROM drive. (Read-only is fine.) All other editions need a CD/DVD drive for installation.
- **Graphics**—To display Vista's basic interface, you'll need a 3D video card that's compatible with DirectX 9. To display the Aero interface, your PC's video card must support DirectX 9 with Pixel Shader 2, have a minimum of 128MB graphics memory, and offer 32 bits per pixel, Windows Display Driver Model (WDDM) support.

If your PC doesn't meet any of these requirements, you can upgrade those components necessary to run Vista—or just keep using Windows XP. As I said before, if it's not broke, don't fix it!

THE ABSOLUTE MINIMUM

As you just learned, Windows XP works a lot like Windows Vista, with some minor operating differences here and there. Here are the key points to remember:

- Windows XP is the direct predecessor to Windows Vista, having been on the market for more than five years.

- Most functions in Windows XP are similar to those in Windows Vista, save for those that require Vista's higher-powered graphics engine.

- Windows XP uses the My Documents folder to store and manage document files, instead of Vista's various Explorers.

- The My Documents and similar folders incorporate a Tasks panel, which provides easy access to common operations.

- Windows XP contains many of the same applications as Vista, with the notable exceptions of Windows Photo Gallery, Windows Calendar, and Windows DVD Maker.

- Windows XP versions of Internet Explorer and Windows Media Player have been updated to offer the same features as Windows Vista versions of these programs.

- If you want to upgrade to Windows Vista, make sure your PC meets the minimum system requirements—or upgrade those components necessary to make the upgrade.

6

PERSONALIZING WINDOWS

When you first turn on your new computer system, you see the Windows desktop as Microsoft (or your computer manufacturer) set it up for you. If you like the way it looks, great. If not, you can change it.

Windows presents a lot of different ways to personalize the look and feel of your desktop. In fact, one of the great things about Windows is how quickly you can make the desktop look like *your* desktop, different from anybody else's.

Getting to Know the Windows Control Panel

Virtually all of Windows' settings are configured via the Control Panel. You open the Control Panel by clicking the Start button and selecting Control Panel; from there, what you see depends on which version of Windows you're using.

In Windows Vista, the Control Panel looks like the one shown in Figure 6.1. You can click a major category, such as System and Maintenance or Security, to access related configuration settings. Or you can click one of the key settings under a major heading to go directly to that setting.

FIGURE 6.1

The Windows Vista Control Panel.

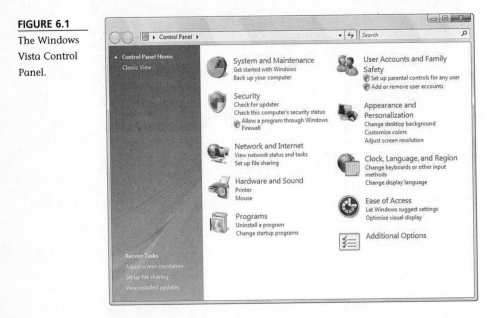

In Windows XP, the Control Panel looks a bit different. As you can see in Figure 6.2, the XP Control Panel also organizes configuration settings by type but doesn't let you go directly to any individual setting. And, of course, XP's and Vista's configuration settings are organized differently, so you'll have a different path to get to any specific setting; it's all fairly logical, however.

After you click through the various links, you eventually end up with a specific configuration utility displayed onscreen. Each type of configuration setting uses a different utility; you may see a full-fledged window full of controls, or a smaller dialog box with a few options to check. Whatever you see onscreen, select those options you want; then click OK. This applies the settings you selected.

FIGURE 6.2

The Windows XP
Control Panel.

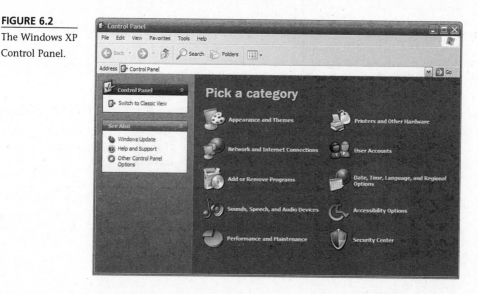

Changing the Look of Your Desktop in Windows Vista

One of the first things that most users want to personalize is the look of the Windows desktop itself. This is a little different in Windows Vista than in Windows XP, due to Vista's added visual features. Read on to learn how to customize your Vista desktop.

Personalizing the Desktop Background

Don't like the default background picture on your desktop? Then change it!

Windows Vista offers a wide selection of pictures you can use for your desktop background; you can also opt to have a plain-colored background, or choose any other picture on your PC. All you have to do is follow these steps:

1. From the Start menu, select Control Panel.

2. When the Control Panel opens, select Change Desktop Background (in the Appearance and Personalization section).

3. This opens the Desktop Background window, shown in Figure 6.3. Click the Picture Location list and select what kind of background you want—Windows Wallpapers, Pictures, Sample Pictures, Public Pictures, or Solid Colors.

tip

To select another picture stored elsewhere on your computer, click the Browse button and browse for the picture you want.

FIGURE 6.3

Choosing a new background for your Windows Vista desktop.

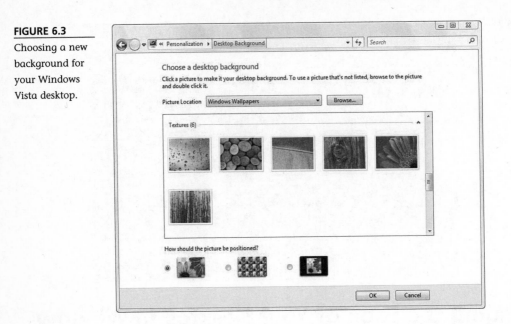

4. Scroll through the list of options until you find the background you want. Select by the background by clicking it; this automatically applies the background to your desktop.

5. For all backgrounds except solid colors, you can position the picture three ways on your desktop—stretched, tiled, or centered. Check the desired How Should the Picture Be Positioned? option at the bottom of the dialog box.

6. Click OK.

Changing the Color Scheme

The primary Windows Vista interface is called the Aero interface, and it's a nice combination of translucent (see-through) colors. You can change the color scheme, however, as well as the level of translucency used in windows and other onscreen elements.

To change the color and translucency in Windows Vista, follow these steps:

1. From the Start menu, select Control Panel.

2. When the Control Panel opens, select Customize Colors (in the Appearance and Personalization section).

3. When the Window Color and Appearance window appears, as shown in Figure 6.4, click the color scheme you want. Alternately, you can click the Show Color Mixer button to fine-tune the selected hue, saturation, and brightness.

FIGURE 6.4

Choosing a new color scheme and transparency for your Windows Vista desktop.

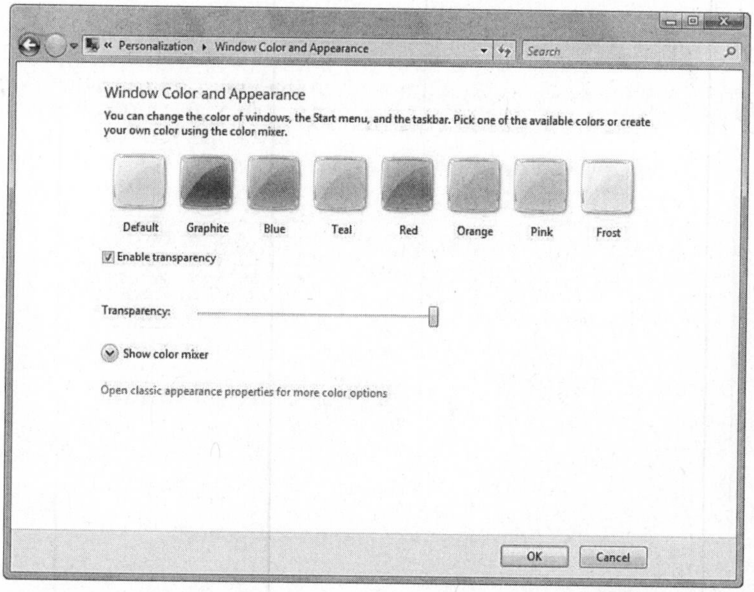

4. To make the onscreen windows more transparent, move the Transparency slider to the left. To make the windows more solid, move the slider to the right.

5. Click OK when finished.

Changing the Desktop Size

You can also configure your computer's display so that the desktop is larger or smaller than normal. A larger desktop lets you view more things onscreen at the same time—even though each item is smaller than before. A smaller desktop displays fewer items, but they're larger. (This is great if your eyesight is less than perfect.)

Changing the size of the desktop is accomplished by changing Windows' *screen resolution*. You do this by following these steps:

1. From the Start menu, select Control Panel.

2. When the Control Panel opens, select Adjust Screen Resolution (in the Appearance and Personalization section).

note

If your PC doesn't have enough graphics horsepower, it won't display the translucent Aero interface. In this instance, you'll see the Windows Vista Basic interface instead—which looks similar but doesn't have the translucency and many of the three-dimensional effects. (The Basic interface is also what you'll see if you're running the Vista Home Basic edition, which doesn't include the Aero interface.)

3. When the Display Settings dialog box appears, as shown in Figure 6.5, adjust the Resolution slider. Move the slider to the right (High) to put more items on the desktop; move it to the left (Low) to create a smaller desktop with larger individual items.

4. Click OK to apply your changes.

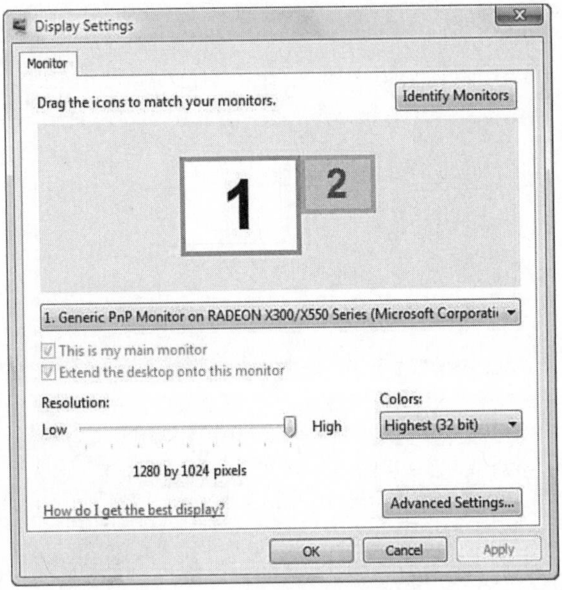

FIGURE 6.5

Use the Display Properties dialog box to configure Windows' display settings.

By the way, while you are in the Display Settings dialog box, you can also change the number of colors displayed by your monitor. (More is better.) Just choose the desired setting from the Colors drop-down list and then click OK when finished.

Choosing a Screensaver

Screensavers display moving designs on your computer screen when you haven't typed or moved the mouse for a while. This prevents static images from burning into your screen—and provides some small degree of entertainment if you're bored at your desk.

tip

To best use all the features of Windows Vista, go for a 1024×768 or higher resolution. If this setting makes things look too small (a problem if you have a smaller monitor), try the 800×600 resolution. As for color, go for 32-bit if your graphics card lets you; if you don't see that option, choose 16-bit instead.

To activate one of the screensavers included with Windows Vista, follow these steps:

1. From the Start menu, select Control Panel.

2. When the Control Panel opens, select Appearance and Personalization.

3. When the next window appears, select Change Screen Saver (in the Personalization section).

4. When the Screen Saver Settings dialog box appears, as shown in Figure 6.6, pull down the Screen Saver list and select the screensaver you want. (You can preview any selected screensaver by clicking the Preview button.)

5. Click the Settings button to configure that screensaver's specific settings (if available).

6. Click OK when finished.

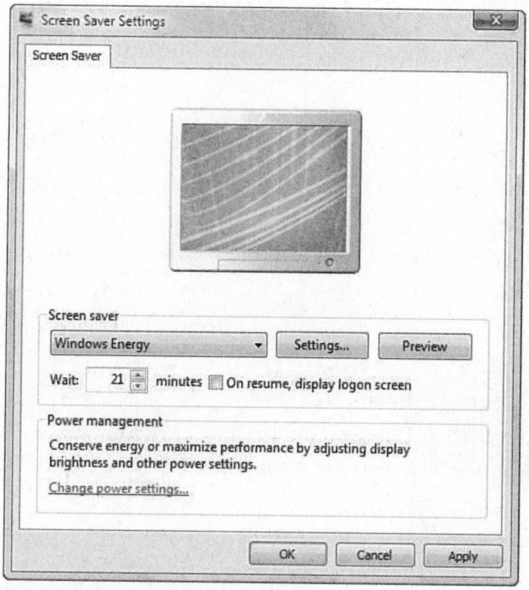

FIGURE 6.6

Selecting a
Windows Vista
screensaver.

Customizing the Windows Sidebar

One of the cool new features in Windows Vista is the Windows Sidebar, shown in Figure 6.7. The Sidebar is an area of the desktop (typically docked on the right side of the screen) used to hold a variety of "gadgets." These gadgets are actually small utility applications that perform a single simple function. For example, the Clock gadget displays the current time, the Weather gadget reports the current weather conditions and forecast for your area, and so on.

FIGURE 6.7

The Windows
Sidebar, with
gadgets
attached.

These gadgets can stay docked to the Sidebar, or they can be dragged off with your
mouse to sit on the desktop itself, as shown in Figure 6.8. In either position, you can
configure their opacity—each gadget can have a solid background, or it can be see-
through, to match the Vista interface.

FIGURE 6.8

The Weather
gadget, undocked
on the desktop.

The Sidebar should be displayed by default in Windows Vista. If it isn't, you can display it by clicking the Start button and selecting All Programs, Accessories, Windows
Sidebar.

To add gadgets to the Sidebar, right-click anywhere on an empty section of the
Sidebar and select Add Gadgets from the pop-up menu. When the next window
appears, as shown in Figure 6.9, double-click any gadget you want to add. To view
even more gadgets, click Get More Gadgets Online; this launches Internet Explorer
and takes you to the Windows Vista Gadgets Gallery online. Browse through the
available gadgets, and click the Download button when you find one you want.

FIGURE 6.9

Adding new
gadgets to the
Sidebar.

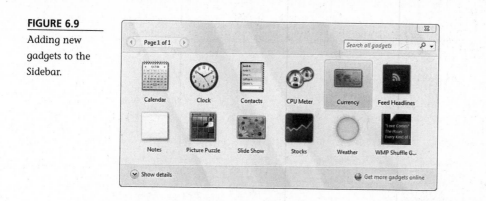

To configure an individual gadget, right-click it and select Options; to change the
opacity, right-click the gadget, select Opacity, and then select a percent. To change
the position of the gadgets in the Sidebar, use your mouse to drag a gadget up or
down in the Sidebar.

Changing the Look of Your Desktop in Windows XP

If your computer is running Windows XP, you can change many of the same desktop options as you can with Windows Vista. This section explains how.

Personalizing the Desktop Background

To change the desktop background in Windows XP, follow these steps:

1. From the Start menu, select Control Panel.

2. When the Control Panel opens, select
   Appearance and Themes; then select
   Change the Desktop Background.

3. When the Display Properties dialog box
   appears, select the Desktop tab, shown in
   Figure 6.10.

4. To choose one of Windows' built-in backgrounds, make a selection from the
   Background list. Or, to select your own
   graphics file, click the Browse button and
   navigate to the file you want to use.

> **tip**
>
> If you would rather display
> a solid background color
> with no graphic, select None
> from the Background list and
> select a color from the Color
> list.

FIGURE 6.10

Use the Display Properties dialog box to select a new desktop background.

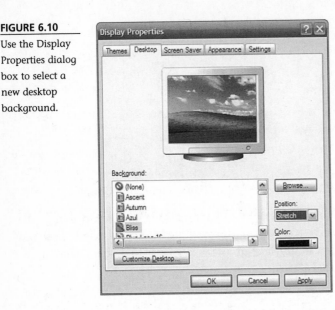

5. To determine how the image file is displayed on your desktop, select one of the items from the Position pull-down list: Center, Tile, or Stretch.

6. Click OK to register your changes.

Changing the Desktop Size

To change the screen resolution in Windows XP, follow these steps:

1. From the Start menu, select Control Panel.

2. When the Control Panel opens, select Appearance and Themes; then select Change the Screen Resolution.

3. When the Display Properties dialog box appears, select the Settings tab.

4. Adjust the Screen Resolution slider to left for a lower resolution (smaller desktop with larger items), or to the right for a higher resolution (bigger desktop with smaller items).

5. Click OK when finished.

As with Windows Vista, you can also change the number of colors displayed while you're on this tab. More is better, of course.

Choosing a Screensaver

Windows XP also has its own collection of screensavers. To choose a screensaver, follow these steps:

1. From the Start menu, select Control Panel.
2. When the Control Panel opens, select Appearance and Themes; then select Choose a Screen Saver.
3. When the Display Properties dialog box appears, select the Screen Saver tab.
4. Pull down the Screen Saver list and select the screensaver you want. (You can preview any selected screensaver by clicking the Preview button.)
5. Click the Settings button to configure that screensaver's specific settings (if available).
6. Click OK when finished.

Organizing Desktop Icons

Both Windows Vista and Windows XP display a variety of desktop icons—those little pictures on your desktop that function as shortcuts for starting applications and opening documents. Placing a shortcut on your desktop is an alternative to launching items from the Start menu.

Creating New Shortcuts on the Desktop

To put a new shortcut on your desktop, follow these steps:

1. From within any Windows Explorer (Vista) or from within any folder (XP), navigate to the application or document for which you want to create a shortcut.
2. Right-click the file icon and then select Send To, Desktop (Create Shortcut).

To remove a shortcut icon from the desktop, just drag it into the Recycle Bin.

Changing the Name of a Shortcut

When you create a new shortcut icon, the word "Shortcut" (or, in XP, "Shortcut to   ") is automatically added to the icon's name. You can get rid of this, if you want.

tip

You can also create a shortcut by right-dragging a file icon directly to the desktop, or by right-clicking on the desktop and selecting New, Shortcut from the pop-up menu.

To change the name of a shortcut, follow these steps:

1. Right-click the shortcut on your desktop.

2. When the pop-up menu appears, select Rename.

3. The shortcut's name is now highlighted on your desktop. Use the Delete or Backspace keys to erase parts of the existing name, and then type a new name. Press Enter when you've finished entering the new name.

Arranging Icons on the Desktop

All those desktop icons let you quickly open your most-used programs, but they can really clutter up the look of your Windows desktop. To better arrange your icons, right-click a blank area of the desktop, select View, Sort By (or, in Windows XP, select Arrange Icons By), and choose from one of the following options:

- **Name**—Sorts items alphabetically by filename

- **Size**—Sorts items by file size, from smallest to largest

- **Type**—Sorts items by file type so that files with the same extension are grouped together

- **Date Modified**—Sorts items by date, from oldest to most recent

In addition, you can click the View option and choose to Auto Arrange the items, which automatically arranges the icons along the left side of your desktop, or Align to Grid, which makes all your icons snap to an invisible grid.

Changing the Way the Start Menu Works

You use the Start menu every time you launch a program. Windows offers a few ways for you to customize the way the Start menu works for you.

> **tip**
>
> You can't choose Align to Grid and Auto Arrange at the same time. If you want to spread your icons across the desktop (but aligned to the invisible grid), turn off Auto Arrange and Keep Align to Grid on.

Displaying More—or Fewer—Programs on the Start Menu

By default, the Start menu displays the five most-recent applications you've run. You can reconfigure the Start menu to display more (up to nine) or fewer (as few as zero) applications at a time.

To display more or fewer programs, follow these steps:

1. Right-click the Start button and select Properties from the pop-up menu.
2. When the Taskbar and Start Menu Properties dialog box appears, select the Start Menu tab.
3. Click the Customize button to display the Customize Start Menu dialog box. (If you're using Windows XP, you should now select the General tab.)
4. Select a new number from the Number of Recent Programs to Display (or, in XP, the Number of Programs on Start Menu) list.
5. Click OK when finished.

Adding a Program to the Start Menu—Permanently

If you're not totally comfortable with the way programs come and go from the Start menu, you can add any program to the Start menu—*permanently*. All you have to do is follow these steps:

1. Click the Start button to display the Start menu.
2. Click All Programs to open the Programs menu.
3. Navigate to a specific program.
4. Right-click that program to display the pop-up menu.
5. Select Pin to Start Menu.

The program you selected now appears on the Start menu, just below the browser and email icons.

Resetting the Time and Date

The time and date for your system should be automatically set when you first turn on your computer. If you find that you need to change or reset the time or date settings, all you have to do is follow these steps; it's easy.

In Windows Vista, click the time display in the notification area of the taskbar; then select Change Date and Time Settings. This opens the Date and Time dialog box. Select the Date and Time tab; then click the Change Date and Time button.

> **note**
>
> To remove a program you've added to the Start menu, right-click its icon and select Unpin from Start Menu.

When the Date and Time Settings dialog box appears, select the correct month and year; then use the clock control to set the correct time. Click OK when finished.

While you're in the Date and Time dialog box, you can also set your time zone. Just click the Change Time Zone button and select your time zone from the pull-down list.

This process is similar in Windows XP. If you're an XP user, double-click the time display in the system tray; then, when the Date and Time Properties dialog box appears, make the appropriate date, time, and time zone selections.

Setting Up Additional Users

Chances are you're not the only person using your computer; it's likely that you'll be sharing your PC to some degree with your spouse and kids. Fortunately, you can configure Windows so that different people using your computer sign on with their own custom settings—and access to their own personal files.

You should assign each user in your household his own password-protected *user account*. Anyone trying to access another user's account and files without the password will then be denied access.

You can establish two different types of user accounts on your computer—computer administrator and standard user. (In XP, this is called a limited account.) Only an administrator account can make systemwide changes to your PC, install software, and access all the files on the system.

When you first configured Windows on your PC, you were set up as an administrator. The other members of your household should be set up with standard accounts; they'll be able to use the computer and access their own files but won't be able to install software or mess up the main settings.

> **tip**
>
> You can have more than one administrator account per PC, so you might want to set up your spouse with an administrator account, too.

Creating a New Account

Only the computer administrator can add a new user to your system. To set up a new account on a Windows Vista machine, follow these steps:

1. From the Start menu, select Control Panel.
2. When the Control Panel opens, select Add or Remove User Accounts (in the User Accounts and Family Safety section).
3. When the next window appears, click Create a New Account.
4. When prompted, enter a name for the new account; then select whether this account is for a standard user or an account administrator.
5. Click the Create Account button.

Windows now creates the new account and randomly assigns a picture that will appear next to the user-name.

Changing an Account

If you don't like the picture assigned to an account, you can change this picture at any time by opening the Control Panel and selecting Add or Remove User Accounts. When the Manage Accounts window appears, as shown in Figure 6.11, select the account you want to change; then select the Change the Picture option.

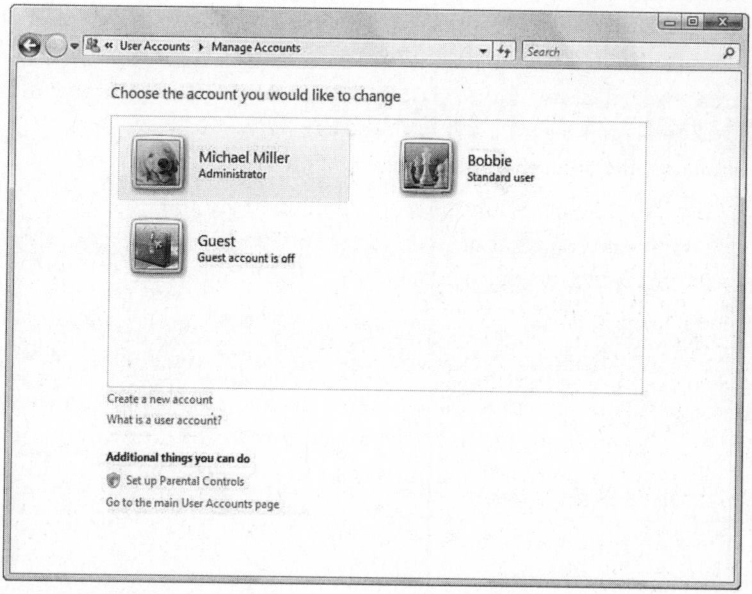

note

In Windows XP, open the Control Panel, select User Accounts, and then select Create a New Account. The rest of the process is similar.

FIGURE 6.11

Managing user accounts in Windows Vista.

By default, no password is assigned to the new account. If you want to assign a password, return to the Manage Accounts window, select the account, and then select the Create a Password option.

Setting Up Parental Controls in Windows Vista

If you set up an account for one of your children, you may want to take advantage of Windows Vista's new Parental Controls feature. Parental Controls let you determine how your children will use your computer. You can set time limits for when they can use the PC, and you can select which websites they can visit, which PC games they can play (based on game ratings), and which specific programs they can or cannot use. You can even have Vista create activity reports for each chosen user.

caution

If you create a password for your account, you better remember it. You won't be able to access Windows—or any of your applications and documents—if you forget the password!

To activate and configure the various Parental Controls, open the Control Panel and select Set Up Parental Controls for Any User (in the User Accounts and Family Safety section). When the next screen appears, select the user that you want to monitor; then follow the onscreen instructions to configure the desired controls.

THE ABSOLUTE MINIMUM

Here are the key points to remember from this chapter:

- Most Windows settings are configured via the Control Panel.
- In Windows Vista, you can change the desktop background, color scheme, and window transparency.
- Windows Vista and Windows XP both let you activate a screensaver, which displays when your system is inactive for a period of time.
- If you have multiple users in your household, you can create a user account for each person and assign each user his own password. (Just make sure that you remember your password—or you won't be able to log in to Windows!)

7

WORKING WITH FILES, FOLDERS, AND DISKS

Managing the data stored on your computer is vitally important. After you've saved a file, you may need to copy it to another computer, move it to a new location on your hard drive, rename it, or even delete it. You have to know how to perform all these operations—which means learning how to work with Windows' files, folders, and disks.

Understanding Files and Folders

All the information on your computer is stored in *files*. A file is nothing more than a collection of digital data. The contents of a file can be a document (such as a Word memo or Excel spreadsheet), a digital photo or music track, or the executable code for a software program. The contents of a file can be a document from an application (such as a Works worksheet or a Word document), or they can be the executable code for the application itself.

Every file has its own unique name. A defined structure exists for naming files, and its conventions must be followed for Windows to understand exactly what file you want when you try to access one. Each filename must consist of two parts, separated by a period—the *name* (to the left of the period) and the *extension* (to the right of the period). A filename can consist of letters, numbers, spaces, and characters and looks something like this: `filename.ext`.

Windows stores files in *folders*. A folder is like a master file; each folder can contain both files and additional folders. The exact location of a file is called its *path* and contains all the folders leading to the file. For example, a file named `filename.doc` that exists in the `system` folder, that is itself contained in the `windows` folder on your `c:\` drive, has a path that looks like this:

`c:\windows\system\filename.doc`

tip

By default, Windows hides the extensions when it displays filenames. To display extensions in Windows Vista, open the Control Panel, select Appearance and Personalization, and then select Folder Options. When the Folder Options dialog box appears, select the View tab; then, in the Advanced Settings list, *uncheck* the Hide Extensions for Known File Types option. Click OK when finished.

Learning how to use files and folders is a necessary skill for all computer users. You might need to copy files from one folder to another or from your hard disk to a floppy disk. You certainly need to delete files every now and then. To do this in Windows Vista, you use Windows Explorer; in Windows XP, you use the My Documents folder.

Viewing Folders and Files

In Windows Vista you can open any Windows Explorer to view the folders and files on your system. Perhaps the easiest Explorer to use is the Documents Explorer, which you open by clicking the Documents icon on the Start menu. The Documents Explorer opens automatically to display the contents of the Documents folder on your computer's hard disk.

note

In Windows XP, use the My Documents folder to view your files and folders.

As you can see in Figure 7.1, the Documents Explorer displays not only individual files but also other folders—called *subfolders*—that themselves contain other files. You can perform most file-related operations by clicking the Organize button to display the Organize menu, or by right-clicking a file icon to display the context-sensitive pop-up menu.

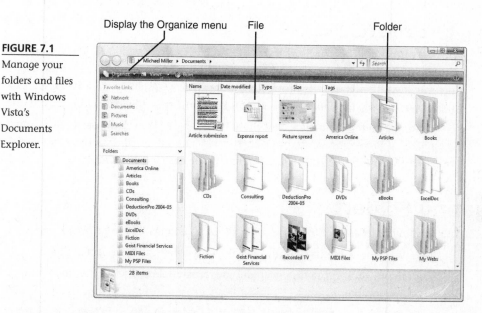

Display the Organize menu   File   Folder

FIGURE 7.1
Manage your folders and files with Windows Vista's Documents Explorer.

Changing the Way Files Are Displayed

You can choose to view the contents of a folder in a variety of ways. To change the file view, click the Views button on the Explorer toolbar; this displays a pull-down menu. You can then select from the available views: Extra Large Icons, Large Icons, Medium Icons, Small Icons, List, Details, or Tiles. You can also move the slider up and down to change the size of the file/folder icons.

Sorting Files and Folders

When viewing files in the Documents Explorer, you can sort your files and folders in a number of ways. To do this, right-click anywhere in the Explorer window, select the Sort By option, and then choose to sort by Name, Date Modified, Type, Size, or Tags. You can also choose to sort the items in either ascending or descending order.

tip

Any of the icon views are good for working with graphics files, or for getting a quick thumbnail glance at a file's contents. The Details view is better if you're looking for files by date or size.

If you want to view your files in alphabetical order, choose to sort by Name. If you want to see all similar files grouped together, choose to sort by Type. If you want to sort your files by the date and time they were last edited, choose the Date Modified option. And if you want to sort by a user-applied file tag (assuming you've done this in the file's host program), choose the Tags option.

Grouping Files and Folders

You can also configure Windows to group the files in your folder, which can make it easier to identify particular files. For example, if you sorted your files by time and date modified, they'll now be grouped by date (Today, Yesterday, Last Week, and so on). If you sorted your files by type, they'll be grouped by file extension, and so on.

To turn on grouping, right-click anywhere in the Explorer window, select the Group By option, and then choose to group by Name, Date Modified, Type, Size, or Tags. Windows now groups your files and folders by the selected criteria.

Navigating Folders

You can navigate through all your folders and subfolders in several ways:

■ To view the contents of a disk or folder, double-click the selected item.

■ To move back to the disk or folder previously selected, click the Back button on the toolbar.

■ To choose from the history of disks and folders previously viewed, click the down arrow in the Address bar at the top of the Explorer window and select a disk or folder.

■ If you've moved back through multiple disks or folders, you can move forward to the next folder by clicking the Forward button on the toolbar.

■ Go directly to any disk or folder by entering the path in the Address Bar (in the format `x:\folder\subfolder`) and pressing Enter.

■ Move backward through the "bread crumb" path in the Address bar. Click any previous folder location (separated by arrows) to display that particular folder.

You can also go directly to key locations by using the list of locations in the navigation pane on the left side of the Explorer window. This pane displays the most common locations for files on your system. The top part of the pane displays your Favorite Links—including the Documents, Pictures,

note

The My Documents folder in Windows XP has a similar treelike display called the Folders pane. To display this pane, click the Folders button.

and Music folders. The Folders section on the bottom of the pane displays all the contents of your system in a treelike outline. Double-click any section of the tree to display that item's contents.

Searching for Files

As organized as you might be, you may not always be able to find the specific files you want. Fortunately, Windows Vista offers an easy way to locate difficult-to-find files, via the new Instant Search function. Instant Search indexes all the files stored on your hard disk (including email messages) by type, title, and contents. So you can search for a file by extension, filename, or keywords within the document.

To use the Instant Search feature, follow these steps:

1. From within the Explorer window, locate the Search box at the top right of the window, as shown in Figure 7.2.

2. Enter one or more keywords into the search box.

3. Press Enter, or click the Go button (looks like a magnifying glass).

FIGURE 7.2
The Search box in Windows Explorer.

Vista now displays a list of files that match your search criteria. Double-click any icon to open that file.

Creating New Folders

The more files you create, the harder it is to organize and find things on your hard disk. When the number of files you have becomes unmanageable, you need to create more folders—and subfolders—to better categorize your files.

To create a new folder, follow these steps:

1. Navigate to the drive or folder where you want to place the new folder.

2. Click the Organize button to display the drop-down menu; then select New Folder.

tip

You can also search for files from Vista's main Instant Search window, accessible by clicking the Search icon on the Start menu. This window offers more advanced search options than are available from the Windows Explorer Search box.

3. A new, empty folder now appears within the Explorer window, with the file-name New Folder highlighted.

4. Type a name for your folder (which overwrites the New Folder name), and press Enter.

Renaming Files and Folders

When you create a new file or folder, it helps to give it a name that somehow describes its contents. Sometimes, however, you might need to change a file's name. Fortunately, Windows makes it relatively easy to rename an item.

To rename a file (or folder), follow these steps:

1. Click the file or folder you want to rename.

2. Click the Organize button and then select Rename from the pull-down menu (or just press the F2 key on your keyboard); this highlights the filename.

3. Type a new name for your folder (which overwrites the current name), and press Enter.

caution

Folder and filenames can include up to 255 characters—including many special characters. Some special characters, however, are "illegal," meaning that you *can't* use them in folder or filenames. Illegal characters include the following: \ / : * ? " < > |.

Copying Files

Now it's time to address the most common things you do with files—copying and moving them from one location to another.

It's important to remember that copying is different from moving. When you *copy* an item, the original item remains in its original location—plus you have the new copy. When you *move* an item, the original is no longer present in the original location—all you have is the item in the new location.

caution

The one part of the filename you should never change is the extension—the part that comes after the "dot." That's because Windows and other software programs recognize different types of program files and documents by their extension. This is why, by default, Windows hides these file extensions—so you can't change them by mistake.

The Easy Way to Copy

To copy a file or a folder with Windows Vista, follow these steps:

1. Select the item you want to copy.

2. Click the Organize button and select Copy from the pull-down menu.

3. Use Windows Explorer to navigate to the new location for the item.

4. Click the Organize button and select Paste from the pull-down menu.

That's it. You've just copied the file from one location to another.

Other Ways to Copy

The method just presented is just one of many ways to copy a file. Windows Vista provides several other methods, including

- Right-click a file and select Copy from the pop-up menu, then paste to the new location.

- Right-click a file and select Send To from the pop-up menu, then select a location from the choices listed.

- Hold down the Ctrl key and then use your mouse to drag the file or folder from one location to another within the Explorer window.

- Drag the file or folder while holding down the *right* mouse button. When you drop the file into a new location, you see a pop-up menu that asks whether you want to move it or copy it. Select the copy option.

Moving Files

Moving a file (or folder) is different from copying it. Moving cuts the item from its previous location and places it in a new location. Copying leaves the original item where it was *and* creates a copy of the item elsewhere.

In other words, when you copy something you end up with two of it. When you move something, you only have the one thing.

The Easy Way to Move

To move a file, follow these steps:

1. Select the item you want to move.

2. Click the Organize button and select Cut from the pull-down menu.

3. Use Windows Explorer to navigate to the new location for the item.

4. Click the Organize button and select Paste from the pull-down menu.

Other Ways to Move a File

Just as Windows provides several other ways to copy a file, you also have a choice of alternative methods for moving a file, including the following:

- Right-click a filename and select Cut from the pop-up menu; then paste it to the new location.
- Use your mouse to drag the file from one location to another.
- Drag the file or folder while holding down the *right* mouse button. When you drop the file into a new location, you see a pop-up menu that asks whether you want to move it or copy it. Select the move option.

Deleting Files

Too many files eat up too much hard disk space—which is a bad thing, because you only have so much disk space. (Music and video files, in particular, can chew up big chunks of your hard drive.) Because you don't want to waste disk space, you should periodically delete those files (and folders) you no longer need.

The Easy Way to Delete

Deleting a file is as easy as following these two simple steps:

1. Select the file.
2. Click the Organize button and select Delete from the pull-down menu.

This simple operation sends the file to the Windows Recycle Bin, which is kind of a trash can for deleted files. (It's also a trash can that periodically needs to be dumped—as discussed later in this activity.)

Other Ways to Delete a File

As you might expect, there are other ways to delete files in Windows Vista. In particular, you can do the following:

- Highlight the file and press the Del key on your keyboard.
- Drag the file from the Explorer window onto the Recycle Bin icon on your desktop.

Restoring Deleted Files

Have you ever accidentally deleted the wrong file? If so, you're in luck. For a short period of time, Windows stores the files you delete in the Recycle Bin. The Recycle Bin is actually a special folder on your hard disk; if you've recently deleted a file, it should still be in the Recycle Bin folder.

To "undelete" a file from the Recycle Bin, follow these steps:

1. Double-click the Recycle Bin icon on your desktop (shown in Figure 7.3) to open the Recycle Bin folder.

2. Click the file(s) you want to restore.

3. Click the Restore This Item button on the toolbar.

This copies the deleted file back to its original location, ready for continued use.

FIGURE 7.3

The Recycle Bin, where all your deleted files end up.

Managing the Recycle Bin

Deleted files do not stay in the Recycle Bin indefinitely. By default, the deleted files in the Recycle Bin can occupy 10% of your hard disk space. When you've deleted enough files to exceed this 10%, the oldest files in the Recycle Bin are automatically and permanently deleted from your hard disk.

If you'd rather dump the Recycle Bin manually (and thus free up some hard disk space), follow these steps:

1. Double-click the Recycle Bin icon on your desktop to open the Recycle Bin folder.

2. Click the Empty the Recycle Bin button on the toolbar.

3. When the confirmation dialog box appears, click Yes to completely erase the files, or click No to continue storing the files in the Recycle Bin.

Working with Compressed Folders

Really big files can be difficult to move or copy. They're especially difficult to transfer to other users, whether by email or portable disk drive.

Fortunately, Windows includes a way to make big files smaller. *Compressed folders* take big files and compress their size, which makes them easier to copy or move. After the file has been transferred, you can then uncompress the file back to its original state.

Compressing a File

Compressing one or more files is a relatively easy task from within any Windows folder. Just follow these steps:

1. Select the file(s) you want to compress.
2. Right-click the file(s) to display the pop-up menu.
3. Select Send to, Compressed (zipped) Folder.

Windows now creates a new folder that contains compressed versions of the file(s) you selected. (This folder is distinguished by a little zipper on the folder icon, as shown in Figure 7.4.) You can now copy, move, or email this folder, which is a lot smaller than the original file(s).

note

The compressed folder is actually a file with a .ZIP extension, so it can be used with other compression/decompression programs, such as WinZip.

FIGURE 7.4
A compressed folder containing one or more files.

Extracting Files from a Compressed Folder

The process of decompressing a file is actually an *extraction* process. That's because you *extract* the original file(s) from the compressed folder.

In Windows XP and Windows Vista, this process is eased by the use of the Extraction Wizard. Follow these steps:

1. Right-click the compressed folder to display the pop-up menu.
2. Select Extract All.
3. When the Extraction Wizard launches, select a location for the extracted files and then click the Extract button to complete the process.

Copying Files to Another Computer

Of course, you're not limited to copying and moving files from one location to another on a single PC. You can also copy files to other PCs via either a network connection or some sort of portable disk drive.

Copying Files Over a Network

We talk more about network operations in Chapter 9, "Setting Up a Home Network." For now, it's important to know that if your PC is connected to a network and has file sharing activated, you can copy and move files from one network computer to another just as you can within folders on a single computer.

In Windows Vista, you access the other computers on your network by opening the Start menu and selecting Network. As you can see in Figure 7.5, each computer on your network is displayed in this window; double-click a PC's icon to view the public (sharable) folders on this computer. You can then copy files to or from any public folder on your network.

FIGURE 7.5

Viewing all the PCs on your home network in Windows Vista.

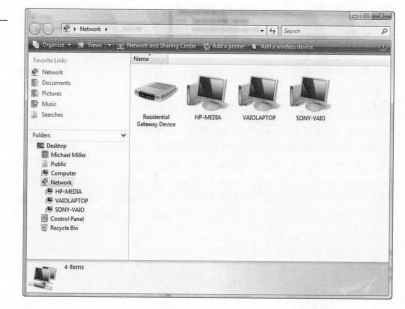

In Windows XP, all the publicly accessible folders on your network are displayed in the My Network Places window, shown in Figure 7.6. You open this window by clicking the My Network Places icon on the Start menu. Double-click any network place to copy files to or from that location.

tip

Your network computers are also accessible from the Network icon in the Windows Explorer Folders tree.

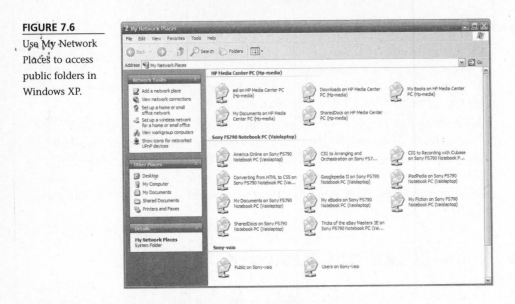

Copying Files with a Portable Drive

If you're not on a network, you can use a portable drive to transport files from one computer to another. The most popular type of portable drive today is the USB drive, such as the one shown in Figure 7.7, which stores computer data in flash memory. The drive itself is small enough to fit on a keychain, hence the nickname of "keychain drive." (Some people also called them "thumb drives.") You can find USB drives with capacities up to 4GB—more than big enough to hold even your biggest files.

FIGURE 7.7

Use a USB drive to transport files from one computer to another.

To use a USB drive, simply insert the device into an open USB port on your computer. Once inserted, the drive appears as a new drive in the Computer Explorer (My Computer in Windows XP). Double-click the USB drive icon to view the contents of the drive; you can then copy and paste files from your hard drive to the USB drive and vice versa. When you're finished copying files, just remove the USB device. It's that simple.

Copying Files Via Email

Another popular way to send files from one computer to another is via email. You can send any file as an email *attachment*; a file is literally attached to an email message. When the message is sent, the recipient can open or save the attached file when reading the message.

To learn how to send files as email attachments, turn to Chapter 20, "Sending and Receiving Email."

Backing Up Your Important Files

Then there's the issue of protecting your files. What do you do if your computer crashes, or your hard disk dies—are all your important files and documents totally lost?

Not so if you're prescient enough to back up your key files on a regular basis. The easiest way to do this is by connecting an external hard disk drive to your computer. Get a big enough external disk (200GB or larger), and you can copy your entire hard disk to the external drive. Then, if your system ever crashes, you can restore your backed-up files from the external drive to your computer's system unit.

External hard drives can be purchased for as little as $100 and are easy to connect via either USB or FireWire. You can use the proprietary backup software that comes with most external drives, or use Vista's Windows Backup utility. Whichever program you use, you should back up your data at least weekly—if not daily. That way you won't lose much fresh data if the worst happens.

note

Learn more about Windows Backup in Chapter 10, "Performing Routine Maintenance."

THE ABSOLUTE MINIMUM

Here are the key points to remember from this chapter:

- In Windows Vista, you manage your files and folders from the Documents Explorer; in Windows XP, you use the My Documents folder.

- Most of the operations you'll want to perform are accessible from the Windows Explorer Organize pull-down menu.

- If you accidentally delete a file, you may be able to recover it by opening the Recycle Bin window.

- If you need to share a really big file, consider compressing it into a compressed folder (also called a .ZIP file).

- To copy a file to another PC, you can copy the file over a network, send the file as an email attachment, or copy the file to a portable USB drive.

- You should back up your important files to an external hard drive, using Windows Backup or a similar backup utility.

PART III

UPGRADING AND MAINTAINING YOUR SYSTEM

8

ADDING NEW HARDWARE AND DEVICES TO YOUR SYSTEM

If you just purchased a brand-new, right-out-of-the-box personal computer, it probably came equipped with all the components you could ever want—or so you think. At some point in the future, however, you might want to expand your system—by adding a second printer, a scanner, an external hard drive, better speakers, a different keyboard, or something equally new and exciting.

Adding new hardware to your system is relatively easy if you know what you're doing. That's where this chapter comes in.

Most Popular Peripherals

When it comes to adding stuff to your PC, what are the most popular peripherals? Here's a list of hardware you can add to or upgrade on your system:

- **Hard drive**—To add more storage capacity to your system, or to perform periodic backups from your main hard disk. You can add either an internal hard drive (inside your PC's system unit) or an external model. (External hard drives are easiest to add and are great for backing up your data; they connect to your PC via either USB or FireWire cable and cost just a few hundred bucks.)

- **Memory card reader**—So you can read data from devices (such as digital cameras) that use various types of flash memory cards.

- **USB memory device**—To provide gigabytes of removable storage; you can transport the USB memory device from one computer to another, connecting to each PC's USB port.

- **Monitor**—To upgrade to a larger viewing area or even to a widescreen display—great for viewing DVD movies.

- **Video card**—To display higher-resolution pictures and graphics, provide smoother playback with visually demanding PC games, or power a second monitor for some high-end programming or development activities.

- **Sound card**—To improve the audio capabilities of your systems; this is particularly important if you're playing state-of-the-art PC games, listening to CDs or MP3 files, watching surround-sound DVD movies, or mixing and recording your own digital audio.

- **Speakers**—To upgrade the quality of your computer's sound system. (Surround-sound speaker systems with subwoofers are particularly popular.)

- **Keyboard**—To upgrade to a more ergonomic or wireless model.

- **Mouse**—To upgrade to a different type of controller (such as a trackball), a more fully featured unit, or a wireless model.

- **Joystick or other game controller**—To get better action with your favorite games.

- **Broadband modem**—To obtain high-speed DSL or cable Internet service.

- **CD-R/RW drive (burner)**—To add recordable/rewritable capabilities to your system.

- **DVD**—To add DVD capability to your system. (DVD drives can also play CDs.)

- **DVD-R/RW (burner)**—To burn your own DVD movies or to back up entire hard disks. (DVD burners can also be used to burn CDs, so you don't need two separate burners in your system.)
- **Printer**—To improve the quality of your printouts, to add color to your printouts, or to add photo-quality printing to your system. You can even add specialty label printers, which are great if you do a lot of mailing or eBay shipping.
- **Scanner**—So that you can scan photographs and documents into a digital format to store on your computer's hard drive.
- **PC camera**—So that you can send real-time video to friends and family or create your own Webcam on the Internet.
- **Network card**—So that you can connect your computer to other computers in a small home network.
- **Wireless router**—So that you can create a wireless network in your home—and share your broadband Internet connection among multiple computers.
- **Wireless network adapter**—So that you can connect your computer to any wireless network.
- **Digital media server**—To connect your PC to your home audio system so that you can listen to digital audio files and Internet radio on your home system.
- **Media Center extender**—Another way to listen to your PC's music on your home audio system—or even share recorded TV shows.

Understanding Ports

Everything that's hooked up to your PC is connected via some type of *port*. A port is simply an interface between your PC and another device—either internally (inside your PC's system unit) or externally (via a connector on the back of the system unit).

Internal ports are automatically assigned when you plug a new card in to its slot inside the system unit. As for external ports, many types are available—each optimized to send and receive specific types of data. Different types of hardware connect via different types of ports.

The most common types of external ports are shown in Table 8.1.

Table 8.1 External Ports

Connector	Type	Uses	Description
	USB	Almost anything—iPods, other portable audio players, digital cameras, PC cameras, printers, scanners, WiFi adapters, modems, external sound cards, mice, keyboards, joysticks, external hard drives, external CD/DVD drives, and USB memory devices	The most common type of connector in use today; USB is a faster, more intelligent form of the older serial port. USB devices can be added while your computer is still running, which you can't do with older types of ports.
	FireWire	Digital camcorders, external hard drives, external CD/DVD burners, and professional digital audio workstations	Also called IEEE 1394, the FireWire interface enables hot pluggable, high-speed data transmission.
	Keyboard/Mouse	Keyboards, mice, and other input devices	Sometimes called a PS/2 port, used to connect both wired and wireless input devices.
	Parallel	Printers, scanners	An older type of port, still used for some types of printers, that enables communications going in two directions at once.
	Serial	Modems, printers, mice	No longer widely used, serial ports enable communication one bit at a time, in one direction at a time.
	Gameport	Joysticks and other game controllers, as well as MIDI devices and musical instruments	This port is typically used to connect gaming controllers; it can also function as a MIDI port with the appropriate adapter.
	SCSI	Hard drives, CD/DVD drives	The *small computer system interface* (SCSI) port is a high-speed parallel interface, typically used for fast external data storage.

Adding New External Hardware

The easiest way to add a new device to your system is to connect it externally—which saves you the trouble of opening your PC's case.

Connecting Via a USB or FireWire Port

The most common external connector today is the USB port. USB is a great concept (and truly "universal") in that virtually every type of new peripheral comes in a USB version. Want to add a second hard disk? Don't open the PC case; get the USB version. Want to add a new printer? Forget the parallel port; get the USB version. Want to add a wireless network adapter? Don't bother with Ethernet cards; get the USB version.

USB is popular because it's so easy to use. When you're connecting a USB device, not only do you not have to open your PC's case, but also you don't even have to turn off your system when you add the new device. That's because USB devices are *hot swappable*. That means you can just plug the new device in to the port, and Windows will automatically recognize it in real-time.

The original USB standard, version 1.1, has been around for awhile and, if your PC is more than four or five years old, is probably the type of USB you have installed. The newer USB 2.0 protocol is much faster than USB 1.1 and is standard on all newer computers. For what it's worth, newer USB 2.0 ports are fully backward compatible with older USB 1.1 devices. You want to use newer USB 2.0 connections when you're installing devices that transfer a lot of data, such as external hard drives.

And let's not forget FireWire. Like USB devices, FireWire devices are hot-swappable, and very easy to connect. Like USB 2.0, FireWire is a very fast standard, which makes it ideal for connecting devices that move a lot of data, such as hard drives and camcorders. (It's also a little more expensive, which is why USB is still preferred for most devices.)

note

No matter how you're connecting a new device, make sure to read the installation instructions for the new hardware and follow the manufacturer's instructions and advice.

tip

If you connect too many USB devices, it's possible to run out of USB connectors on your PC. If that happens to you, buy an add-on USB hub, which lets you plug multiple USB peripherals into a single USB port.

To connect a new USB or FireWire device, follow these steps:

1. Find a free USB or FireWire port on your system unit and connect the new peripheral, as shown in Figure 8.1.

2. Windows should automatically recognize the new peripheral and either install the proper device driver automatically or prompt you to provide a CD or disk containing the driver file. Follow the onscreen instructions to finish installing the driver.

FIGURE 8.1
Connecting an external device via USB.

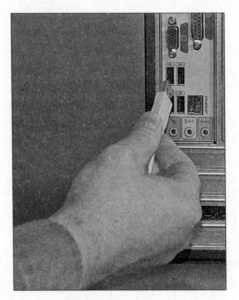

That's it! The only variation on this procedure is if the peripheral's manufacturer recommends using its own installation program, typically provided on an installation CD. If this is the case, follow the manufacturer's instructions to perform the installation and setup.

Connecting Via a Parallel or Serial Port

Connecting a new device to a parallel or serial port is slightly more involved than using USB or FireWire. These ports are *not* hot-swappable, which means that you have to turn off your system first, connect the new device, and then restart your system. Follow these steps:

note

A *device driver* is a small software program that enables your PC to communicate with and control a specific device. Windows XP includes built-in device drivers for many popular peripherals. If Windows doesn't include a particular driver, you typically can find the driver on the peripheral's installation disk or on the peripheral manufacturer's website.

1. Close Windows and turn off your computer.
2. Find an open port on the back of your system unit and connect the new peripheral.
3. Restart your system.
4. As Windows starts, it should recognize the new device and either install the proper drivers automatically or ask you to supply the device drivers (via CD-ROM or disk).
5. Windows installs the drivers and finishes the startup procedure. Your new device should now be operational.

Adding New Internal Hardware

Adding an internal device—usually through a plug-in card—is much more difficult than adding an external device primarily. That's because you have to use a screwdriver and get "under the hood" of your system unit. Other than the extra screwing and plugging, however, the process is much the same as with external devices.

Follow these steps to add a new card to your system:

1. Turn off your computer, and unplug the power cable.
2. Take the case off your system unit, per the manufacturer's instructions, as shown in Figure 8.2.
3. If the new card has switches or jumpers that need to be configured, do this before inserting the card into your system unit.
4. Find an open card slot inside the system unit and insert the new card according to the manufacturer's instructions, as shown in Figure 8.3.
5. After the card is appropriately seated and screwed in, put the case back on the system unit, plug back in the power, and restart your system.
6. After Windows starts, it should recognize the new device and automatically install the appropriate driver.

caution

You probably want to see whether the new component configures properly and works fine before you close up your system unit. For that reason, you might want to leave the case off until you're convinced everything is working okay and you don't need to do any more fiddling around inside your PC.

FIGURE 8.2
Removing your
system unit's
case.

FIGURE 8.3
Carefully insert-
ing a new inter-
nal card.

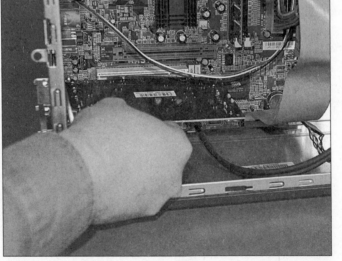

Connecting Portable Devices to Your PC

These days, a lot of the devices you connect to your PC really aren't computer
peripherals. Instead, these are gadgets that you use on their own but plug in to your
PC to share files.

What kinds of portable devices are we talking about? Here's a short list:

- Portable music players, such as Apple's popular iPod player
- Digital cameras
- Digital camcorders
- USB keychain memory devices
- Personal digital assistants (PDAs), such as Palm and Pocket PC devices

Most of these devices connect to a USB port on your PC; some camcorders use a FireWire connection instead. As you remember, both USB and FireWire ports are hot-swappable, which means that all you have to do is connect the device to the proper port—no major configuration necessary. In most cases, the first time you connect your device to your PC, you'll need to run some sort of installation utility to install the device's software on your PC's hard drive. Each subsequent time you connect the device, your PC should recognize it automatically and launch the appropriate software program.

Once your portable device is connected to your PC, what you do next is up to you. Most of the time, you'll be transferring files either from your PC to the portable device, or vice versa. Use the device's software program to perform these operations, or use Windows Explorer to copy files back and forth.

For example, you can use a USB memory device as a removable and portable memory storage system. One of these USB drives is smaller than a pack of chewing gum and can hold several gigabytes worth of data in electronic flash memory. Plug a USB memory device into your PC's USB port, and your PC recognizes it just as if it were another disk drive. You can then copy files from your PC to the USB drive to take your work (or your digital music or photo files) with you.

For more detailed information, see the instructions that came with your portable device.

note

Learn more about connecting a digital camera in Chapter 30, "Using Your PC with a Digital Camera." Learn more about connecting a portable music player in Chapter 35, "Using Your PC with an iPod or MP3 Player."

THE ABSOLUTE MINIMUM

Here's what you need to know if you're adding new equipment to your computer system:

- The easiest way to connect a new peripheral is via an external USB or FireWire connection.

- When you're installing an internal card, make sure that you turn off your PC before you open the system unit's case.

- In most cases, Windows automatically recognizes your new hardware and automatically installs all the necessary drivers.

- Connecting a portable device, such as a portable music player or digital camera, is typically done via an external USB port.

9

SETTING UP A HOME NETWORK

When you need to connect two or more computers together, you need to create a computer *network*.

Why would you want to connect two computers together? Maybe you want to transfer files or digital photos from one computer to another. Maybe you want to share an expensive piece of hardware (such as a printer) instead of buying one for each PC. Maybe you want to connect all your computers to the same Internet connection. Whatever your reasons, it's easy to set up and configure a simple home network. Read on to learn how!

How Networks Work

When it comes to physically connecting your network, you have two ways to go—wired or wireless. A wireless network is more convenient (no wires to run), but a wired network is faster. Which you choose depends on how you use the computers you network together.

If you use your network primarily to share an Internet connection or a printer or to transfer the occasional word processing file, wireless should work just fine. However, if you plan on transferring a lot of big files from one PC to another, or using your network for multiplayer gaming, you'll want to stick to a faster wired network.

Wired Networks

A *wired network* is the kind that requires you to run a bunch of cables from each PC to a central hub or router. In a wired network, you install a *network interface card (NIC)* in each PC and connect the cards via Ethernet cable. (Note that many new PCs come with built-in Ethernet capability, so you don't have to purchase an additional card.) Although this type of network is fast and easy enough to set up, you still have to deal with all those cables—which can be a hassle if your computers are in different areas of your house.

note

How quickly data is transferred across a network is measured in megabits per second, or Mbps. The bigger the Mbps number, the faster the network—and faster is always better than slower.

Most newer wired networks transfer data at 100Mbps; some older equipment works at a slower 10Mbps rate. The 100Mbps rate is ideal for transferring really big files, or for playing real-time PC games.

Wireless Networks

The alternative to a wired network is a *wireless network*. Wireless networks use radio frequency (RF) signals to connect one computer to another. The advantage of wireless, of course, is that you don't have to run any cables. This is a big plus if you have a large house with computers on either end or on different floors.

note

Wi-Fi is short for *wireless fidelity*.

The most popular wireless networks use the Wi-Fi standard. The original Wi-Fi standard, known as 802.11b, transferred data at 11Mbps—slower than

Fast Ethernet, but fast enough for most practical purposes. The current 802.11g standard transfers data at 54Mbps and is more than fast enough for most home networking needs.

Even faster is the upcoming new 802.11n standard (available in some "pre-n" equipment now on the market), which promises a blazing 540Mbps data transmission with a substantially longer range than current equipment. Current 802.11b and g equipment has a range of about 100 feet between transmitter and receiver; 802.11n promises a 160-foot range, with less interference from other wireless household devices.

> **caution**
>
> Any "pre-n" equipment purchased before the standard is finalized (sometime in 2008, perhaps) may not be fully compatible with the final technical standard.

In addition, you can combine wired and wireless technologies into a single network. Some PCs can connect directly to a wireless router via Ethernet, while others can connect via wireless WiFi signals. This type of mixed network is quite common.

Connecting and Configuring

Whether you're going wired or wireless, the setup is surprisingly easy. You have to assemble the appropriate cards, cables, and hubs, and then install and connect them all. After everything is hooked up properly, you then have to configure all the PCs on your network. The configuration can be made from within Windows or via the configuration utility provided with your network router or wireless adapter. You run this utility on each computer you connect to your network and then configure the network within Windows itself.

Setting Up a Wired or Wireless Network

Connecting multiple computers in a wired network is actually fairly simple. Just make sure that you do the proper planning beforehand and buy the appropriate hardware and cables; everything else is a matter of connecting and configuration.

How It Works

If you're setting up a wired network, you'll need to install a network interface card (NIC) in each computer you intend to connect. Each NIC then connects, via Ethernet cable, to the network *router*, which is a simple device that functions like the hub of a wheel and serves as the central point in your network. Then, after you make the physical connections, each computer has to be configured to function as part of the network and to share designated files, folders, and peripherals.

In a wireless network, the hub function is performed by a *wireless router*, sometimes called a *base station*. This device can make both wireless and wired connections; most base stations include four or more Ethernet connectors in addition to wireless capabilities.

You still need to connect your broadband modem and your main PC to the router via Ethernet cables, but all the other PCs on your network will connect wirelessly, via wireless adapters. These devices function as mini-transmitters/receivers to communicate with the base station. Wireless adapters can be small external devices that connect to the PC via USB, expansion cards that install inside your system unit, or PC cards that insert into a portable PC's card slot.

When complete, your network should look something like the one in Figure 9.1.

note

On a desktop PC, the wireless adapter connects to the PC's USB port; on a laptop PC, the wireless adapter is typically built into the computer.

FIGURE 9.1

A typical wireless network.

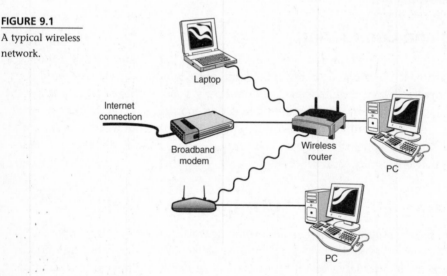

What You Need

Here's the specific hardware you'll need to set up your network:

- Network interface cards (on a wired network, one for each PC; on a wireless network, just one for the main PC)
- Network router (one for the entire network; use a wireless router for a wireless network)

■ Ethernet cables (on a wired network, one for each PC and another for your broadband modem; on a wireless network, one for the main PC and a second for the broadband modem)

■ Wireless network adapters (one for each client PC; these may already be built into notebook PCs)

Making the Connections

Naturally, you should follow the instructions that come with your networking hardware to properly set up your network. In general, however, here are the steps to take:

1. Power down your main computer and remove the system unit case.

2. Install a network interface card into an open expansion slot.

3. Close up the case, reboot the computer, and run the NIC installation software.

4. Run an Ethernet cable from your broadband modem to your router.

5. Run an Ethernet cable from the router to your main computer.

6. Connect your network router to a power source.

7. On your main computer, configure Windows to recognize your new network. (See "Configuring Windows for Your New Network," later in this chapter, for more details.)

note

If your host PC has built-in Ethernet networking, you can skip steps 1–3.

8. If you're connecting a wired network, connect each of the other computers to your network router via Ethernet cables.

9. If you're connecting a wireless network, move on to the second computer in your network and install a wireless networking adapter—either internally, via an expansion card, or externally, via USB. (Or, if your second PC is a laptop and doesn't have built-in wireless networking, insert a wireless networking PC card.)

10. Run the installation software to properly configure the wireless adapter.

11. On the second computer, configure Windows to recognize your new network.

12. Repeat steps 9–11 for each additional computer on your wireless network.

After you've connected all the computers on your network, you can proceed to configure any devices (such as printers) you want to share over the network. For example, if you want to share a single printer over the network, it connects to one of the network PCs (*not* directly to the router), and then is shared through that PC.

Configuring Windows for Your New Network

After your network hardware is all set up, you have to configure Windows to recognize and work with your new network. This is done differently depending on which version of Windows you have running on your computer.

caution

Some DSL and cable modems include a built-in router and firewall that might interfere with your regular wireless router. You may need to disable the router capabilities of your modem, or reconfigure your wireless router to avoid the conflict. Consult with your broadband Internet service provider and router manufacturer if you run into problems.

Configuring Windows Vista

Configuring Windows Vista for your new network is a piece of cake. First, open the Control Panel and select Network and Internet. When the next window appears, select Connect to a Network (in the Network and Sharing Center section) and let Windows do its thing; it should recognize the existing network and walk you through any necessary configuration. (This is one of the great things about Windows Vista; networking is much easier and more automatic than in previous versions.)

Configuring Windows XP

Configuring Windows XP for your new network is a little more complicated—although the task is made easier via the Network Setup Wizard. You start by opening the Control Panel and clicking Network and Internet Connections. When prompted, select Set Up or Change Your Home or Small Office Network. This launches the Network Setup Wizard.

Click the Next button to move through the introductory screens. When the Select a Connection Method screen appears, select This Computer Connects to the Internet Through a Residential Gateway or Through Another Computer on My Network and then click Next. When the next screen appears, enter a description for this PC (make and model is good), along with a unique name (such as "Main Computer"); then click Next. When the next screen appears, enter a name for your network and then click Next. Finally, on the next screen, check Turn On File and Printer Sharing. Continue clicking Next to finish the wizard, and Windows will be properly configured.

Setting Up Wireless Security

One of the issues with a wireless network is that all your data is just out there, broadcast over the air via radio waves, for anyone to grab. Fortunately, to keep outsiders from tapping into your wireless network, you can add wireless security to your network. This is done by assigning a fairly complex encryption code to your network; in order to tap into the network, a computer must know the code.

You can assign security codes to all the PCs in your network in one of several ways. First, most wireless hubs, routers, and adapters come with configuration utilities that let you activate this type of wireless security. If your wireless equipment has this type of configuration utility, use it.

Otherwise, you can use Windows' built-in wireless security. As you might suspect, this feature is different in Windows Vista than in Windows XP.

Wireless Security in Windows Vista

In Windows Vista, you enable wireless security via the Set Up a Wireless Router or Access Point Wizard. (Boy, is that a long name!) To get to this wizard, open the Control Panel, select Network and Internet, select Network and Sharing Center, and then choose Set Up a Connection or Network (in the Tasks panel). In the next window, select Set Up a Wireless Router or Access Point. This launches the wizard.

Click the Next button until Windows automatically detects your network hardware and settings. From here you can give your network an SSID name (different from the name assigned in the Network Setup Wizard) and then either automatically assign or manually enter a network key. The type and length of the key you choose depends on the type of encryption you choose; the strongest encryption comes from a 26-character WEP key.

note

SSID stands for *Service Set Identifier*, which is a set of letters or numbers that identify a particular wireless network.

After the key is assigned, write it down. You'll need to run this wizard on all the other PCs on the network and manually enter this same key for each computer. (Alternatively, Windows lets you save the key to a USB drive, which you can then transfer to your other PCs.) After all the work is done, only those PCs that have been assigned this specific key can connect to your wireless network—which means no more neighbors leeching off your wireless connection.

Wireless Security in Windows XP

In Windows XP, you configure wireless security via the Wireless Network Setup Wizard. To run the wizard, open the Control Panel and click the Wireless Network Setup Wizard icon.

After you've launched the wizard, you proceed just as you do with the similar wizard in Windows Vista. You'll choose an SSID name and then set your network key. As with the Vista wizard, make sure that you write down the key; you'll need it to activate the wireless security on the other PCs on your network.

Sharing Files and Folders Across the Network

After you have your network up and running, it's time to take advantage of it—by copying or moving files from one computer to another. To share files between the PCs on your network, you have to enable file sharing on the PC that contains those files. As with most networking functions, this is done differently in Windows Vista than in Windows XP.

caution

Be cautious about turning on file sharing. When you allow a folder to be shared, anyone accessing your network can access the contents of the folder.

File Sharing in Windows Vista

In Windows Vista, file sharing is activated from the Network and Sharing Center, shown in Figure 9.2. You access the Network and Sharing Center from the Windows Control Panel.

To turn on file sharing, simply click the down arrow next to the Public Folder Sharing option in the Sharing and Discovery section; then check the Turn On File Sharing option. You'll also want to click the down arrow next to the Public Folder Sharing option and select either the first or second option; the first option lets other users view but not change your files, whereas the second option lets other users fully edit the files in your Public folder.

With Windows Vista, the files you share are those located in the Public folder. If you want to share a file, just save it to the Public folder when you're finished.

File Sharing in Windows XP

With Windows XP, you can share files stored in the Shared Documents folder or in any other folder you specify. By default, file sharing is turned on for the Shared Documents folder; you have to manually activate file sharing for any other folder you want to use. You do this by following these steps:

1. Use My Computer to navigate to the folder that contains the file you want to share.

2. Right-click the folder icon and select Sharing and Security from the pop-up menu; this displays the Properties dialog box.

3. Select the Sharing tab, shown in Figure 9.3.

4. Check the Share This Folder on the Network option.

5. Click OK when done—then repeat this procedure for every folder you want to share on every computer connected to your network.

FIGURE 9.2

Activating file sharing in Windows Vista.

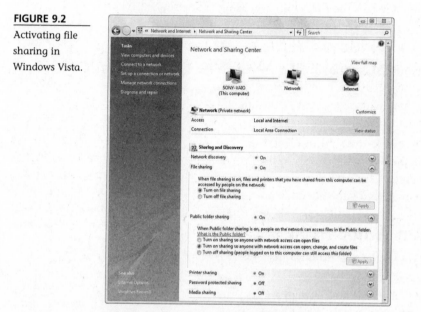

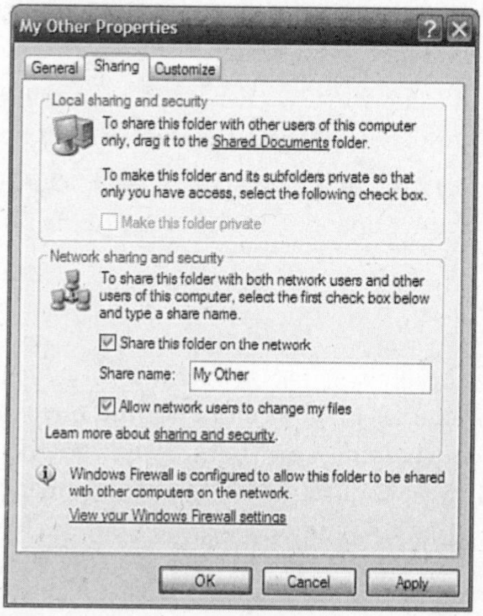

FIGURE 9.3

Activating file sharing on a folder-by-folder basis in Windows XP.

Sharing a Printer Across Your Network

To share a printer connected to one computer with all the other computers on your network, you have to activate printer sharing on the computer to which the printer is connected. You then have to manually install that printer on all the computers on your network.

As you've come to expect, this process is slightly different in Windows XP than in Windows Vista.

Printer Sharing in Windows Vista

Activating printer sharing in Windows Vista is quick and easy. It's done from the Network and Sharing Center, which you access from the Windows Control Panel.

After the Network and Sharing Center window is open, click the down arrow next to the Printer Sharing option. Check the Turn On Printer Sharing option, and you're good to go.

Printer Sharing in Windows XP

In Windows XP, the process is slightly more involved. Follow these steps:

1. Click the Start button to open the Start menu; then select Control Panel.

2. From the Control Panel, double-click Printers and Other Hardware; then select View Installed Printers or Fax Printers.

3. When the Printers and Faxes window opens, select the printer that you want to share; then click Share This Printer in the Printer Tasks panel.

4. When the printer Properties dialog box appears, select the Sharing tab and check the Share This Printer option. Edit the name of the printer if you want and then click OK.

note

Network configuration in Windows Vista is different from network configuration in Windows XP because Microsoft completely revamped Vista's networking functions. In Vista, networking is both easier to implement and more stable than in any previous version of Windows.

Installing a Shared Printer

After you've enabled printer sharing on your main PC, you have to install that shared printer on all the other computers on your network. You do this on a Windows Vista PC by opening the Control Panel, selecting Printer (in the Hardware and Sound section), and then clicking the Add a Printer button. (On Windows XP, open the Printers and Faxes window and select Add a Printer.) When prompted, opt to add a network printer; then follow the onscreen instructions from there to identify and select the network printer to install.

Sharing an Internet Connection

The other thing you're likely to share over your network is your Internet connection, especially if you have a broadband (cable or DSL) connection. For many users, this is the primary—and sometimes the sole—reason to set up a home network.

Sharing an Internet connection is relatively automatic, as soon as you connect your broadband Internet modem to your network router. Most broadband modems connect to the router via an Ethernet cable. Just plug the modem into the router, and the Internet connection is available to all computers connected to the network. It's that simple.

note

Learn more about sharing an Internet connection in Chapter 19, "Connecting to the Internet—At Home and on the Road."

THE ABSOLUTE MINIMUM

Here are the key things to remember about networking and the Internet:

- To share information or hardware between two or more computers, you have to connect them in a network.

- There are two basic types of networks—wired and wireless (WiFi).

- After all the networking hardware is installed and connected, you have to configure Windows to recognize your new network.

- If you've set up a wireless network, you should add wireless security to protect the network from outside intruders.

- To share folders between computers on your network, enable Windows' file sharing feature.

- All of these networking operations are easier in Windows Vista than they are in Windows XP; Microsoft significantly upgraded Vista to make networking easier and more stable.

- You can also use your home network to share a single printer and to share your broadband Internet connection.

10

PERFORMING ROUTINE MAINTENANCE

"An ounce of prevention is worth a pound of cure."

That old adage might seem trite and clichéd, but it's also true—especially when it comes to your computer system. Spending a few minutes a week on preventive maintenance can save you from costly computer problems in the future.

To make this chore a little easier, Windows includes several utilities to help you keep your system running smoothly. You should use these tools as part of your regular maintenance routine—or if you experience specific problems with your computer system.

Free Up Disk Space by Deleting Unnecessary Files

Even with today's humongous hard disks, you can still end up with too many useless files taking up too much hard disk space. Fortunately, Windows includes a utility that identifies and deletes unused files. The Disk Cleanup tool is what you want to use when you need to free up extra hard disk space for more frequently used files.

To use Disk Cleanup, follow these steps:

1. Click the Start button to display the Start menu.

2. Select All Programs, Accessories, System Tools, Disk Cleanup.

3. If prompted, select the drive you want to clean up.

4. Disk Cleanup automatically analyzes the contents of your hard disk drive.

5. When Disk Cleanup is finished analyzing, it presents its results in the Disk Cleanup dialog box, shown in Figure 10.1.

FIGURE 10.1

Use Disk Cleanup to delete unused files from your hard disk.

6. Select the Disk Cleanup tab.

7. You now have the option of permanently deleting various types of files: downloaded program files, temporary Internet files, offline web pages, deleted files in the Recycle Bin, and so forth. Select which files you want to delete.

8. Click OK to begin deleting.

note

You can safely choose to delete all these files *except* the setup log, Content Indexer, and Office Setup files, which are often needed by the Windows operating system.

Make Your Hard Disk Run Better by Defragmenting

If you think that your computer is taking longer than usual to open files or notice that your hard drive light stays on longer than usual, you might need to *defragment* your hard drive.

File fragmentation is sort of like taking the pieces of a jigsaw puzzle and storing them in different boxes along with pieces from other puzzles. The more dispersed the pieces are, the longer it takes to put the puzzle together. Spreading the bits and pieces of a file around your hard disk occurs whenever you install, delete, or run an application or when you edit, move, copy, or delete a file.

If you notice that your system takes longer and longer to open and close files or run applications, it's because these file fragments are spread all over the place. You fix the problem when you put all the pieces of the puzzle back in the right boxes— which you do by defragmenting your hard disk.

To defragment your hard disk, use Windows' Disk Defragmenter utility. In Windows Vista, Disk Defragmenter runs constantly in the background, automatically defragging your hard disk whenever your computer is turned on. In Windows XP, however, you have to run Disk Defragmenter manually—which you should do at least once a month. (You can also run the utility manually in Windows Vista, if you want to perform more immediate maintenance.)

To run Disk Defragmenter manually, follow these steps:

1. Click the Start button to display the Start menu.
2. Select All Programs, Accessories, System Tools, Disk Defragmenter to open the Disk Defragmenter utility.
3. If prompted, select the drive you want to defragment, typically drive C:.
4. In Windows Vista, you're shown Disk Defragmenter's current schedule; to defragment your hard disk now, click the Defragment Now button.

Defragmenting your drive can take awhile, especially if you have a large hard drive or your drive is really fragmented. So, you might want to start the utility and let it run while you are at lunch.

Perform a Hard Disk Checkup with ScanDisk

Any time you run an application, move or delete a file, or accidentally turn the power off while the system is running, you run the risk of introducing errors to your hard disk. These errors can make it harder to open files, slow down your hard disk, or cause your system to freeze when you open or save a file or an application.

Fortunately, you can find and fix most of these errors directly from within Windows. All you have to do is run the built-in ScanDisk utility.

To find and fix errors on your hard drive, follow these steps:

1. Click the Start button to display the Start menu.
2. Select Computer to open the Computer Explorer. (Or, in Windows XP, select My Computer to open the My Computer folder.)
3. Right-click the icon for the drive you want to scan, and then select the Properties option from the pop-up menu.
4. When the Properties dialog box appears, select the Tools tab.
5. Click the Check Now button to display the Check Disk dialog box.
6. Check both the options (Automatically Fix File System Errors and Scan for and Attempt Recovery of Bad Sectors).
7. Click Start.

Windows now scans your hard disk and attempts to fix any errors it encounters.

Keep Your Hardware in Tip-Top Condition

There's also a fair amount of preventive maintenance you can physically perform on your computer hardware. It's simple stuff, but can really extend the life of your PC.

System Unit

Your PC system unit has a lot of sensitive electronics inside—everything from memory chips to disk drives to power supplies. Check out these maintenance tips to keep your system unit from flaking out on you:

- Position your system unit in a clean, dust-free environment. Keep it away from direct sunlight and strong magnetic fields. In addition, make sure that your system unit and your monitor have plenty of air flow around them to keep them from overheating.
- Hook up your system unit to a surge suppressor to avoid damaging power spikes.
- Avoid turning on and off your system unit too often; it's better to leave it on all the time than incur frequent "power on" stress to all those delicate components. However...
- Turn off your system unit if you're going to be away for an extended period—anything longer than a few days.
- Check all your cable connections periodically. Make sure that all the connectors are firmly connected and all the screws properly screwed—and make

sure that your cables aren't stretched too tight or bent in ways that could damage the wires inside.

Keyboard

Even something as simple as your keyboard requires a little preventive maintenance from time to time. Check out these tips:

- Keep your keyboard away from young children and pets—they can get dirt and hair and Silly Putty all over the place, and they have a tendency to put way too much pressure on the keys.

- Keep your keyboard away from dust, dirt, smoke, direct sunlight, and other harmful environmental stuff. You might even consider putting a dust cover on your keyboard when it's not in use.

- Use a small vacuum cleaner to periodically sweep the dirt from your keyboard. (Alternately, you can use compressed air to *blow* the dirt away.) Use a cotton swab or soft cloth to clean between the keys. If necessary, remove the keycaps to clean the switches underneath.

- If you spill something on your keyboard, disconnect it immediately and wipe up the spill. Use a soft cloth to get between the keys; if necessary, use a screwdriver to pop off the keycaps and wipe up any seepage underneath. Let the keyboard dry thoroughly before trying to use it again.

Mouse

If you're a heavy Windows user, you probably put thousands of miles a year on your mouse. Just like a car tire, anything turning over that often needs a little tender loving care. Check out these mouse maintenance tips:

- If you use a mouse that has a roller ball mechanism, periodically open up the bottom of your mouse and remove the roller ball. Wash the ball with water (or perhaps a mild detergent). Use a soft cloth to dry the ball before reinserting it.

- While your mouse ball is removed, use compressed air or a cotton swab to clean dust and dirt from the inside of your mouse. (In extreme cases, you might need to use tweezers to pull lint and hair out of your mouse—or use a small knife to scrape packed crud from the rollers.)

note

If you have an optical mouse, you can skip these steps; there aren't any mouse balls to clean. (However, you still might need to keep pieces of lint from clogging the optical sensor.)

■ Always use a mouse pad—they really do help keep things rolling smoothly; plus, they give you good traction. (And while you're at it, don't forget to clean your mouse pad with a little spray cleaner—it can get dirty, too.)

Monitor

If you think of your monitor as a little television set, you're on the right track. Just treat your monitor as you do your TV, and you'll be okay. That said, look at these preventive maintenance tips:

■ As with all other important system components, keep your monitor away from direct sunlight, dust, and smoke. Make sure that it has plenty of ventilation, especially around the back; don't cover the rear cooling vents with paper or any other object, and don't set anything bigger than a small plush toy on top of the cabinet.

■ Don't place any strong magnets in close proximity to your monitor. (This includes external speakers.)

■ *With your monitor turned off*, periodically clean the monitor screen. For a traditional CRT monitor, spray standard glass cleaner on a soft cloth (antistatic type, if possible), and then wipe the screen clean. For an LCD flat-panel monitor, use water to dampen a lint-free cloth, and then wipe the screen; do not spray liquid directly on the screen. Do not use any cleaner that contains alcohol or ammonia; these chemicals may damage an LCD screen. (You can, however, use commercial cleaning wipes specially formulated for LCD screens.)

■ Don't forget to adjust the brightness and contrast controls on your monitor every now and then. Any controls can get out of whack—plus, your monitor's performance will change as it ages, and simple adjustments can often keep it looking as good as new.

Printer

Your printer is a complex device with a lot of moving parts. Follow these tips to keep your printouts in good shape:

■ Use a soft cloth, mini-vacuum cleaner, and/or compressed air to clean the inside and outside of your printer on a periodic basis. In particular, make sure that you clean the paper path of all paper shavings and dust.

■ If you have an ink-jet printer, periodically clean the ink jets. Run your printer's cartridge cleaning utility, or use a small pin to make sure that they don't get clogged.

- If you have a laser printer, replace the toner cartridge as needed. When you replace the cartridge, remember to clean the printer cleaning bar and other related parts, per the manufacturer's instructions.
- *Don't* use alcohol or other solvents to clean any rubber or plastic parts—you'll do more harm than good!

Backing Up Your Important Data with Windows Backup

One more piece of maintenance can make or break the way you use your computer. I'm talking about the necessity of backing up your data files so that if your computer ever crashes or goes dead, you have backup copies of everything that's important to you—including your work documents, music files, digital photos, and the like.

Choosing a Backup Device

The easiest way to back up your data files is to use an external hard disk. These run anywhere from $100 to a few hundred dollars, depending on the size of the hard disk. You should get an external hard disk that's about as big as the hard disk in your main PC; if you have a 200GB hard drive on your PC, get a 200GB external hard disk.

> **caution**
>
> For many users, the scariest thing about a PC data disaster is losing all their valuable digital photographs. If you don't have backups of your digital files, you could lose several years' worth of photos if your hard disk crashes.

Most external hard drives connect to your PC via USB; some bigger disks use the faster FireWire connection. Either type of connection is fine, and both are easy enough to connect and install.

After the external hard drive is connected, you need to run a software program that automates the backup process. Most external hard drives come with their own proprietary backup programs; these are typically easy to use and get the job done. You can also use one of the many third-party backup programs sold at your local computer or electronics store, such as Acronis True Image (www.acronis.com) or CMS Bounceback Professional (www.cmsproducts.com/product_bounceback_software.htm). You'll typically pay from $50 to $100 for one of these programs.

Automatic Backup in Windows Vista

If your PC is running Windows Vista, you have a backup program built into the operating system. Windows Backup (on all but the Home Basic edition) lets you schedule automatic backups of your key data. You launch Windows Backup by clicking the Start button and then selecting All Programs, Accessories, System Tools, Backup Status, and Configuration.

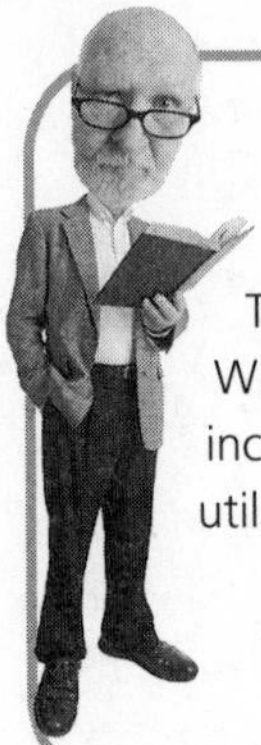

When the window shown in Figure 10.2 appears, click the Back Up Files button; then click the Set Up Automatic File Backup option. Windows scans your system for a backup device (typically an external hard disk) and asks you to select that device for your backup.

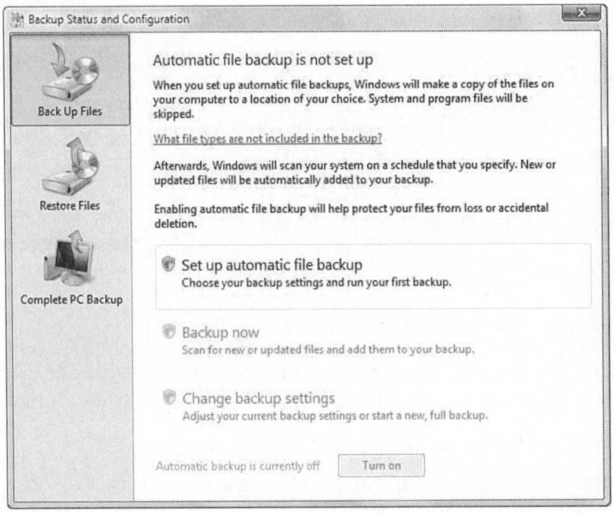

tip

The Home Edition of Windows XP does not include a built-in backup utility.

FIGURE 10.2

Use Windows Backup (in Windows Vista) to back up your valuable data files.

The next screen, shown in Figure 10.3, asks you what types of files you want to back up. You can choose from picture, music, video, email, and other common types of files.

Click Next, and select how often (and when) you want to back up your files. As shown in Figure 10.4, you can choose to back up daily, weekly, or monthly; the more often you back up, the better. When finished, click the Save Settings and Start Backup button. Vista starts your first disk backup.

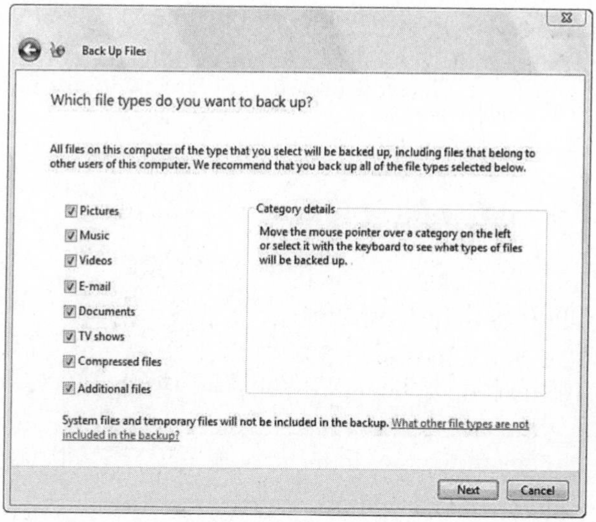

FIGURE 10.3

Select which types of files you want to back up.

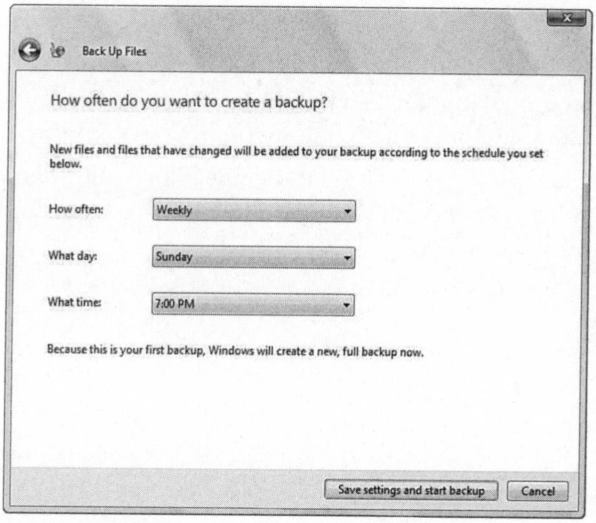

FIGURE 10.4

Setting your backup schedule

CompletePC Backup

In addition to this standard Windows Backup utility, the Business, Enterprise, and Ultimate versions of Vista come with an enhanced type of backup, dubbed CompletePC, that creates an exact image of all the files on your system—including program and system files. Most backups copy only data files; a system image backup copies every file on your hard drive. When you recover from a system failure, a system image backup lets you restore your complete system exactly the way it was before the crash. (With a traditional data backup, you'll have to reinstall your operating system and programs from their installation disks before you restore your backed-up data files.)

If you're running the Business, Enterprise, or Ultimate editions of Vista and you have a big enough external hard drive, doing a CompletePC full-system backup is the way to go. Otherwise, protect your data files (only) with the normal Windows Backup utility.

THE ABSOLUTE MINIMUM

Here are the key points to remember from this chapter:

- Dedicating a few minutes a week to PC maintenance can prevent serious problems from occurring in the future.
- To delete unused files from your hard disk, use the Disk Cleanup utility.
- To defragment a fragmented hard disk, use the Disk Defragmenter utility (which automatically runs in the background with Windows Vista).
- To find and fix hard disk errors, use the ScanDisk utility.
- Make sure that you keep all your computer hardware away from direct sunlight, dust, and smoke, and make sure that your system unit has plenty of ventilation.
- Invest in a small handheld vacuum cleaner or a can of compressed air to better clean dust out of the small spaces in your system.
- Protect your valuable files by backing them up to an external hard disk— using either a third-party backup program or, in Windows Vista, the Windows Backup utility.

11

DEALING WITH COMMON PROBLEMS

Computers aren't perfect. It's possible—although unlikely—that at some point in time, something will go wrong with your PC. It might refuse to start, it might freeze up, it might crash and go dead. Yikes!

When something goes wrong with your computer, there's no need to panic. (Even though that's what you'll probably feel like doing.) Most PC problems have easy-to-find causes and simple solutions. The key thing is to keep your wits about you, and attack the situation calmly and logically—following the advice you'll find in this chapter.

How to Troubleshoot Computer Problems

No matter what kind of computer-related problem you're experiencing, there are six basic steps you should take to track down the cause of the problem. Work through these steps calmly and deliberately, and you're likely to find what's causing the current problem—and then be in a good position to fix it yourself:

1. **Don't panic!**—Just because there's something wrong with your PC is no reason to fly off the handle. Chances are there's nothing seriously wrong. Besides, getting all panicky won't solve anything. Keep your wits about you and proceed logically, and you can probably find what's causing your problem and get it fixed.

2. **Check for operator errors**—In other words, something *you* did wrong. Maybe you clicked the wrong button, or pressed the wrong key, or plugged something into the wrong jack or port. Retrace your steps and try to duplicate your problem. Chances are the problem won't recur if you don't make the same mistake twice.

3. **Check that everything is plugged into the proper place and that the system unit itself is getting power**—Take special care to ensure that all your cables are *securely* connected—loose connections can cause all sorts of strange results.

4. **Make sure you have the latest versions of all the software installed on your system**—While you're at it, make sure you have the latest versions of device drivers installed for all the peripherals on your system.

5. **Try to isolate the problem by *when* and *how* it occurs**—Walk through each step of the process to see if you can identify a particular program or driver that might be causing the problem.

6. **When all else fails, call in professional help**—If you think it's a Windows-related problem, contact Microsoft's technical support department. If you think it's a problem with a particular program, contact the tech support department of the program's manufacturer. If you think it's a hardware-related problem, contact the manufacturer of your PC or the dealer you bought it from. (And don't rule out where you purchased the computer—many computer dealers have helpful tech support

note

Does a particular computer problem have you stumped? Then learn more about troubleshooting computer problems in my companion book, *Absolute Beginner's Guide to Upgrading and Fixing Your PC* (Que, 2003), available wherever computer books are sold.

departments.) The pros are there for a reason—when you need technical support, go and get it.

Using Windows Troubleshooters

Windows includes several interactive utilities that can help you diagnose and fix common system problems. These utilities are called Troubleshooters, and they walk you step-by-step through a series of questions. All you have to do is answer the questions in the Troubleshooter, and you'll be led to the probable solution to your problem.

To run a Troubleshooter, open the Start menu and select Help and Support. In Windows Vista, click the Troubleshooting icon; in Windows XP, click the Fixing a Problem link. When the next screen appears, click the link for the type of problem you're having, and then click the link to start a specific Troubleshooter. All you have to do now is follow the interactive directions to troubleshoot your particular hardware problem.

Troubleshooting in Safe Mode

If you're having trouble getting Windows to start, it's probably because some setting is set wrong or some driver is malfunctioning. The problem is, how do you get into Windows to fix what's wrong, when you can't even start Windows?

The solution is to hijack your computer before Windows gets hold of it and force it to start *without* whatever is causing the problem. You do this by watching the screen as your computer boots up and pressing the F8 key just before Windows starts to load. This displays the Windows startup menu, where you select Safe mode.

Safe mode is a special mode of operation that loads Windows in a very simple configuration. Once in Safe mode, you can look for device conflicts, restore incorrect or corrupted device drivers, or restore your system to a prior working configuration (using the System Restore utility, discussed later in this chapter).

note

Depending on the severity of your system problem, Windows might start in Safe mode automatically.

What to Do When Windows Freezes

Probably the most common computer trouble is the freeze-up. That's what happens when your PC just stops dead in its tracks. The screen looks normal, but nothing works—you can't type onscreen, you can't click any buttons, nothing's happening.

If your system happens to freeze up, the good news is that there's probably nothing wrong with your computer hardware. The bad news is that there's probably something funky happening with your operating system.

This doesn't mean your system is broken. It's just a glitch. And you can recover from glitches. Just remember not to panic and to approach the situation calmly and rationally.

What Causes Windows to Freeze?

What causes Windows to freeze? There can be many different causes of a Windows freeze, including the following:

- You might be running an older software program or game that isn't compatible with your version of Windows. If so, upgrade the program.

- A memory conflict might exist between applications, or between an application and Windows itself. Try running fewer programs at once, or running problematic programs one at a time to avoid potential memory conflicts.

- You might not have enough memory installed on your system. Upgrade the amount of memory in your PC.

- You might not have enough free hard disk space on your computer. Delete any unnecessary files from your hard drive.

- Your hard disk might be developing errors or bad sectors. Check your hard disk for errors. (See the ScanDisk section in Chapter 10, "Performing Routine Maintenance.")

Dealing with Frozen Windows

When Windows freezes, you need to get it unfrozen and up and running again. The way to do this is to shut down your computer. You may be able to do this by pressing Ctrl+Alt+Del to display the Windows Task Manager, and then selecting Shut Down from the toolbar. If that doesn't work, press and hold down the power button on the front of your PC's system unit until your system shuts off. You can then start up your computer again; chances are everything will be working just fine this time around.

If your system crashes or freezes frequently, however, you should call in a pro. These kinds of problems can be tough to track down by yourself when you're dealing with Windows.

note

Just to give you an idea as to what kinds of problems can cause a computer crash, the three most recent crashes I've had to deal with (on my own PC, and on friends' units) were caused by (1) a bad power supply, (2) a bad motherboard, and (3) a bad auxiliary hard disk. All three computers had the same symptoms, which were caused by three completely different problems!

Dealing with a Frozen Program

Sometimes Windows works fine but an individual software program freezes. Fortunately, Windows XP is an exceptionally safe environment. When an individual application crashes or freezes, it seldom messes up your entire system. You can use a utility called the Windows Task Manager to close the problem application without affecting other Windows programs.

When a Windows application freezes or crashes, press Ctrl+Alt+Del; this opens the Windows Task Manager, shown in Figure 11.1. Select the Applications tab and then select the frozen application from the list. Now click the End Task button. After a few seconds, a Wait/Shutdown window appears; confirm that you want to shut down the selected application; then, click the End Task button.

FIGURE 11.1
Use the Windows Task Manager to end nonresponding programs.

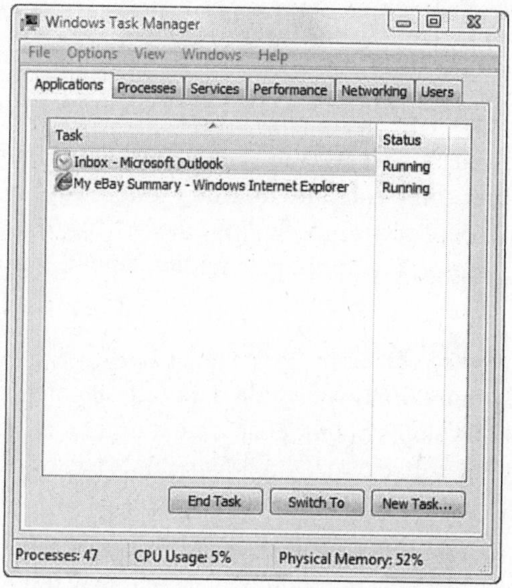

This closes the offending application and lets you continue your work in Windows.

If you have multiple applications that crash on a regular basis, the situation probably can be attributed to insufficient memory. See your computer dealer about adding more RAM to your system.

Dealing with a Major Crash

Perhaps the worst thing that can happen to your computer system is that it crashes—completely shuts down, without any warning. If this happens to you, start by not panicking. Stay calm, take a few deep breaths, and then get ready to get going again.

You should always wait about 60 seconds after a computer crashes before you try to turn on your system again. This gives all the components time to settle down and—in some cases—reset themselves. Just sit back and count to 60 (slowly), then press your system unit's "on" button.

Nine times out of ten, your system will boot up normally, as if nothing unusual has happened. If this is what happens for you, great! If, on the other hand, your system doesn't come back up normally, you'll need to start troubleshooting the underlying problem, as discussed later in this chapter.

Even if your system comes back up as usual, the sudden crash might have done some damage. A system crash can sometimes damage any software program that was running at the time, as well as any documents that were open when the crash occurred. You might have to reinstall a damaged program or recover a damaged document from a backup file.

Undoing the Damage with System Restore

Perhaps the best course of action when your system crashes is to use Microsoft's System Restore utility. This utility can automatically restore your system to the state it was in before the crash occurred—and save you the trouble of reinstalling any damaged software programs. It's a great safety net for when things go wrong.

Setting System Restore Points

System Restore works by monitoring your system and noting any changes that are made when you install new applications. Each time it notes a change, it automatically creates what it calls a *restore point*. A restore point is basically a "snapshot" of key system files just before the new application is installed.

Just to be safe, System Restore also creates a new restore point after every 10 hours of system use. You can also choose to manually create a new restore point at any moment in time. It's a good idea to do this whenever you make any major change to your system, such as installing a new piece of hardware.

To set a manual restore point, follow these steps:

1. Click the Start button to display the Start menu.
2. Select All Programs, Accessories, System Tools, System Restore to open the System Restore window.
3. Select Create a Restore Point and click Next.
4. You are prompted to enter a description for this new restore point; do this.
5. Click the Create button.

That's all you have to do. Windows notes the appropriate system settings and stores them in its System Restore database.

Restoring Your System

If something in your system goes bad, you can run System Restore to set things right. Pick a restore point before the problem occurred (such as right before a new installation), and System Restore will then undo any changes made to monitored files since the restore point was created. This restores your system to its pre-installation—that is, *working*—condition.

To restore your system from a restore point, follow these steps:

1. Click the Start button to display the Start menu.

2. Select All Programs, Accessories, System Tools, System Restore to open the System Restore window.

3. When the System Restore window appears, as shown in Figure 11.2, you can choose to restore to Windows' recommended restore point or to a different restore point. Make your choice and click Next.

4. If you select Choose a Different Restore Point, you are presented with a list of available restore points. Make your choice and click Next.

5. When the confirmation screen appears, click the Finish button.

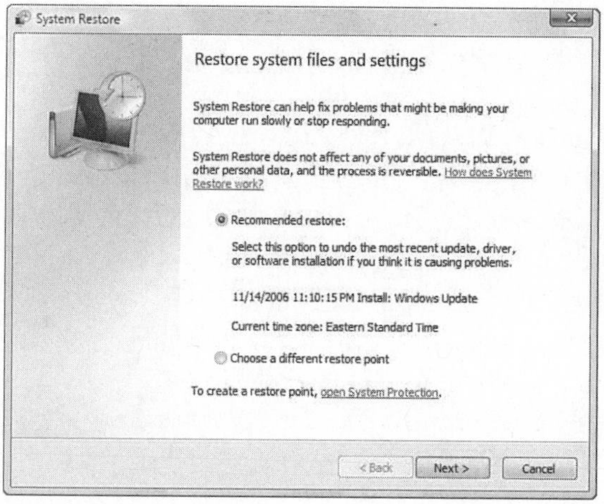

FIGURE 11.2

Use the System Restore utility to restore damaged programs or system files.

Windows now starts to restore your system. You should make sure that all open programs are closed because Windows will need to be restarted during this process.

When the process is complete, your system should be back in tip-top shape. Note, however, that it might take a half-hour or more to complete a system restore—so you'll have time to order a pizza and eat dinner before the operation is done!

caution

System Restore will help you recover any damaged programs and system files, but it won't help you recover any damaged documents or data files.

THE ABSOLUTE MINIMUM

Here are the key points to remember from this chapter:

- If something strange happens to your computer system, the first thing to do is *not panic!*

- Most so-called computer problems are actually caused by operator error, so back up and do whatever it is you did one more time—carefully, this time.

- You can shut down frozen programs from the Windows Task Manager, which you display by pressing Ctrl+Alt+Del.

- You can also use the Windows Task Manager to manually reboot your computer—and if this doesn't work, simply press and hold down the power button on the front of your PC's system unit.

- Some problems can be fixed from Windows Safe mode; to enter Safe mode, restart your computer and press F8 before the Windows start screen appears.

- If your system misbehaves after installing new software or hardware, use the System Restore utility to return your system to its pre-installation state.

12

PROTECTING YOUR PC FROM VIRUSES, SPAM, AND OTHER ONLINE NUISANCES

Not all computer problems come from software bugs and hardware glitches. When you connect your PC to the Internet, you open up a whole new world of potential dangers—viruses, spam, computer attacks, and more.

Fortunately, it's easy to protect your computer and your family from these dangers. All you need are a few software utilities—and a lot of common sense!

Safeguarding Your System from Computer Viruses

A *computer virus* is a malicious software program designed to do damage to your computer system by deleting files or even taking over your PC to launch attacks on other systems. A virus attacks your computer when you launch an infected software program, launching a "payload" that oftentimes is catastrophic.

Signs of Infection

How do you know whether your computer system has been infected with a virus?

In general, whenever your computer starts acting different from normal, it's possible that you have a virus. You might see strange messages or graphics displayed on your computer screen or find that normally well-behaved programs are acting erratically. You might discover that certain files have gone missing from your hard disk or that your system is acting sluggish—or failing to start at all. You might even find that your friends are receiving emails from you (that you never sent) that have suspicious files attached.

If your computer exhibits one or more of these symptoms—especially if you've just downloaded a file from the Internet or received a suspicious email message—the prognosis is not good. Your computer is probably infected.

How to Catch a Virus

Whenever you share data with another computer or computer user, you risk exposing your computer to potential viruses. There are many ways you can share data and many ways a virus can be transmitted:

- Opening an infected file attached to an email message or instant message
- Launching an infected program file downloaded from the Internet
- Sharing a data CD, USB memory drive, or floppy disk that contains an infected file
- Sharing over a network a computer file that contains an infected file

Of all these methods, the most common means of virus infection is via email—with instant messaging close behind. Whenever you open a file attached to an email message or instant message, you stand a good chance of infecting your computer system with a virus—even if the file was sent by someone you know and trust. That's because many viruses "spoof" the sender's name, thus making you think the file is from a friend or colleague. The bottom line is that no email or instant message attachment is safe unless you were expressly expecting it.

Practicing Safe Computing

Because you're not going to completely quit doing any of these activities, you'll never be 100% safe from the threat of computer viruses. There are, however, some steps you can take to reduce your risk:

- Don't open email attachments from people you don't know—or even from people you *do* know, if you aren't expecting them. (That's because some viruses can hijack the address book on an infected PC, thus sending out infected email that the owner isn't even aware of.)
- Don't accept any files sent to you via instant messaging.
- Download files only from reliable file archive websites, such as Download.com (www.download.com) and Tucows (www.tucows.com).
- Don't execute programs you find in Usenet newsgroups or posted to web message boards or blogs.
- Don't click links sent to you from strangers via instant messaging or in a chat room.
- Share disks and files only with users you know and trust.
- Use antivirus software—and keep it up-to-date with the most recent virus definitions.

> **caution**
>
> If you remember nothing else from this chapter, remember this: *Never open an unexpected file attachment.* Period!

These precautions—especially the first one about not opening email attachments—should provide good insurance against the threat of computer viruses.

Disinfecting Your System with Antivirus Software

Antivirus software programs are capable of detecting known viruses and protecting your system against new, unknown viruses. These programs check your system for viruses each time your system is booted and can be configured to check any programs you download from the Internet. They're also used to disinfect your system if it becomes infected with a virus.

The most popular antivirus programs include

- AVG Anti-Virus (www.grisoft.com)
- Kaspersky Anti-Virus Personal (www.kaspersky.com)
- McAfee VirusScan (www.mcafee.com)
- Norton AntiVirus (www.symantec.com)
- PC-cillin (www.trendmicro.com)
- Windows Live OneCare (www.windowsonecare.com)

All of these programs do a good job—although their prices vary considerably. For example, AVG Anti-Virus is available for free (and does a great job), Norton AntiVirus costs $39.99 for a one-year subscription, and Windows Live OneCare costs $49.95 per year—although you can use it on up to three different PCs, which makes it a real bargain for multiple-PC households.

Whichever antivirus program you choose, you'll need to go online periodically to update the virus definition database the program uses to look for known virus files. As new viruses are created every week, this file of known viruses must be updated accordingly.

> **caution**
>
> Your antivirus software is next to useless if you don't update it at least weekly. An outdated antivirus program won't be capable of recognizing—and protecting against—the very latest computer viruses.

Fighting Email Spam

Viruses aren't the only annoying things delivered via email. If you're like most users, well over half the messages delivered to your email inbox are unsolicited, unauthorized, and unwanted—in other words, *spam*. These spam messages are the online equivalent of the junk mail you receive in your postal mailbox, and it's a huge problem.

Although it's probably impossible to do away with 100% of the spam you receive (you can't completely stop junk mail, either), there are steps you can take to reduce the amount of spam you have to deal with. The heavier your spam load, the more steps you can take.

Protecting Your Email Address

Spammers accumulate email addresses via a variety of methods. Some use high-tech methods to harvest email addresses listed on public web pages and message board postings. Others use the tried-and-true approach of buying names from list brokers. Still others automatically generate addresses using a "dictionary" of common names and email domains.

One way to reduce the amount of spam you receive is to limit the public use of your email address. It's a simple fact: The more you expose your email address, the more likely it is that a spammer will find it—and use it.

To this end, you should avoid putting your email address on your web page, or your company's web page. You should also avoid including your email address in any postings you make to web-based message boards or Usenet newsgroups. In addition, you should most definitely not include your email address in any of the conversations you have in chat rooms or via instant messaging.

Another strategy is to actually use *two* email addresses. Take your main email address (the one you get from your ISP) and hand it out only to a close circle of friends and family; do *not* use this address to post any public messages or to register at any websites. Then obtain a second email address (you can get a free one at www.hotmail.com, mail.yahoo.com, or gmail.google.com) and use that one for all your public activity. When you post on a message board or newsgroup, use the second address. When you order something from an online merchant, use the second address. When you register for website access, use the second address. Over time, the second address will attract the spam; your first email address will remain private and relatively spam-free.

Blocking Spammers in Your Email Programs

Most email programs include some sort of spam filtering. As you might suspect, newer programs have more robust spam filters than do older programs.

For example, the older Outlook Express program doesn't even have a spam filter built in. Instead, the program lets you manually block messages from known spammers by using the Blocked Senders List feature. When you receive a spam message in your inbox, select the message and then select Message, Block Sender. In the future, all messages from this sender will automatically be deleted.

For more robust spam fighting, you can upgrade to Microsoft Outlook. Outlook 2003 includes four levels of spam filtering, which you can access by selecting Actions, Junk E-Mail, Junk E-Mail Options. The four levels are Low (blocks the obvious spam messages), High (blocks most spam messages, but might also block some nonspam email), Safe Lists Only (blocks all email except from people on your Safe Senders List), and No Automatic Filtering (turns off the spam filter).

tip

If you do have to leave your email address in a public forum, you can insert a *spamblock* into your address—an unexpected word or phrase that, although easily removed, will confuse the software spammers use to harvest addresses. For example, if your email address is johnjones@myisp.com, you might change the address to read johnSPAMBLOCKjones@myisp.com. Other users will know to remove the SPAMBLOCK from the address before emailing you, but the spam harvesting software will be foiled.

note

Outlook Express doesn't actually block any email messages; the messages are still received by your computer, but sent immediately to the Delete folder—where they can still be viewed until you delete the contents of the folder. In fact, it's a good idea to browse through the Delete folder, just in case a "good" message has accidentally been tagged as spam, which sometimes happens.

Outlook 2007 features an even more advanced junk email filter, as does Windows Mail, the email program included with Windows Vista. Bottom line: The newer the email program, the better its spam-fighting capabilities. This may be reason enough to upgrade from Outlook Express in Windows XP to Windows Mail in Windows Vista, or from Outlook 2003 to Outlook 2007.

Using Anti-Spam Software

If the amount of spam in your inbox becomes particularly onerous, you might want to consider using an anti-spam software program. Most anti-spam software uses some combination of spam blocking or content filtering to keep spam messages from ever reaching your inbox; their effectiveness varies, but they will decrease the amount of spam you receive to some degree.

The most popular anti-spam software includes

- ANT 4 MailChecking (www.ant4.com)
- MailWasher (www.mailwasher.net)
- RoadBlock (www.roadblock.net)

In addition, many antivirus and content filtering programs also include anti-spam modules. If you're already using an antivirus program or security suite, check whether it offers spam email filtering.

Resisting Phishing Scams

Phishing is a technique used by online scam artists to steal your identity by tricking you into disclosing valuable personal information, such as passwords, credit card numbers, and other financial data. If you're not careful, you can mistake a phishing email for a real one—and open yourself up to identity theft.

A phishing scam typically starts with a phony email message that appears to be from a legitimate source, such as your bank, eBay, or PayPal. (Figure 12.1 shows just such a fake message.) When you click the link in the phishing email, you're taken to a fake website masquerading as the real site, complete with logos and official-looking text. You're encouraged to enter your personal information into the forms on the web page; when you do so, your information is sent to the scammer, and you're now a victim of identity theft. When your data falls into the hands of criminals, it can be used to hack into your online accounts, make unauthorized charges on your credit card, and maybe even drain your bank account.

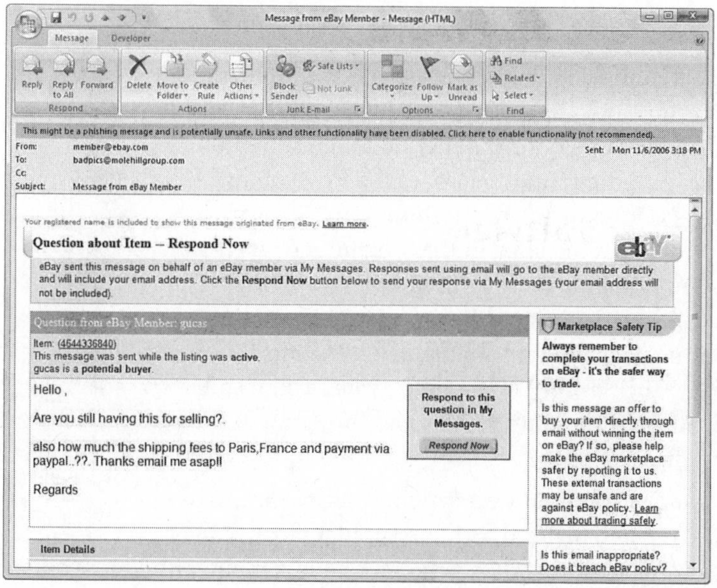

FIGURE 12.1

A phony phishing message—it looks just like the real thing!

Until recently, the only guard against phishing scams was common sense. That is, you should never click through a link in an email message that asks for any type of personal information—whether that be your bank account number or eBay password. Even if the email *looks* official, it probably isn't; legitimate institutions and websites never include this kind of link in their official messages. Instead, you should access your personal information only by using your web browser to go directly to the website in question. Don't link there!

This all changes in Windows Vista, which includes a new feature called the Microsoft Phishing Filter. This filter works within both Windows Mail and Internet Explorer 7 and compares all the links in your Windows Mail email messages to an online list of known phishing websites. If the link matches a fraudulent site, Windows Mail displays a warning message at the top of the message.

If you attempt to click a link to a known phishing site, the Microsoft Phishing Filter blocks access to the site, changes the Address Bar to red, navigates to a neutral page, and displays a warning message. If you attempt to click a link to a site that is not on the list of known fraudulent sites but behaves similarly to such sites, the Microsoft Phishing Filter changes the Address Bar to yellow and cautions you about potentially suspicious content.

But whether you're using Windows Mail or any other email program, use your head. Don't click through suspicious email links, and don't give out your personal information and passwords unless you're sure you're dealing with an official (and not just an official-looking) site!

Hunting Down Spyware

Another growing online nuisance is the proliferation of *spyware* programs. These are programs that install themselves on your computer and then surreptitiously send information about the way you use your PC to some interested third party. Spyware typically gets installed in the background when you're installing another program. One of the biggest sources of spyware are peer-to-peer music-trading networks (*not* legitimate online music stores, such as the iTunes Store); when you install the file-trading software, the spyware is also installed.

note

Learn more about music-trading networks in Chapter 34, "Downloading and Playing Digital Music."

Having spyware on your system is nasty, almost as bad as being infected with a computer virus. Some spyware programs will even hijack your computer and launch pop-up windows and advertisements when you visit certain web pages. If there's spyware on your computer, you definitely want to get rid of it.

Unfortunately, most antivirus programs won't catch spyware because spyware isn't a virus. To track down and uninstall these programs, then, you need to run an anti-spyware utility, such as Windows Defender (shown in Figure 12.2), which is included free with Windows Vista—and available as a free download for Windows XP users.

FIGURE 12.2

Finding hidden spyware programs with Windows Defender.

Here are some of the best of these spyware fighters:

- Ad-Aware (www.lavasoftusa.com)
- Windows Defender (www.microsoft.com/athome/security/spyware/software/)
- Spy Sweeper (www.webroot.com)
- Spybot Search & Destroy (www.safer-networking.org)
- ZoneAlarm Anti-Spyware (www.zonelabs.com)

In addition, some of the major Internet security suites, such as Norton Internet Security and the McAfee Internet Security Suite, include anti-spyware modules. Check the program's feature list before you buy.

Defending Against Computer Attacks

Connecting to the Internet is a two-way street—not only can your PC access other computers online, but other computers can also access *your* PC. Which means that, unless you take proper precautions, malicious hackers can read your private data, damage your system hardware and software, and even use your system (via remote control) to cause damage to other computers.

You protect your system against outside attack by blocking the path of attack with a *firewall*. A firewall is a software program that forms a virtual barrier between your computer and the Internet. The firewall selectively filters the data that is passed between both ends of the connection and protects your system against outside attack.

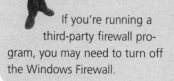

caution

The risk of outside attack is even more pronounced if you have an always-on broadband Internet connection, such as that offered with DSL and cable modems.

Using the Windows Firewall

If you're running Windows Vista or Windows XP, you already have a firewall program installed on your system. The Windows Firewall is activated by default, although you can always check to make sure that it's up and working properly. In Windows Vista, open the Control Panel and select Security, Windows Firewall (see Figure 12.3). In Windows XP, open the Control Panel and go to the Windows Security Center; all Windows security settings are visible there.

note

If you're running a third-party firewall program, you may need to turn off the Windows Firewall.

FIGURE 12.3

Checking Windows' firewall and security settings in the Security Center.

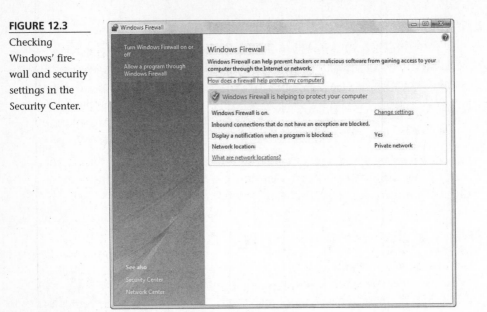

Using Third-Party Firewall Software

For most users, the Windows Firewall is more than enough protection against computer attacks. That said, a number of third-party firewall programs also are available, most of which are more robust and offer more protection than Windows' built-in firewall. The best of these programs include

- BlackICE PC Protection (blackice.iss.net)
- McAfee Personal Firewall (www.mcafee.com)
- Norton Personal Firewall (www.symantec.com)
- ZoneAlarm (www.zonelabs.com)

Shielding Your Children from Inappropriate Content

The Internet contains an almost limitless supply of information on its tens of billions of web pages. Although most of these pages contain useful information, it's a sad fact that the content of some pages can be quite offensive to some people—and that there are some Internet users who prey on unsuspecting youths.

As a responsible parent, you want to protect your children from any of the bad stuff (and bad people) online, while still allowing access to all the good stuff. How do you do this?

Using Content-Filtering Software

If you can't trust your children to always click away from inappropriate web content, you can choose to install software on your computer that performs filtering functions for all your online sessions. These safe-surfing programs guard against either a preselected list of inappropriate sites or a preselected list of topics—and then block access to sites that meet the selected criteria. Once you have the software installed, your kids won't be able to access the really bad sites on the Web.

The most popular filtering programs include the following:

- CyberPatrol (www.cyberpatrol.com)
- Cybersitter (www.cybersitter.com)
- Net Nanny (www.netnanny.com)

In addition, many of the big Internet security suites (such as those from McAfee and Norton/Symantec) offer built-in content-filtering modules.

Kids-Safe Searching

If you don't want to go to all the trouble of using content-filtering software, you can at least steer your children to some of the safer sites on the Web. The best of these sites offer kid-safe searching so that all inappropriate sites are filtered out of the search results.

The best of these kids-safe search and directory sites include

- AltaVista—AV Family Filter (www.altavista.com; go to the Settings page and click the Family Filter link)
- Ask for Kids (www.askforkids.com)
- Fact Monster (www.factmonster.com)
- Google SafeSearch (www.google.com; go to the Preferences page and then choose a SafeSearch Filtering option)
- Yahooligans! (www.yahooligans.com)

tip

Kids-safe search sites are often good to use as the start page for your children's browser because they are launching pads to guaranteed safe content.

Encouraging Safe Computing

Although your using content-filtering software and kids-safe websites are good steps, the most important thing you can do, as a parent, is to create an environment that encourages appropriate use of the Internet. Nothing replaces traditional parental supervision, and at the end of the day, you have to take responsibility for your children's online activities. Provide the guidance they need to make the Internet a fun and educational place to visit—and your entire family will be better for it.

Here are some guidelines you can follow to ensure a safer surfing experience for your family:

- Make sure that your children know never to give out any identifying information (home address, school name, telephone number, and so on) or to send their photos to other users online.

- Provide each of your children with an online pseudonym so they don't have to use their real names online.

- Don't let your children arrange face-to-face meetings with other computer users without parental permission and supervision. If a meeting is arranged, make the first one in a public place and be sure to accompany your child.

- Teach your children that people online might not always be who they seem; just because someone says that she's a 10-year-old girl doesn't necessarily mean that she really is 10 years old, or a girl.

- Consider making Internet surfing an activity you do together with your younger children—or turn it into a family activity by putting your kids' PC in a public room (such as a living room or den) rather than in a private bedroom.

- Set reasonable rules and guidelines for your kids' computer use. Consider limiting the number of minutes/hours they can spend online each day.

- Monitor your children's Internet activities. Ask them to keep a log of all websites they visit; oversee any chat sessions they participate in; check out any files they download; even consider sharing an email account (especially with younger children) so that you can oversee their messages.

- Don't let your children respond to messages that are suggestive, obscene, belligerent, or threatening—or that make them feel uncomfortable in any way. Encourage your children to tell you if they receive any such messages, and then report the senders to your ISP.

- Install content-filtering software on your PC, and set up one of the kid-safe search sites (discussed earlier in this section) as your browser's start page.

Teach your children that Internet access is not a right; it should be a privilege earned by your children and kept only when their use of it matches your expectations.

tip

In Windows Vista, you can use the Parental Controls feature to monitor and regulate your children's computer use. Learn more in Chapter 6, "Personalizing Windows."

THE ABSOLUTE MINIMUM

Here are the key points to remember from this chapter:

- Avoid computer viruses by not opening unsolicited email attachments and by using an anti-spam software program.

- Fight email spam by keeping your email address as private as possible, upgrading to a newer or more fully featured mail program, and using anti-spam software.

- Avoid falling for phishing scams characterized by fake—but official-looking—email messages.

- Use anti-spyware tools, such as Microsoft Defender, to track down and remove spyware programs from your computer.

- Protect your computer from Internet-based attack by turning on the Windows Firewall, or using a third-party firewall program.

- To protect against inappropriate content on the Internet, install content-filtering software—and make sure that your children use kids-safe websites.

Using Computer Software

13

INSTALLING NEW SOFTWARE

Your new computer system probably came with a bunch of programs preinstalled on its hard disk. As useful as these programs are, at some point you're going to want to add something new. Maybe you want to upgrade from Microsoft Works to the more full-featured Microsoft Office. Maybe you want to add some educational software for the kids or a productivity program for yourself. Maybe you just want to play some new computer games.

Whatever type of software you're considering, installing it on your computer system is easy. In most cases software installation is so automatic you don't have to do much more than stick a disc in the CD-ROM drive and click a few onscreen buttons. Even when it isn't that automatic, Windows will walk you through the installation process step-by-step—and you'll be using your new software in no time!

Automatic Installation

Almost all software programs have their own built-in installation programs. Installing the software is as easy as running this built-in program.

If the program you're installing comes on a CD-ROM or DVD, just insert the program's main or installation CD/DVD in your computer's CD/DVD drive. The program's installation program should then start automatically, and all you have to do is follow the onscreen instructions.

Manual Installation

If the installation program *doesn't* start automatically, you have to launch it manually. To do this, open Computer Explorer (in Windows Vista) or My Computer (in Windows XP) and double-click the icon for your CD or DVD drive. This opens the drive and displays the contents of the installation disc. Look for file called setup.exe or install.exe; then double-click that file's icon. This launches the software's installation program; follow the onscreen instructions from there.

Installing Software from the Internet

Nowadays, many software publishers make their products available via download from the Internet. Some users like this because they can get their new programs immediately. However, downloading software like this can take quite a long time, especially if you have a dial-up Internet connection, because the program files are so big.

When you download a program from a major software publisher, the process is generally easy to follow. You probably have to read a page of do's and don'ts, agree to the publisher's licens-

> **tip**
>
> Most software publishers that offer downloadable software also let you order CD versions of their software—although you might have to pay extra to get a physical copy.

ing agreements, and then click a button to start the download. After you specify where (which folder on your hard disk) you want to save the downloaded file, the download begins.

When the download is complete, you should be notified via an onscreen dialog box. When prompted, choose to Run the program you just downloaded. Follow the onscreen instructions from there.

Sometimes, programs you download from the Internet require the use of ActiveX controls—something that Internet Explorer normally blocks, for security reasons. If you go to install a program and nothing happens, look for a message underneath your browser's address bar. If you're sure that this is a legitimate part of the program you're installing, click the message and select Install ActiveX Control from the pop-up menu. The installation should proceed normally from this point.

Removing Old Programs

Chances are you got a *lot* of different software programs with your new PC. Chances are also that some of these are programs you'll never use—and are just taking up space on your hard disk.

> **caution**
>
> Unless you're download-ing a program from a trusted download site, the downloaded file could contain a computer virus. See Chapter 12, "Protecting Your PC from Viruses, Spam, and Other Online Nuisances," for more information.

For example, your new computer might have come with both Microsoft Money and Quicken installed—and you'll only use one of these two programs. Or your new system came with a lot of junk programs installed—trial versions and demos of applications that you'll never use.

If you're sure you won't be using a particular program, Windows can easily remove the software from your hard disk. This frees up hard disk space for other programs you might install in the future.

To remove a software program from your PC in Windows Vista, follow these steps:

1. From the Start menu, open the Control Panel.
2. Select Uninstall a Program (in the Programs section).
3. Windows displays a list of installed pro-grams, as shown in Figure 13.1. Select the program you want to uninstall from this list.
4. Click the Uninstall button.
5. If prompted, confirm that you want to con-tinue to uninstall the application. Answer any other prompts that appear onscreen; then the uninstall process will start.

> **note**
>
> In Windows XP, you use the Add or Remove Programs utility to uninstall soft-ware programs. You open this util-ity from the Control Panel.

FIGURE 13.1
Choose a program to remove from your system.

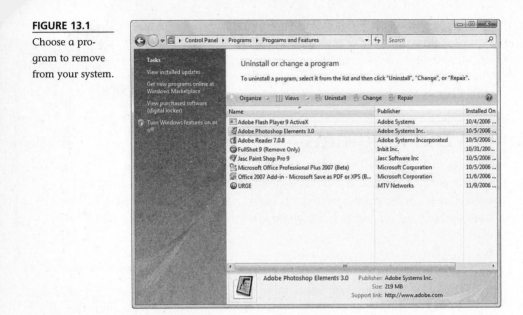

THE ABSOLUTE MINIMUM

Here are the key points to remember from this chapter:

- Most programs come with their own built-in installation programs; the installation should start automatically when you insert the program's installation CD.

- You also can download some programs from the Internet—just be careful about catching a computer virus!

- To remove unwanted programs from your PC, go to the Windows Vista Control Panel and select Uninstall a Program.

14

THE SUITE SPOT: WORKING WITH MICROSOFT WORKS AND MICROSOFT OFFICE

When you first turned on your new PC, you might have been surprised to see your desktop already populated with a bunch of shortcut icons for different programs. These are the programs that were preinstalled by your PC's manufacturer. Which particular programs were pre-installed on your PC depends on what sort of arrangements the PC manufacturer made with the software publishers.

Many PC manufacturers preinstall some sort of software "suite," which is basically a bundle of useful productivity programs. For many users, this suite of programs will be all you need to perform basic computer tasks such as letter writing and number crunching.

The most common software bundle installed on new computer systems is Microsoft Works, which includes a variety of different functions—word processor, spreadsheet, and the like. Alternatively, some higher-priced computers have Microsoft Office installed, which is a more fully featured suite than Microsoft Works. We'll take a quick look at both.

Different Versions of Works

Microsoft sells several different versions of Works. Which version you have installed on your PC depends on what the PC manufacturer chose.

Basic Works

The most basic version of Microsoft Works is a suite of five basic applications, all tied together by an interface called the Task Launcher (discussed later in this chapter). The key components of Works are

- **Works Word Processor**—A simple word processing program you can use to write letters, memos, and notes.
- **Works Spreadsheet**—A simple spreadsheet program that lets you enter rows and columns of numbers and other data, and then performs basic calculations and analysis on those numbers.
- **Works Database**—A simple database program that functions more-or-less like a giant electronic filing cabinet.
- **Works Calendar**—A schedule management program.
- **Address Book**—An all-purpose contact manager you can use to store names, addresses, phone numbers, and email addresses.

Works with Word

Some versions of Works take out the Works Word Processor and substitute the more powerful Microsoft Word program. All the other applications are the same, you just have Word instead of the Works Word Processor.

Works Suite

Another popular version of Works is called Microsoft Works Suite. Works Suite takes the basic Microsoft Works program and supplements it with a variety of other software programs, all tied

note

Learn more about Microsoft Word in Chapter 15, "Letters, Memos, and More: Working with Microsoft Word."

together by the Task Launcher. The programs that Microsoft packages in Works Suite differ from year to year, but typically include

- **Microsoft Money Standard**—A personal finance program that lets you write checks and manage your banking and investment accounts. (Learn more in Chapter 18, "Banking and Beyond: Working with Microsoft Money and Quicken.")
- **Microsoft Digital Image Standard**—A graphics program that lets you edit and manage your digital photos.
- **Microsoft Streets & Trips Essentials**—Used to generate maps and driving directions.
- **Microsoft Encarta Encyclopedia Standard**—A first-class electronic encyclopedia.

Of course, you'll still get the basic Works applications, including Works Spreadsheet, Works Database, Works Calendar, Address Book, and the Microsoft Word word processor.

Working with Works

Microsoft's goal with Microsoft Works is to provide an easy-to-use interface to its most-used applications. To that end, when you launch Microsoft Works, the Works Task Launcher appears onscreen. Along the top of the Task Launcher are buttons that link to five different pages; each page represents a different way to enter a program or document.

The Task Launcher's main pages include

- **Home**—The Home page, shown in Figure 14.1, is what you see when you first launch Works Suite. The Home page includes tabs to view your Calendar and Contacts, as well as a Quick Launch bar that lets you launch any Works Suite application directly.
- **Templates**—Use the Templates page to identify a particular type of document you want to create—select the template, and the Task Launcher will launch the appropriate program, with the appropriate template already loaded.
- **Programs**—Use the Programs page to launch a specific Works Suite program—then select the task you want that program to perform.
- **Projects**—Use the Tasks page to create large-scale projects or open preexisting projects—select the project, and the Task Launcher will launch the appropriate program along with a step-by-step wizard to get you started.
- **History**—Use the History page to reload any document you've recently edited with any Works Suite application.

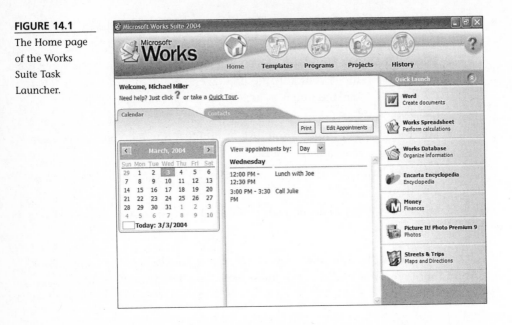

When Task Launcher is launched, select a page, select a program or task, and then you're ready to work!

Launching a Program

You use the Programs page to launch individual Works Suite applications. Just follow these steps:

1. From the Works Task Launcher, select the Programs page (shown in Figure 14.2).
2. From the Choose a Program list, select a program.
3. From the tasks displayed for that program, click a task.

The Task Launcher now launches the program you selected with the appropriate task-based template or wizard loaded.

Creating a New Document

To create a specific type of document—and have Works load the right program for that task, automatically—you use the Templates page, as shown in Figure 14.3. Just follow these steps:

1. From the Works Task Launcher, select the Templates page.
2. From the Choose a Category list, select a particular type of template.
3. From the templates displayed for that category, click a specific template.

FIGURE 14.2

Use the Programs page to launch a specific Works Suite program.

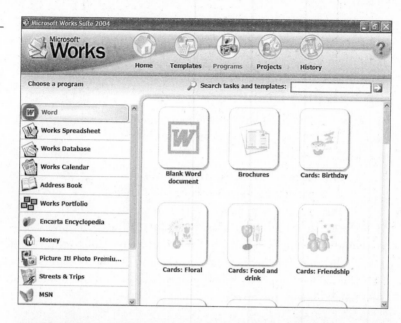

FIGURE 14.3

Click the Templates page to get started with a specific task—and let Works Suite figure out which program to launch.

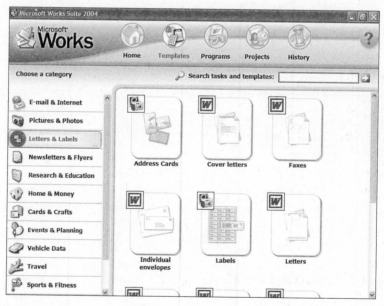

The Task Launcher now launches the appropriate program for your selected template with that template already loaded.

Opening an Existing Document

If you've been working with Works for awhile, you can use the History page to reopen documents you previously created.

The History page, shown in Figure 14.4, lists all your recently used files, newest files first. For each file, the Task Launcher includes the filename, the date it was originally created, the type of template

note

In older versions of Works, the Templates page is called the Tasks page.

it's based on (when known), and the program associated with that file. You can re-sort the list of files by any column by clicking on the column header. For example, if you wanted to sort files by name, you would click on the Name header; click a second time to sort in the reverse order.

FIGURE 14.4

Click the History page to view a list of recent files—click a column header to sort items by that column.

Name	Date	Template	Program
105301c	1/27/2004	N/A	Word
ABG Std Table	1/31/2003	N/A	Word
896629x	10/14/2002	N/A	Word
896633x	10/14/2002	N/A	Word
896634x	10/14/2002	N/A	Word
896635x	10/14/2002	N/A	Word
896636x	10/14/2002	N/A	Word
896609x	10/3/2002	N/A	Word
896610x	10/3/2002	N/A	Word
PB280024	11/30/2002	N/A	Picture It! Pho...
Bargain06	2/1/2004	N/A	Word
3510_02c	2/12/2003	N/A	Word
Bargain-Part IV	2/19/2004	N/A	Word

Microsoft Works Suite 2004

Microsoft Works

Home Templates Programs Projects History

Clear History

Use the History list

To open a document, click its name.

To sort by name, date, template, or program, click a heading.

If you do not see the file you are looking for in this History list, you can search your computer for files and folders by clicking the link below.

Find files and folders

To open a file listed in the History pane, just click its name. Task Launcher will launch the program associated with that file, and then load the selected file into the program.

Managing a Big Project

Moving? Planning a party? Getting ready for the holidays? Microsoft Works helps you with many big projects by offering a ready-made project planner, complete with suggested tasks for each project. Here's what you do:

1. From the Works Task Launcher, open the Projects page, shown in Figure 14.5.

2. Click the button for the project you want to start.

3. When the individual page appears, as shown in Figure 14.6, click an item in the To Do list to set a Due Date.

4. Click the New To Do button to add new items to the To Do list.

tip

If the file you want isn't listed on the History tab, Task Launcher lets you search for that file. When you click the Find Files and Folders link, Task Launcher displays a Windows file/folder window with the search function enabled. You can use this window to search your entire system for specific files.

FIGURE 14.5

Open the Projects page to create and manage big projects.

To Do	Due Date
Keep club members database	<none>
Track club finances	<none>
Schedule club meeting events	<none>
Design club newsletter	<none>
Record club meeting agenda	<none>
Design club event flyer	<none>
Track contacts	<none>
List prices for club merchandise	<none>
Assemble club photo album	<none>

Name: Manage Club and Group Activities

Schedule club meeting events:
Due date
Set due date: <date>
Delete
Associated item
New document from template
Open
Remove association
Replace with:
Works template
Document
Web link
Notes

FIGURE 14.6
Managing the to-do list of a specific project.

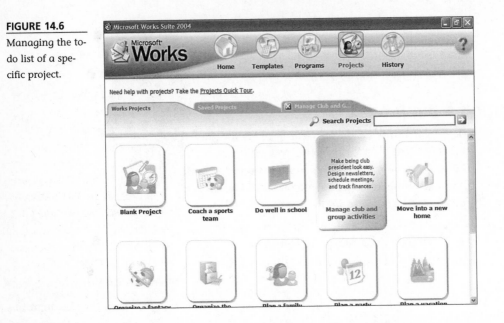

Introducing Microsoft Office

Microsoft Works isn't the only software suite available today. Some manufacturers opt to include other software suites with their new PCs; you can also buy these other applications in standalone versions.

The most-used software suite, especially in the corporate environment, is Microsoft Office, a suite of professional-level applications that are more fully featured than the ones in Works. The latest version of Microsoft Office is Office 2007, although the older Office 2003 version is still widely used.

tip

If a specific type of project isn't listed on the Projects page, click the Blank Project button to build your own custom project and To Do list.

Office Editions

If you're looking to upgrade to Microsoft Office, know that Microsoft sells several different "editions" of the suite. Each edition contains a different bundle of programs; which Office programs you get depends on the edition of Office you have:

- **Microsoft Office 2007 Basic**—Includes Microsoft Word (word processor), Excel (spreadsheet), and Outlook (email and scheduling)

- **Microsoft Office 2007 Standard**—Includes Word, Excel, Outlook, and PowerPoint (presentations)

- **Microsoft Office 2007 Home and Student—** Includes Word, Excel, PowerPoint, and OneNote (note organizer)

- **Microsoft Office 2007 Small Business—** Includes Word, Excel, PowerPoint, Outlook (with Business Contact Manager), Publisher (desktop publishing), and Accounting Express (small-business accounting)

- **Microsoft Office 2007 Professional—** Includes Word, Excel, PowerPoint, Outlook (with Business Contact Manager), Publisher, Accounting Express, and Access (database management)

- **Microsoft Office 2007 Professional Plus—** Includes Word, Excel, PowerPoint, Outlook, Publisher, Access, OneNote, Communicator (instant messaging), InfoPath (information gathering), and server-based content and forms management

> **note**
>
> Another office suite you might find preinstalled on some PCs is Corel's WordPerfect suite, which includes the WordPerfect word processor, Quattro Pro spreadsheet, and Paradox database program. Some versions of the WordPerfect suite also add Intuit's Quicken personal finance software.

- **Microsoft Office 2007 Ultimate—**Includes Word, Excel, PowerPoint, Outlook (with Business Contact Manager), Accounting Express, Publisher, Access, InfoPath, Groove (workgroup collaboration), OneNote, and various enterprise-oriented tools

- **Microsoft Office 2007 Enterprise—**Includes Word, Excel, PowerPoint, Outlook, Publisher, Access, InfoPath, Groove, OneNote, Communicator, and various enterprise-oriented tools

If your new PC comes with Office 2007 included, chances are it's the Basic edition. You can always update to another version to obtain additional Office applications.

The New Office 2007 Interface

Although Microsoft Office doesn't have a unified launch page, as Works does, all the Office applications share a common interface. In the older Office 2003, this interface looked a lot like that of most other Windows applications, as you can see in Figure 14.7.

In Office 2007, however, Microsoft has upped the ante and provided a completely revamped program interface. As you can see in Figure 14.8, all Office 2007 interfaces do away with toolbars and menu bars, instead offering a collection of function buttons in a context-sensitive *Ribbon*. Each Ribbon has a series of tabs; select a different tab to view a different collection of function buttons. The Ribbon changes automatically depending on what type of task you're currently performing, so the most common operations should always be at the top of the screen. And all the Office 2007 applications feature a similar Ribbonized experience; whether you use Word, Excel, PowerPoint, or Outlook, the operation is similar.

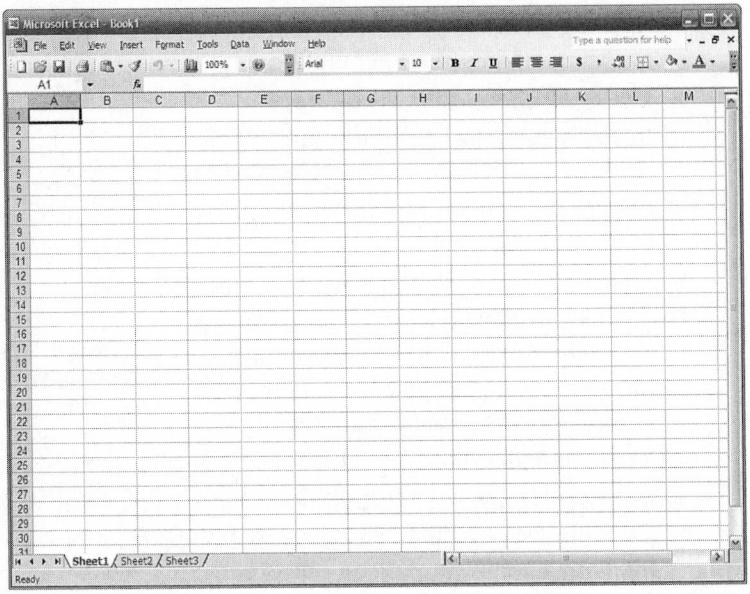

FIGURE 14.7

The Office 2003 interface, shown in Microsoft Excel.

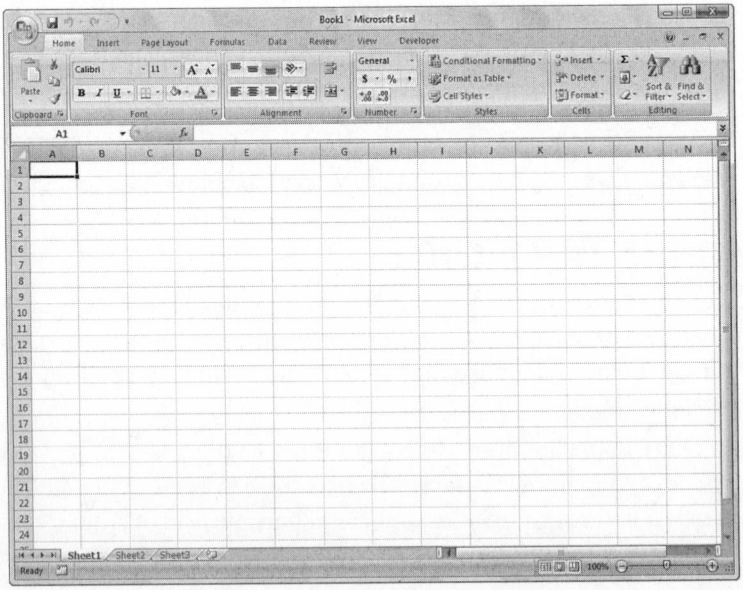

FIGURE 14.8

The Office 2007 interface (in Excel), complete with context-sensitive Ribbon.

If you're used to Office 2003, the Ribbon approach might be a little confusing at first because almost everything is in a different place. For example, where's the much-used File menu? Well, in Office 2007, most of the File menu functions are found somewhere on the Ribbon, or by clicking the round Office button in the top-left corner. In fact, the menu that's displayed when you click the Office button is pretty much the same as the old File menu—although it's probably just as easy to access the operations directly from the Ribbon.

After you get used to the new interface, using Office 2007 applications is much the same as using their Office 2003 counterparts. And whichever version you're using, Office is a lot more fully featured than Microsoft Works. So if you're using Works but find it somewhat limiting (that is, you can't always get it to do what you want), consider making the upgrade to Office—it's probably worth the money.

THE ABSOLUTE MINIMUM

Here are the key points to remember from this chapter:

- Most new PCs come with a suite or bundle of applications preinstalled—the most popular of which is Microsoft Works.

- Works' Task Launcher lets you launch individual programs, create new documents by choosing a particular template or project, open old documents you've worked on, or create and manage big projects.

- If Works can't do what you need it to, upgrade to Microsoft Office—which is Microsoft's more fully featured office suite.

- Different editions of Office include different sets of programs; the Basic edition, preinstalled on most new PCs, includes Microsoft Word, Excel, and Outlook.

- Microsoft Office 2007 sports a completely revamped interface, substituting a context-sensitive Ribbon for the traditional menus and toolbars.

LETTERS, MEMOS, AND MORE: WORKING WITH MICROSOFT WORD

When you want to write a letter, fire off a quick memo, create a report, or create a newsletter, you use a type of software program called a *word processor*. For most computer users, Microsoft Word is the word processing program of choice. Word is a full-featured word processor, and it's included with Microsoft Office and many versions of Microsoft Works. You can use Word for all your writing needs—from basic letters to fancy newsletters, and everything in between.

Word isn't the only word processor out there, of course. For very basic word processing, the Works Word Processor included in Microsoft Works is often adequate. And if you're not a Microsoft fan, Corel's WordPerfect offers the same kind of professional features you find in Microsoft Word, and works in a similar fashion. But it you want maximum document compatibility with your friends, family, and co-workers, Word is the way to go.

Exploring the Word Interface

Before we get started, let's take a quick tour of the Word workspace—so you know what's what and what's where.

You start Word either from the Windows Start menu (with Word 2007, select Start, All Programs, Microsoft Office, Microsoft Office Word 2007; with Word 2003, select Start, All Programs, Microsoft Word) or, if you're using Microsoft Works (with Word installed), from the Works Task Launcher. When Word launches, a blank document appears in the Word workspace.

What's Where in Word 2007

When you open a new document in Word 2007, you see a document contained within a workspace. The key features of the workspace, shown in Figure 15.1, include

- **Title bar**—This is where you find the filename of the current document, as well as buttons to minimize, maximize, and close the window for the current Word document.
- **Ribbon**—In Word 2007, Microsoft has abandoned the traditional menus, toolbars, and sidebars found in previous versions of the program. Instead, it puts all of its functions on what it calls the *Ribbon*, which is a collection of buttons and controls that run along the top of the Word workspace. Different tabs on the Ribbon display different collections of functions.

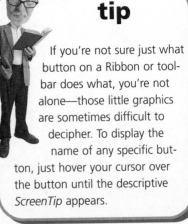

note

The version of Word sold in the Office 2007 suite is Word 2007; the version of Word included with Microsoft Works on new PCs is Word 2003. Even though they look a bit different, they both perform essentially the same functions.

tip

If you're not sure just what button on a Ribbon or toolbar does what, you're not alone—those little graphics are sometimes difficult to decipher. To display the name of any specific button, just hover your cursor over the button until the descriptive *ScreenTip* appears.

- **Document**—This main space displays your current Word document.
- **Scrollbars**—The scrollbar at the bottom of the page lets you scroll left and right through the current page; the scrollbar along the side of the workspace lets you scroll through a document from top to bottom.

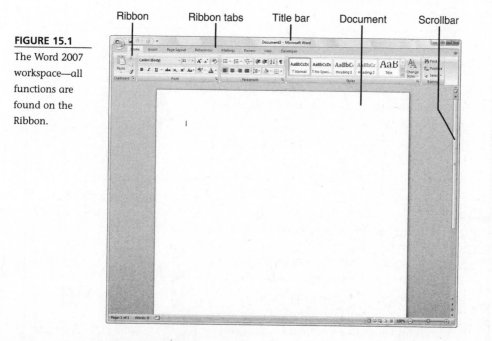

Ribbon   Ribbon tabs   Title bar   Document   Scrollbar

FIGURE 15.1
The Word 2007 workspace—all functions are found on the Ribbon.

What's Where in Word 2003

If you're using Word 2003, the previous version of the program, the workspace looks a bit different. For one thing, there's no Ribbon; all the functions are found on traditional pull-down menus, toolbars, and a useful sidebar found on the right side of the screen. Figure 15.2 details the parts of the Word 2003 workspace, includes many of the same elements found in Word 2007, along with the following unique elements:

- **Menu bar**—This collection of pull-down menus contains virtually all of Word 2003's commands. Use your mouse to click a menu item, and then the menu pulls down to display a full range of commands and options.

tip

If two toolbars docked side-by-side are longer than the available space, buttons at the end of one or both of the toolbars will not be displayed. Instead, you'll see a More Buttons arrow; click this double-arrow to display a submenu of the leftover buttons.

Title bar   Ruler   Menu bar   Toolbars   Scrollbars

FIGURE 15.2

The Word work-space—to perform most tasks, just pull down a menu or click a toolbar button.

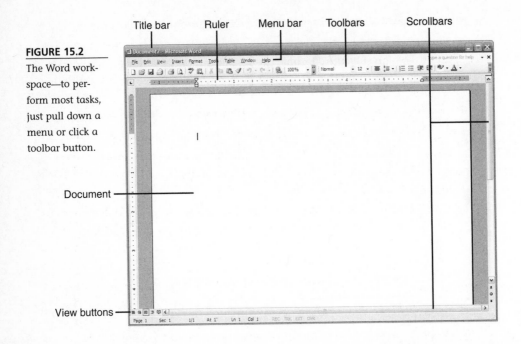

Document

View buttons

■ **Toolbars**—By default, two toolbars—Standard and Formatting—are docked at the top of the workspace, just underneath the menu bar. Word 2003 includes a number of different toolbars that you can display anywhere in the Word workspace. Click a button on any toolbar to initiate the associated command or operation. (To display additional toolbars, pull down the View menu and select Toolbars; when the list of toolbars appears, check those toolbars you want to display, and uncheck those you want to hide.)

■ **View buttons**—The View buttons let you switch between different document views.

tip

Word 2003 will automatically display a Task pane on the right side of the workspace when you're performing particular tasks. It's similar to the Task pane found in Windows XP's My Documents and My Computer folders and contains commands related to what you're currently doing in Word. You can display the Task pane manually by selecting View, Task Pane—or by pressing Ctrl+F1.

Viewing a Word Document—in Different Ways

Word can display your document in one of five different *views*. You select a view by clicking one of the View buttons at the bottom of the Word window.

Each view is a particular way of looking at your document:

- **Draft (Normal** in Word 2003)—This is primarily a text-based view, because certain types of graphic objects—backgrounds, headers and footers, and some pictures—aren't displayed. This is *not* a good view for laying out the elements on your page.

- **Print Layout**—This is the view you use to lay out the pages of your document—with *all* elements visible, including graphics and backgrounds.

- **Full Screen Reading (Reading** in Word 2003)—This view makes it easier to read documents that you don't need to edit by hiding all toolbars and resizing the text for better viewing.

- **Web Layout**—This is the view you use when you're creating a document to be displayed on the Web. In this view all the elements in your document (including graphics and backgrounds) are displayed as they would be if viewed by a web browser.

- **Outline**—This is a great view for looking at the structure of your document, presenting your text (but *not* graphics!) in classic outline fashion. In this view you can collapse an outlined document to see only the main headings or expand a document to show all (or selected) headings and body text.

Zooming to View

If Word displays a document too large or too small for your tastes, it's easy to change the size of the document display. In Word 2007, you can zoom the display with the Zoom slider at the bottom-right corner of the screen. In Word 2003, use the pull-down Zoom list on the Standard toolbar. Choose the setting that fits as much of the document onscreen as you want.

Working with Documents

Anything you create with Word is called a *document*. A document is nothing more than a computer file that can be copied, moved, and deleted—or edited, from within Word.

Creating a New Document

Any new Word document you create is based on what Word calls a *template*. A template combines selected styles and document settings—and, in some cases, prewritten text or calculated fields—to create the building blocks for a specific type of document. You can use templates to give yourself a head start on specific types of documents.

To create a new document in Word 2007 based on a specific template, follow these steps:

1. Click the Office button and select New.

2. When the New Document window appears, as shown in Figure 15.3, select a type of template from the Templates list on the left side of the window. You can choose from Installed Templates on your PC, or additional templates found on Microsoft Office Online.

3. Available templates for that category are now displayed in the middle pane of the window, and a sample document appears in the preview pane on the right. Double-click the template you want to use.

> **note**
>
> If you select a template from Microsoft Office Online, that template will be downloaded to your PC—which means you must be connected to the Internet to use the selected template.

FIGURE 15.3

Creating a new document from a template in Word 2007.

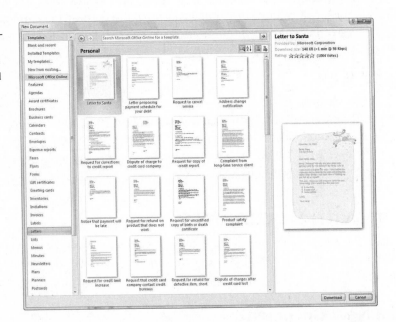

To create a new document in Word 2003, select File, New. This displays the New Document pane; go the Templates section and click On My Computer. When the Templates dialog box appears, select the template you want to use; then click OK.

If you don't know which template to use for your new document, just select Blank and Recent from the Templates list, and then select Blank Document. This opens a new document using Word's Normal template. This is a basic template, with just a few text styles defined—a good starting point for any new document.

Opening an Existing Document

To open a previously created document in Word 2007, click the Office button and select Open; in Word 2003, select File, Open. When the Open dialog box appears, navigate to and select the file you want to open; then click the Open button.

note

If your version of Word 2003 is installed as part of Works Suite, you can view additional Works-related templates by selecting File, New Works Template.

Saving the Document

Every document you make—that you want to keep—must be saved to a file.

The first time you save a file, you have to specify a filename and location. Do this in Word 2007 by clicking the Office button and selecting Save As; in Word 2003, select File, Save As. When the Save As dialog box appears, select a file format, click the Browse Folders button to select a location to save the file, then enter a filename and click the Save button.

When you make additional changes to a document, you must save those changes. Fortunately, after you've saved a file once, you don't need to go through the whole Save As routine again. To "fast save" an existing file, all you have to do is click the Save button on Word 2007's Quick Access toolbar, or Word 2003's Standard toolbar. Alternatively, you can click the Office button (Word 2007) or File menu (Word 2003) and then select Save.

Working with Text

Now that you know how to create and save Word documents, let's examine how you put specific words on paper—or, rather, onscreen.

Entering Text

You enter text in a Word document at the *insertion point*, which appears onscreen as a blinking cursor. When you start typing on your keyboard, the new text is added at the insertion point.

You move the insertion point with your mouse by clicking on a new position in your text. You move the insertion point with your keyboard by using your keyboard's arrow keys.

Editing Text

After you've entered your text, it's time to edit. With Word you can delete, cut, copy, and paste text—or graphics—to and from anywhere in your document, or between documents.

Before you can edit text, though, you have to *select* the text to edit. The easiest way to select text is with your mouse; just hold down your mouse button and drag the cursor over the text you want to select. You also can select text using your keyboard; use the Shift key—in combination with other keys—to highlight blocks of text. For example, Shift+Left Arrow selects one character to the left; Shift+End selects all text to the end of the current line.

Any text you select appears as white text against a black highlight. After you've selected a block of text, you can then edit it in a number of ways, as detailed in Table 15.1.

Table 15.1   Word Editing Operations

Operation	Keystroke
Delete	Del
Copy	Ctrl+Ins or Ctrl+C
Cut	Shift+Del or Ctrl+X
Paste	Shift+Ins or Ctrl+V

Formatting Text

After your text is entered and edited, you can use Word's numerous formatting options to add some pizzazz to your document. It's easiest to edit text when you're working in Print Layout view because this displays your document as it will look when printed. To switch to this view, pull down the View menu and select Print Layout.

Formatting text is easy—and most achievable from the Home Ribbon in Word 2007 or the Formatting toolbar in Word 2003. Both of these items include buttons for bold, italic, and underline, as well as font, font size, and font color. To format a block of text, highlight the text and then click the desired format button.

Checking Spelling and Grammar

If you're not a great speller, you'll appreciate Word's automatic spell checking. You can see it right onscreen; just deliberately misspell a word, and you'll see a squiggly red line under the misspelling. That's Word telling you you've made a spelling error.

When you see that squiggly red line, position your cursor on top of the misspelled word, and then right-click your mouse. Word now displays a pop-up menu with its suggestions for spelling corrections. You can choose a replacement word from the list, or return to your document and manually change the misspelling.

Sometimes Word meets a word it doesn't recognize, even though the word is spelled correctly. In these instances, you can add the new word to Word's spelling dictionary by right-clicking the word and selecting Add from the pop-up menu.

Word also includes a built-in grammar checker. When Word identifies bad grammar in your document, it underlines the offending passage with a green squiggly line. Right-click anywhere in the passage to view Word's grammatical suggestions.

Printing a Document

When you've finished editing your document, you can instruct Word to send a copy to your printer.

Previewing Before You Print

It's a good idea, however, to preview the printed document onscreen before you print it—so you can make any last-minute changes without wasting a lot of paper.

To view your document with Word's Print Preview, click the Office Button and select Print, Print Preview. (In Word 2003, select File, Print Preview.) The to-be-printed document appears onscreen with each page of the document presented as a small thumbnail. To zoom in or out of the preview document, click the Magnifier button and then click the magnifier cursor anywhere on your document. When you're done previewing your document, click the Close button.

Basic Printing

The fastest way to print a document is with Word's quick print option. You activate a fast print by clicking the Office button and selecting Print, Quick Print. (Or, in Word 2003, click the Print button on Word's Standard toolbar.)

When you do a fast print of your document, you send your document directly to your default printer. This bypasses the Print dialog box (discussed next) and all other configuration options.

Changing Print Options

Sometimes fast printing isn't the best way to print. For example, you might want to print multiple copies, or print to a different (non-default) printer. For these and similar situations, you need to use Word's Print dialog box.

You open the Print dialog box, shown in Figure 15.4, by clicking the Office button and selecting Print, Print. (In Word 2003, select File, Print.)

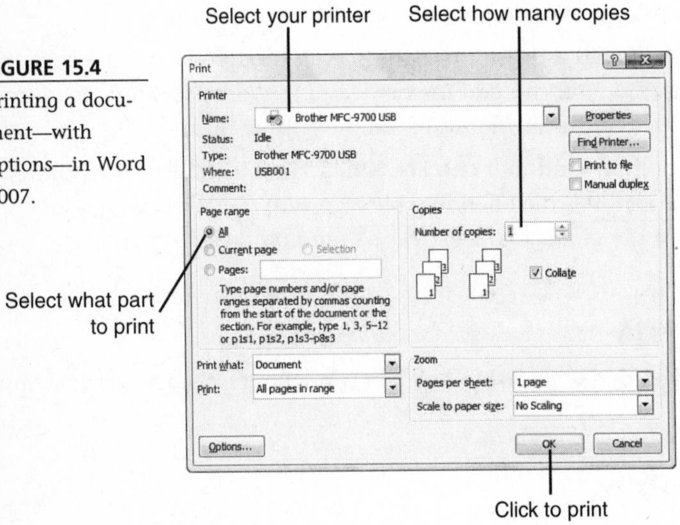

FIGURE 15.4
Printing a document—with options—in Word 2007.

Select your printer   Select how many copies

Select what part to print

Click to print

After you have the Print dialog box displayed, you can choose any one of a number of options specific to this particular print job. After you've made your choices, click the OK button to start printing.

Formatting Your Document

When you're creating a complex document, you need to format more than just a few words here and there.

Formatting Paragraphs

When you need to format complete paragraphs, you use Word 2007's Page Layout Ribbon. Just click the Page Layout tab on the Ribbon, and you'll see all manner of page formatting options—margins, orientation, columns, page color, borders, and so forth.

In Word 2003, most of these same options are found in the Paragraph dialog box. You open this dialog box by positioning your cursor within a paragraph, pulling down the Format menu, and then selecting Paragraph.

Using Word Styles

If you have a preferred paragraph formatting you use over and over and over, you don't have to format each paragraph individually. Instead, you can assign all your formatting to a paragraph *style* and then assign that style to specific paragraphs throughout your document. Most templates come with a selection of predesigned styles; you can modify these built-in styles or create your own custom styles.

Styles include formatting for fonts, paragraphs, tabs, borders, numbering, and more.

To apply a style to a paragraph in Word 2007, position the insertion point anywhere in the paragraph and then click the style you want in the Styles section of the Ribbon. You can select a different set of styles by clicking the Change Styles button, selecting Style Set, and then making a selection.

Working with an Outline

If you have a really long document, you might find it easier to work with the various sections in the form of an outline. For this purpose, Word lets you view your document in Outline view, as shown in Figure 15.5. Just click the Outline button at the bottom of the Word window.

In Word 2003, you apply a style by pulling down the Style list (in the Formatting toolbar) and selecting a style.

FIGURE 15.5

Use Outline view to reorganize the sections of your document.

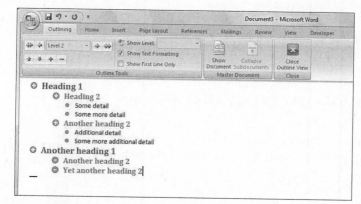

When you're in Outline view, Word displays your headings as different outline levels. Text formatted with the Heading 1 style appears as Level 1 headings in your outline, text formatted as Heading 2 appears as Level 2 headings, and so on.

To make your outline easier to work with, you can select how many levels of headings are displayed. (Just pull down the Outline Level list and select the appropriate level number.) You also can choose to expand or contract various sections of the outline by clicking the plus and minus icons to the side of each Level text in your outline.

Outline view makes rearranging sections of your document extremely easy. When you're in Outline view, you can move an entire section from one place to another by selecting the Level heading and then clicking the up and down arrow buttons. (You also can drag sections from one position to another within the outline.)

Working with Pictures

Although memos and letters might look fine if they contain nothing but text, other types of documents—newsletters, reports, and so on—can be jazzed up with pictures and other graphic elements.

Inserting a Picture from the Clip Art Gallery

The easiest way to add a graphic to your document is to use Word's built-in Clip Art Gallery. The Clip Art Gallery is a collection of ready-to-use illustrations and photos, organized by topic that can be pasted directly into your Word documents.

To insert a piece of clip art in Word 2007, select the Insert Ribbon and click the Clip Art button. (In Word 2003, select Insert, Picture, Clip Art.) This displays the Clip Art pane. Enter one or more keywords into the Search For box; then click Search.

Pictures matching your criteria are now displayed in the Clip Art pane. Double-click a graphic to insert it into your document.

Inserting Other Types of Picture Files

You're not limited to using graphics from the Clip Art Gallery. Word lets you insert any type of graphics file into your document—including GIF, JPG, BMP, TIF, and other popular graphic formats.

To insert a graphics file into your Word 2007 document, select the Insert Ribbon and click the Picture button. (In Word 2003, select Insert, Picture, From File.) When the Insert Picture dialog box appears, navigate to and select the picture you want to insert; then click Insert.

Formatting the Picture

After you've inserted a picture in your document, you might need to format it for best appearance.

note

In Word 2003, most of these effects are selected in the Format Picture dialog box. You open this dialog box by double-clicking the picture.

To format the picture in Word 2007, start by clicking the picture. This displays the Format Ribbon, shown in Figure 15.6. From here you can select different types of picture frames, change the picture's brightness and contrast, edit the position and text wrapping of the picture, and even crop the picture to a new size.

FIGURE 15.6

Use Word 2007's Format Ribbon to edit and format your picture.

To move your picture to another position in your document, use your mouse to drag it to its new position. You also can resize the graphic by clicking the picture and then dragging a selection handle to resize that side or corner of the graphic.

THE ABSOLUTE MINIMUM

Here are the key points to remember from this chapter:

- Microsoft Word is a powerful word processing program included with both Microsoft Works Suite and Microsoft Office.

- The Word 2003 workspace contains the expected assortment of pull-down menus, toolbars, and functional sidebars.

- The Word 2007 workspace replaces menus, toolbars, and sidebars with a tabbed Ribbon; this Ribbon contains buttons and controls for all program functions.

- You can view a Word document in several different ways. The most useful views are the Draft (Normal) and Print Layout views; you can also use the Outline view to display your document as a hierarchical outline.

- If you reuse similar formatting throughout your document, consider using a Word style to apply similar formatting to multiple paragraphs.

- Insert clip art or graphics files by using the Insert Ribbon in Word 2007; you can edit the graphic by using the Format Ribbon.

16

CRUNCHING NUMBERS: WORKING WITH MICROSOFT EXCEL

When you're on your computer and want to crunch some numbers, you use a program called a *spreadsheet*. There are several different spreadsheet programs available for your personal computer. Full-featured spreadsheet programs include Microsoft Excel, Lotus 1-2-3, and Corel's Quattro Pro; for more casual users, there's also the Works Spreadsheet included in Microsoft Works and Works Suite.

The most popular spreadsheet among serious number crunchers is Microsoft Excel, which is included as part of the Microsoft Office suite. That's the spreadsheet we'll look at in this chapter, although the other spreadsheet programs operate in a similar fashion.

Understanding Spreadsheets

A spreadsheet is nothing more than a giant list. Your list can contain just about any type of data you can think of—text, numbers, and even dates. You can take any of the numbers on your list and use them to calculate new numbers. You can sort the items on your list, pretty them up, and print the important points in a report. You can even graph your numbers in a pie, line, or bar chart!

All spreadsheet programs work in pretty much the same fashion. In a spreadsheet, everything is stored in little boxes called *cells*. Your spreadsheet is divided into lots of these cells, each located in a specific location on a giant grid made of *rows* and *columns*. Each single cell represents the intersection of a particular row and column.

As you can see in Figure 16.1, each column has an alphabetic label (A, B, C, and so on). Each row, on the other hand, has a numeric label (1, 2, 3, and so on). The location of each cell is the combination of its column and row locations. For example, the cell in the upper-left corner of the spreadsheet is in column A and row 1; therefore, its location is signified as A1. The cell to the right of it is B1, and the cell below A1 is A2. The location of the selected, or *active*, cell is displayed in the Name box.

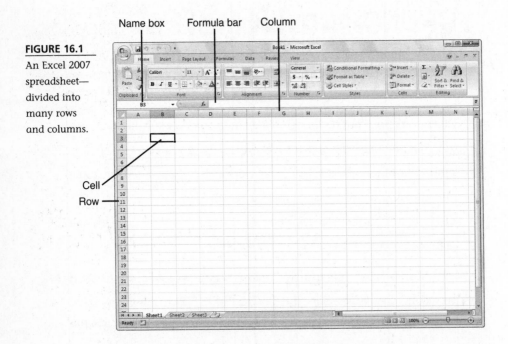

FIGURE 16.1
An Excel 2007 spreadsheet—divided into many rows and columns.

Next to the Name box is the Formula bar, which echoes the contents of the active cell. You can type data directly into either the Formula bar or active cell.

Entering Data

Entering text or numbers into a spreadsheet is easy. Just remember that data is entered into each cell individually—then you can fill up a spreadsheet with hundreds or thousands of cells filled with their own individual data.

To enter data into a specific cell, follow these steps:

1. Select the cell you want to enter data into.
2. Type your text or numbers into the cell; what you type will be echoed in the Formula bar at the top of the screen.
3. When you're done typing data into the cell, press Enter.

Inserting and Deleting Rows and Columns

Sometimes you need to go back to an existing spreadsheet and insert some new information.

Insert a Row or Column

To insert a new row or column in the middle of your spreadsheet, follow these steps:

1. Click the row or column header *after* where you want to make the insertion.
2. In Excel 2007, go to the Cells section of the Ribbon and click the down arrow next to the Insert button; then select either Insert Sheet Rows or Insert Sheet Columns. In Excel 2003, pull down the Insert menu and select either Insert Row or Insert Column.

Excel now inserts a new row or column either above or to the left of the row or column you selected.

Delete a Row or Column

To delete an existing row or column, follow these steps:

1. Click the header for the row or column you want to delete.
2. In Excel 2007, go to the Cells section of the Ribbon and click the Delete button. In Excel 2003, pull down the Edit menu and select Delete.

The row or column you selected is deleted, and all other rows or columns move up or over to fill the space.

Adjusting Column Width

If the data you enter into a cell is too long, you'll only see the first part of that data—there'll be a bit to the right that looks cut off. It's not cut off, of course; it just can't be seen, since it's longer than the current column is wide.

You can fix this problem by adjusting the column width. Wider columns allow more data to be shown; narrow columns let you display more columns per page.

To change the column width, move your cursor to the column header, and position it on the dividing line on the right side of the column you want to adjust. When the cursor changes shape, click the left button on your mouse and drag the column divider to the right (to make a wider column) or to the left (to make a smaller column). Release the mouse button when the column is the desired width.

tip

To make a column the exact width for the longest amount of data entered, position your cursor over the dividing line to the right of the column header and double-click your mouse. This makes the column width automatically "fit" your current data.

Using Formulas and Functions

Excel lets you enter just about any type of algebraic formula into any cell. You can use these formulas to add, subtract, multiply, divide, and perform any nested combination of those operations.

Creating a Formula

Excel knows that you're entering a formula when you type an equal sign (=) into any cell. You start your formula with the equal sign and enter your operations *after* the equal sign.

For example, if you want to add 1 plus 2, enter this formula in a cell: =1+2. When you press Enter, the formula disappears from the cell—and the result, or *value*, is displayed.

Basic Operators

Table 16.1 shows the algebraic operators you can use in Excel formulas.

Table 16.1   Excel Operators

Operation	Operator
Add	+
Subtract	-
Multiply	*
Divide	/

So if you want to multiply 10 by 5, enter `=10*5`. If you want to divide 10 by 5, enter `=10/5`.

Including Other Cells in a Formula

If all you're doing is adding and subtracting numbers, you might as well use a calculator. Where a spreadsheet becomes truly useful is when you use it to perform operations based on the contents of specific cells.

To perform calculations using values from cells in your spreadsheet, you enter the cell location into the formula. For example, if you want to add cells A1 and A2, enter this formula: `=A1+A2`. And if the numbers in either cell A1 or A2 change, the total will automatically change, as well.

An even easier way to perform operations involving spreadsheet cells is to select them with your mouse while you're entering the formula. To do this, follow these steps:

1. Select the cell that will contain the formula.
2. Type =.
3. Click the first cell you want to include in your formula; that cell location is automatically entered in your formula.
4. Type an algebraic operator, such as +, -, *, or /.
5. Click the second cell you want to include in your formula.
6. Repeat steps 4 and 5 to include other cells in your formula.
7. Press Enter when your formula is complete.

Quick Addition with AutoSum

The most common operation in any spreadsheet is the addition of a group of numbers. Excel makes summing up a row or column of numbers easy via the AutoSum function.

All you have to do is follow these steps:

1. Select the cell at the end of a row or column of numbers, where you want the total to appear.
2. Click the AutoSum button in the Editing section of the Ribbon (Excel 2007), as shown in Figure 16.2, or on the Standard toolbar (Excel 2003).

Excel automatically sums all the preceding numbers and places the total in the selected cell.

AutoSum

FIGURE 16.2
Click the
AutoSum (shown
here on the Excel
2007 Ribbon) to
automatically
add a row or col-
umn of numbers.

Other AutoSum Operations

Excel's AutoSum also includes a few other automatic calculations. When you click
the down arrow on the side of the AutoSum button, you can perform the following
operations:

- **Average**, which calculates the average of the selected cells
- **Count Numbers**, which counts the number of selected cells
- **Max**, which returns the largest value in the selected cells
- **Min**, which returns the smallest value in the selected cells

Using Functions

In addition to the basic algebraic operators previously discussed, Excel also includes
a variety of *functions* that replace the complex steps present in many formulas. For
example, if you wanted to total all the cells in column A, you could enter the formula =A1+A2+A3+A4. Or, you could use the *SUM* function, which lets you sum a column or row of numbers without having to type every cell into the formula. (And
when you use AutoSum, it's simply applying the *SUM* function.)

In short, a function is a type of prebuilt formula.

You enter a function in the following format:
=function(argument), where function is the name
of the function and argument is the range of cells
or other data you want to calculate. Using the
last example, to sum cells A1 through A4,
you'd use the following function-based formula:
=sum(A1,A2,A3,A4).

Excel includes hundreds of functions. You can
access and insert any of Excel's functions by following these steps:

1. Select the cell where you want to insert
   the function.

tip

When you're referencing
consecutive cells in a formula, you can just enter the
first and last number or the
series separated by a colon.
For example, cells A1
through A4 can be entered
as A1:A4.

2. In Excel 2007, select the Formulas Ribbon, shown in Figure 16.3.

3. From here you can click a function category to see all the functions of a particular type, or click the Insert Function button to display the Function dialog box. Select the function you want.

4. If the function has related arguments, a Function Arguments dialog box is now displayed; enter the arguments and click OK.

5. The function you selected is now inserted into the current cell. You can now manually enter the cells or numbers into the function's argument.

In Excel 2003, select Insert, Function to display the Function dialog box.

FIGURE 16.3

Choose from hundreds of functions on Excel 2007's Formulas Ribbon.

Sorting a Range of Cells

If you have a list of either text or numbers, you might want to reorder the list for a different purpose. Excel lets you sort your data by any column, in either ascending or descending order.

To sort a range of cells, follow these steps:

1. Select all the cells you want to sort.

2. In Excel 2007, click the Sort & Filter button in the Ribbon; then select how you want to sort—A to Z, Z to A, or in a custom order (Custom Sort).

3. If you select Custom Sort, you'll see the Sort dialog box, shown in Figure 16.4. From here you can select various levels of sorting; select which column to sort by, and the order from which to sort. Click the Add Level button to sort on additional columns.

In Excel 2003, select Data, Sort to display the Sort dialog box.

FIGURE 16.4
Sort your list by
any column, in
any order.

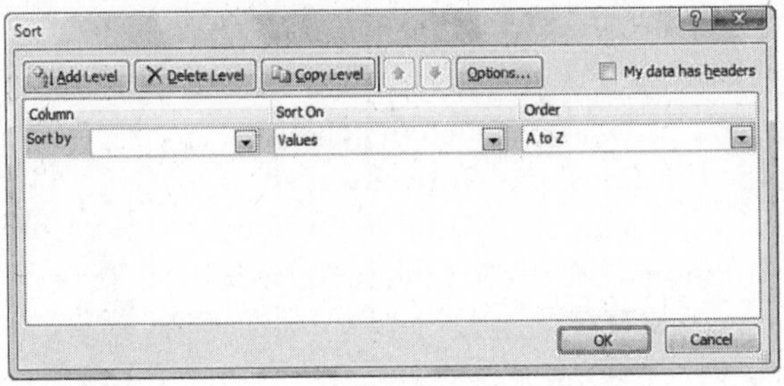

Formatting Your Spreadsheet

You don't have to settle for boring-looking spreadsheets. You can format how the data appears in
your spreadsheet—including the format of any
numbers you enter.

Applying Number Formats

When you enter a number into a cell, Excel
applies what it calls a "general" format to the
number—it just displays the number, right-aligned,
with no commas or dollar signs. You can, however,
select a specific number format to apply to any
cells in your spreadsheet that contain numbers.

In Excel 2007, all the number formatting options
are in the Number section of the Ribbon. Click the
dollar sign button to choose an accounting format,
the percent button to choose a percentage format,
the comma button to choose a comma format, or the
General button to choose from all available formats. You can also click the Increase Decimal and
Decrease Decimal buttons to move the decimal
point left or right.

note

In Excel 2003, you
select Format, Cells to display the Format Cells dialog box.
All available number formatting
options are found on the Number
tab of this dialog box.

Formatting Cell Contents

You can also apply a variety of other formatting
options to the contents of your cells. You can make
your text bold or italic, change the font type or
size, or even add shading or borders to selected
cells.

In Excel 2007, these formatting options are found
in the Font and Alignment sections of the Ribbon.

note

In Excel 2003, select
Format, Cells to display the
Format Cells dialog box. From
there select the Alignment, Font,
Border, or Pattern tabs to format a
particular option.

Just select the cell(s) you want to format; then click the appropriate formatting button.

Creating a Chart

Numbers are fine, but sometimes the story behind the numbers can be better told through a picture. The way you take a picture of numbers is with a *chart*, such as the one shown in Figure 16.5.

FIGURE 16.5

Some numbers are better represented via a chart.

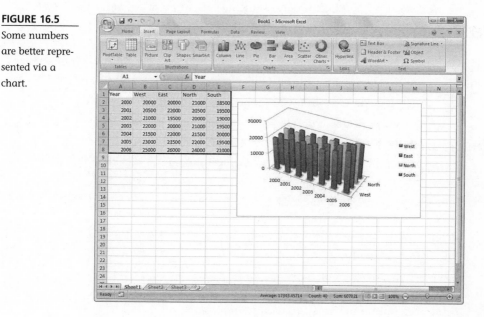

You create a chart based on numbers you've previously entered into your Excel spreadsheet. In Excel 2007, it works like this:

1. Select the range of cells you want to include in your chart. (If the range has a header row or column, include that row or column when selecting the cells.)

2. Select the Insert Ribbon.

3. In the Charts section of the Ribbon, click the button for the type of chart you want to create.

4. Excel now displays a variety of charts within that general category. Select the type of chart you want.

5. When the chart appears in your worksheet, select the Design Ribbon to edit the chart's type, layout, and style; or select the Layout Ribbon to edit the chart's labels, axes, and background.

In Excel 2003, the process is subtly different. After you select the range of cells, click the Chart Wizard button on the Excel toolbar. This wizard walks you through a series of steps that help you choose the type of chart you want and the formatting for that chart.

THE ABSOLUTE MINIMUM

Here are the key points to remember from this chapter:

- Popular spreadsheet programs include Microsoft Excel, Lotus 1-2-3, Corel's Quattro Pro, and the Works Spreadsheet included in Microsoft Works and Works Suite. Of these, Excel is by far the most widely used.

- A spreadsheet is composed of rows and columns; the intersection of a specific row and column is called a cell.

- Each cell can contain text, numbers, or formulas.

- You start an Excel formula with an = sign, and follow it up with specific numbers (or cell locations) and operators—such as +, -, *, and /.

- To graphically display your spreadsheet data, use Excel 2007's Insert Ribbon (or Excel 2003's Chart Wizard).

17

PRESENTING YOURSELF: WORKING WITH MICROSOFT POWERPOINT

When you need to present information to a group of people, the hip way to do it is with a PowerPoint presentation. Whether you use an overhead projector, traditional slides, or a computer projector, PowerPoint can help you create great-looking graphic and bullet-point presentations.

If you work in an office, you probably see at least one PowerPoint presentation a week. Teachers use PowerPoint to present lesson materials in class. Kids even use PowerPoint to prepare what used to be oral reports.

So get with the program—and learn how to create your own great-looking presentations with PowerPoint!

Understanding Microsoft PowerPoint

Microsoft PowerPoint is a presentation program included with most versions of Microsoft Office. We'll look at the latest version of the program, PowerPoint 2007—although the previous version, PowerPoint 2003, works similarly (but with menus and toolbars instead of the 2007 Ribbon).

The PowerPoint Workspace

As you can see in Figure 17.1, PowerPoint 2007 looks like most other Office 2007 applications. The workspace is dominated by the Ribbon at the top of the screen, with the current slide displayed in the middle.

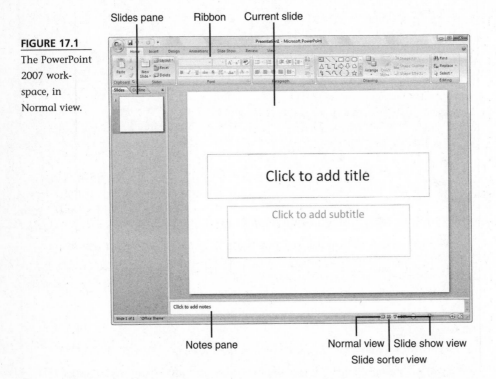

FIGURE 17.1
The PowerPoint 2007 workspace, in Normal view.

One the left side of the workspace is something unique to PowerPoint—the Slides/Outline pane, which displays all the slides in your presentation in either text (Outline) or graphic (Slides) views. Below the current slide is a Notes pane, which lets you enter presentation notes. And at the very bottom of the window, near the right-hand corner, are the View buttons, which you use to switch between different views of your presentation.

Changing Views

The default view of the PowerPoint workspace is called, not surprising, Normal view. PowerPoint offers three different ways to view your presentation, all selectable from either the View buttons or the View menu. These views include

- **Normal**, which is the default view complete with Outline/Slides and Notes panes.
- **Slide Sorter**, which displays thumbnails of all the slides in your presentation.
- **Slide Show**, which launches a live full-screen "slideshow" of your entire presentation.

Creating a New Presentation

When you launch PowerPoint, a blank presentation is loaded and ready for your input. If you'd rather create a presentation based on a predesigned template (more on these next), click the Office button in PowerPoint 2007 and select New; this displays the New Presentation window, which lets you choose from a list of available templates. Click a template to get started.

Applying a Theme

You don't have to reinvent the wheel when it comes to designing the look of your presentation. PowerPoint 2007 includes a number of slide *themes* that you can apply to any presentation, blank or otherwise. A theme specifies the color scheme, fonts, layout, and background for each slide you create in your presentation.

To apply a new theme to your current presentation, select the Design Ribbon (shown in Figure 17.2) and select a new theme from the Themes section. Make sure that you scroll through all available themes; you can also choose to apply only color, font, and effect schemes by using the controls to the right of the Themes section.

note

In PowerPoint 2003, select File, New to display the New Presentation pane. From there, click From Design Template to view a list of available templates.

note

In PowerPoint 2003, themes are called *design templates* and are available by selecting Format, Slide Design.

It's that simple. All the colors, fonts, and everything else from the theme are automatically applied to all the slides in your presentation—and every new slide you
add will also carry the selected design.

Inserting New Slides

When you create a new presentation, PowerPoint
starts with a single slide—the *title slide*. Naturally,
you'll need to insert additional slides to create a
complete presentation. PowerPoint lets you insert
different types of slides, with different types of layouts for different types of information.

To insert a new slide in PowerPoint 2007, follow
these steps:

1. Click the down button next to the New
   Slide button on the Ribbon.

2. A variety of different slide layouts are now
   displayed in a drop-down visual menu;
   click the type of slide you want to insert.

Continue adding as many slides as you need to
complete your presentation.

> **note**
>
> In PowerPoint 2003,
> the New Slide button is on
> the Formatting toolbar. A variety
> of slide layouts are now displayed
> in the Slide Layout pane; choose
> the layout you want.

Working from an Outline

Rather than creating a presentation one slide at a
time, some people find it easier to outline their
entire presentation in advance. To this end,
PowerPoint offers the Outline pane, located at the
left of the workspace. Select the Outline tab and
PowerPoint displays each slide of your presentation, in outline fashion.

To enter text for an outline level, all you have to
do is type. To add another slide in your outline,
press the Enter key. To add bullet text to a slide,
press the Tab key. To add a sub-bullet, press Tab

> **note**
>
> Don't confuse the slide
> *layout*, which defines which
> elements appear on the slide, with
> the slide *template*, which defines
> the colors and fonts used.

again. When you're done entering bullets, press Shift+Tab to move up the hierarchy and create a new slide.

Adding Text

As you've just seen, one way to add text to your slides is via the Outline pane. You can also enter text directly into each slide. When PowerPoint creates a new slide, the areas for text entry are designated with boilerplate text—"Click to add title" (for the slide's title) or "Click to add text" (for regular text or bullet points). Adding text is as easy as clicking the boilerplate text and then entering your own words and numbers. Press Enter to move to a new line or bullet. To enter a sub-bullet, press the Tab key first; to back up a level, press Shift-Tab.

Formatting Your Slides

You've already seen how to use design templates to format your entire presentation in one go. You can also format slides individually.

Formatting Text

Formatting text on a slide is just like formatting text in a word processing document. Select the text you want to format and then click the appropriate button in the Font section of the Ribbon (PowerPoint 2007) or on the Formatting menu (PowerPoint 2003).

Changing Backgrounds

Don't like the slide background from the current template? Then change it! You can create single-color backgrounds, backgrounds that gradate between two different colors, and even backgrounds that incorporate a graphic or photograph.

To apply a new background to all the slides in your PowerPoint 2007 presentation, simply select the Design Ribbon and click the Background Styles button. This displays a variety of different backgrounds; select the one you want, and it will be applied to your entire presentation.

If you want even more background options, click the Background Styles button and then select the

tip

One of the unique formatting operations possible with PowerPoint is the Shadow effect, which you add by clicking the "S" button on the Ribbon or on the Formatting toolbar. This adds a drop shadow behind the selected text, which can really make the text "pop" off a colored or textured background.

note

In PowerPoint 2003, select Format, Background to display the Background dialog box.

Format Background option. This displays the Format Background dialog box, shown in Figure 17.3, where you can choose from various types of fill and picture backgrounds.

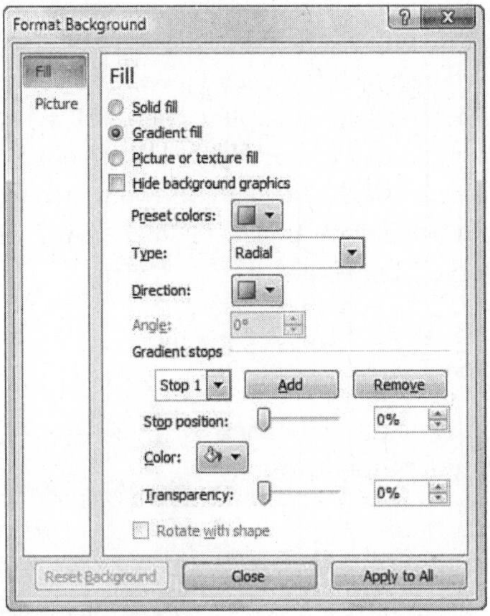

Adding Graphics

An all-text presentation is a little boring. To spice up your slides, you need to add some graphics!

Inserting Pictures

You can insert any type of drawing or photograph into a PowerPoint slide. It's easiest to start with a slide layout that anticipates the addition of a picture, however. Follow these steps:

1. From a blank slide, go to the Slides section of the Ribbon and click the Layout button; then select the Title and Content layout. This formats the slide as shown in Figure 17.4, ready to accept different types of content.

2. To add clip art to the slide, click the Clip Art icon; then search for the clip art you want from the Clip Art pane.

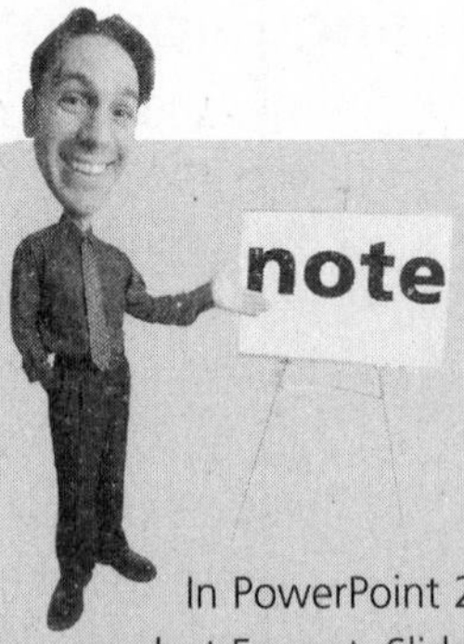

note

In PowerPoint 2003, select Format, Slide Layout to display the Slide Layout pane; select a slide layout from this pane.

FIGURE 17.4

A slide format-
ted with the Title
and Content
layout.

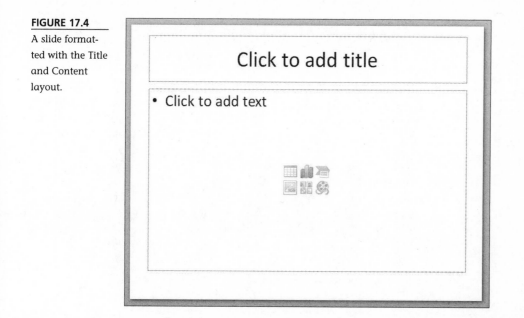

3. To add a picture to your slide, click the Insert Picture from File icon; then navigate to and select a specific picture.

4. To add icons, buttons, and similar graphics to your slide, click the Insert SmallArt Graphic icon; then select a graphic from the resulting dialog box.

After the graphic is added, you can now format it in a number of ways. To rotate the graphic, grab the green handle above the graphic and turn it to the left or right. To recolor the graphic, add a border style, insert a drop shadow, or crop the graphic, select the Design Ribbon and use the options there.

Creating Charts

Another way to spice up your presentation is to display numerical data in chart for-mat, as shown in Figure 17.5. The easiest way to create a chart in PowerPoint 2007 is to start with the Title and Content slide layout and then follow these steps:

1. Click the chart icon.

2. When the Insert Chart dialog box appears, choose a chart type.

3. An Excel spreadsheet now opens onscreen. Enter the data for your chart into this spreadsheet and close the spreadsheet when you're finished.

4. Your chart now appears on the slide. Select the Design Ribbon to select a dif-ferent chart layout or style, or use the Layout Ribbon to format different aspects of the chart.

FIGURE 17.5
Adding a chart to
your presenta-
tion.

FIGURE 17.5
Adding a chart to
your presenta-
tion.

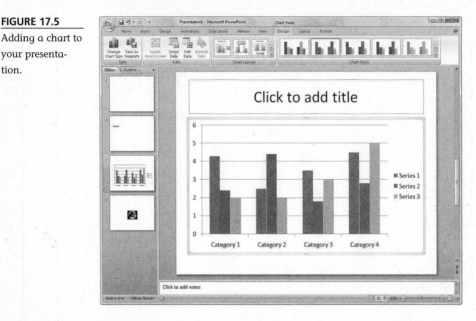

Applying Slide Animations

If you're presenting your slideshow electronically,
via a computer attached to a large monitor or projector, you need to do one more thing—add animated transitions between each slide. PowerPoint
lets you use a wide variety of slide transitions, all
of which are more interesting than just cutting
from one slide to the next.

To apply animated transitions in PowerPoint 2007,
select the Animations Ribbon, shown in Figure
17.6. Select from the wide variety of transitions in
the Transition to This Slide section; make sure that
you click the scrollbar to view all the available
transitions.

> **note**
>
> In PowerPoint 2003,
> animations are called *tran-
> sitions* and are applied from the
> Slide Transition pane. (Select Slide
> Show, Slide Transition.)

FIGURE 17.6
Choosing transi-
tions from
PowerPoint
2007's
Animations
Ribbon.

You can also use the Animations Ribbon to apply a sound to the transition or to adjust the transition speed. You can also apply this transition to all slides or just to selected slides. Have fun!

Start the Show!

To run your slideshow, complete with transitions, click the Slide Show button at the bottom of the PowerPoint workspace, or on the Slide Transition pane. To move from one slide to the next, all you have to do is click your mouse.

tip

You don't have to use the same transitions on every slide. Your presentation will have more visual interest if you use a variety of transitions throughout.

THE ABSOLUTE MINIMUM

Here are the key points to remember from this chapter:

- You use Microsoft PowerPoint to create slides, overhead transparencies, and electronic slideshow presentations.

- The look and feel of your entire presentation is defined by the design template or theme that you choose.

- Each slide you insert can have a different layout, depending on its function.

- A slide can include text, bullets, pictures, and charts.

- When you're presenting an electronic slideshow, add animated transitions between each slide.

18

BANKING AND BEYOND: WORKING WITH MICROSOFT MONEY AND QUICKEN

Most new computers come with at least one personal finance program installed. That program might be Microsoft Money, or it might be Intuit's Quicken. You can use either of these programs to manage your household budgets, track your bank accounts and investments, write checks, and even pay your bills online.

In addition, most banks and credit card companies let you manage all your financial accounts online, from their own websites. You don't have to install any software to do this; just access the bank's website with Internet Explorer and do your banking from within your web browser.

Managing Your Money with Microsoft Money

The personal finance program included with most new PCs (and with Microsoft Works Suite) is Microsoft Money. This program lets you manage all your bank transactions, balance your checkbook, and pay bills online.

Setting Up Your Accounts

Before you can use Microsoft Money, you have to configure it with information about your specific banking and financial accounts. The first time you start the program, Money asks you a series of questions to help you set up the program for your own financial accounts. You'll need to supply your Microsoft Passport information (typically your Hotmail address), as well as information about all your banking and credit card accounts (including financial institution and account number). Obviously, it's easier if you gather this information ahead of time, so you can breeze through the initial setup.

> **tip**
>
> If you don't have a Microsoft Passport account, Money lets you sign up for one (it's free) during the setup process.

Navigating Money

Before you start working with your accounts, it's a good idea to get familiar with the way Money works—starting from the My Money Home page, shown in Figure 18.1. This page is your "home base" for all your Money-related transactions and includes links to different activities; you click a link to access that activity.

Across the top of the My Money Home page are buttons that link to Money's other financial centers. These pages organize tasks and information by specific types of activity.

The buttons across the top of the My Money Home page take you directly to these financial centers:

- **Home**—Takes you back to the My Money Home page, from anywhere in the program.
- **Banking**—Display your account list (for both banking and investment accounts); you can view account balances, add new accounts, manage existing accounts, and link directly to each account's register.
- **Bills**—Set up new payees, pay bills, and register deposits to your banking accounts.
- **Reports**—Create a variety of reports and charts.

■ **Budget**—Access Money's Budget Planner, which lets you create a budget, create a debt reduction plan, and plan your 401(k).

■ **Investing**—View and edit your investment portfolio, record new investment transactions, and go online to get current stock quotes.

■ **Planning**—Plan for various financial scenarios, including retirement, college, savings, and so forth.

■ **Taxes**—Plan and prepare your taxes online.

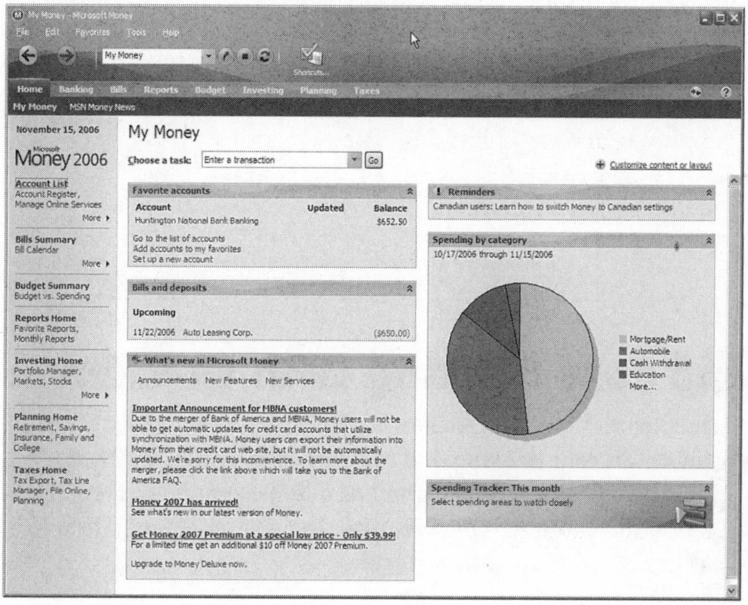

FIGURE 18.1

Start with the My Money Home page, and then click to access different activities and transactions.

Managing Your Bank Account

Many people use Microsoft Money to track their banking transactions. You can enter transactions manually—or, if you're connected to the Internet, download transactions electronically from your banking institution.

To enter a transaction manually, go to the Banking page and click the link for your bank account. This displays that account's register, as shown in Figure 18.2; from here you click the New button to enter a new withdrawal (including bill payments), deposit, or transfer between accounts.

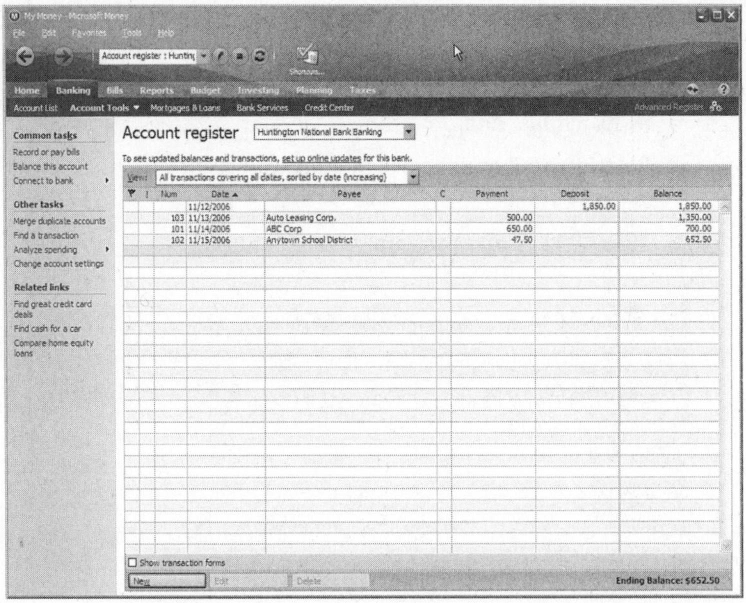

FIGURE 18.2

Enter your Money
transactions from
your bank
account's register
page.

FIGURE 18.2

Enter your Money transactions from your bank account's register page.

Quick and Easy Banking with Quicken

Like Microsoft Money, Quicken is a financial management program that lets you
manage all your banking and investment activities. Quicken has actually been
around longer than Money and has a larger user base. If you have a new PC,
chances are you have Quicken New User edition already installed; other, more fully
featured editions are also available.

Setting Up Your Accounts

Before you can use Quicken, you have to set up the program to recognize all your
bank and financial accounts. This is typically done by following the steps in the wizard that appears when you first start the program; you can also add new accounts
at any time by selecting File, New, and then choosing the New Quicken Account
option.

To set up Quicken to manage your finances, you must have information about all
your financial accounts—bank accounts, credit card accounts, investment accounts,
and so on. The best way to do this is to gather the most recent statements for all
these accounts before you start so that you'll have all the account numbers handy.

Navigating Quicken

The Quicken Home page, shown in Figure 18.3, offers a wealth of information. The main area of the workspace displays a variety of key data about your financial accounts and transactions—including any upcoming bills and scheduled transactions. Click any item to view more detail.

FIGURE 18.3

View key financial information from Quicken's Home page.

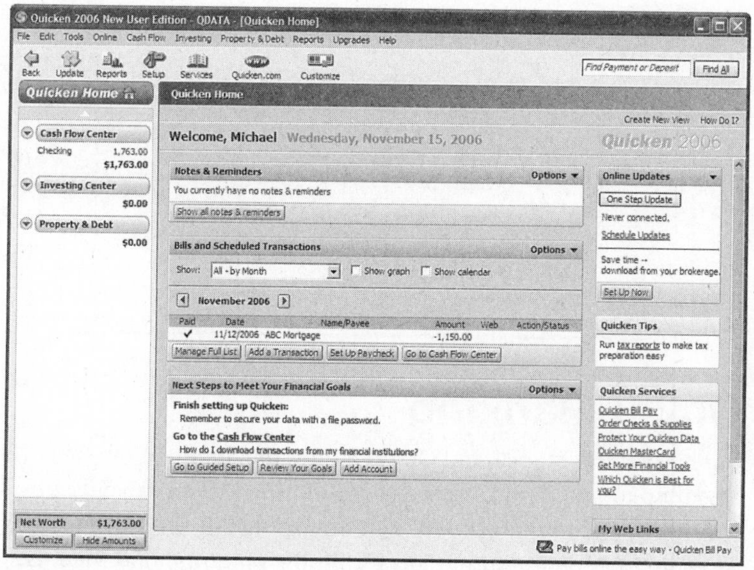

Your key accounts are listed in the sidebar at the left side of the workspace; click any account name to view the register for that account. Along the top of the page is a toolbar that provides pushbutton access to key operations and functions.

Managing Your Bank Account

You perform most financial transactions from the register for a particular account. For example, to write checks and note deposits, open your checking account register by clicking the account name on the Home page. When the register appears, as shown in Figure 18.4, you enter transactions directly into the register, or use the menu options to write checks, transfer funds, or reconcile your account.

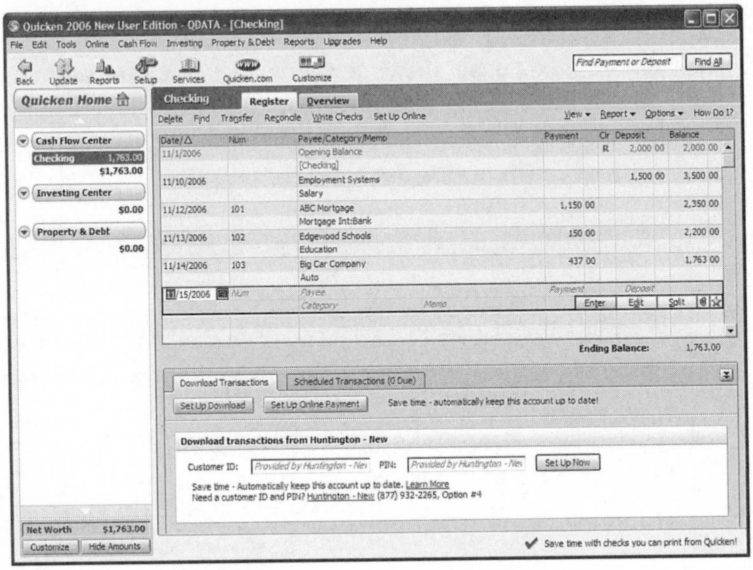

FIGURE 18.4
Entering account
information into
the account
register.

Doing Online Banking

Both Microsoft Money and Quicken offer the option of online banking. You can set them up to automatically download transactions from your bank and other key accounts, and to pay your bills electronically. All you have to do is supply your account and login information within the program, and then use the online update feature to download your latest transactions.

Of course, you don't have to use Money or Quicken to do your banking online. Most banks and credit card institutions let you access and manage your account information online, via their own proprietary websites. All you have to do is register with the website (you'll need your account number, PIN, and other personal information), and then you can access your account from any web browser.

To find out whether your bank or credit card company offers online banking—and to get the website URL—contact your financial institution. Most are eager to move your banking online because it costs them less money than dealing with a physical paper trail. Some banks charge a slight fee to access their online banking services; others offer online access for free. As always, shop around for the best deal.

THE ABSOLUTE MINIMUM

Here are the key points to remember from this chapter:

- You can use any financial management program—including Microsoft Money and Quicken—to manage your banking and investment transactions.

- Both Money and Quicken let you enter transactions manually, or sign up for online banking to automatically download transactions from your bank or credit card company.

- Most banks and credit card companies also offer their own web-based online banking services, either for free or for a slight monthly charge.

- When you do your banking from a bank's website, you don't need to use Money, Quicken, or similar programs; instead, you access the site conveniently from your web browser.

PART V

USING THE INTERNET

19

CONNECTING TO THE INTERNET—AT HOME AND ON THE ROAD

It used to be that most people bought personal computers to do work—word processing, spreadsheets, databases, the sort of programs that still make up the core of Microsoft Works and Microsoft Office. But today, the majority of people also buy PCs to access the Internet—to send and receive email, surf the Web, and chat with other users.

Different Types of Connections

The first step in going online is establishing a connection between your computer and the Internet. To do this, you have to sign up with an Internet service provider (ISP), which, as the name implies, provides your home with a connection to the Internet.

Depending on what's available in your area, you can choose from two primary types of connections—dial-up or broadband. Dial-up is slower than broadband, but it's also lower priced. That said, dial-up connections are going the way of the dodo bird; if you do a lot of web surfing, it's probably worth a few extra dollars a month to get the faster broadband connection.

Whichever type of connection you choose, you'll connect your PC to a *modem*, which will then connect to the phone or cable line coming into your house. Most PCs have a built-in dial-up modem; if you choose broadband service, you'll get an external broadband modem from your ISP. Read on to learn more.

Traditional Dial-Up

A dial-up connection provides Internet service over normal phone lines. The fastest dial-up connections transmit data at 56.6Kbps (kilobits per second), which is okay for normal web surfing but isn't fast enough for downloading music or videos. Most ISPs charge $20 or so per month for normal dial-up service.

Broadband DSL

DSL is a phone line-based technology that operates at broadband speeds. DSL service piggybacks onto your existing phone line, turning it into a high-speed digital connection. Not only is DSL faster than dial-up (384Kbps to 3Mbps, depending on your ISP), you also don't have to surrender your normal phone line when you want to surf; DSL connections are "always on." Most providers offer DSL service for $30–$50 per month. Look for package deals that offer a discount when you subscribe to both Internet and phone services.

Broadband Cable

Another popular type of broadband connection is available from your local cable company. Broadband cable Internet piggybacks on your normal cable television line, providing speeds in the 500Kbps to 30Mbps range, depending on the provider. Most cable companies offer broadband cable Internet for $30–$50 per month. As with DSL, look for package deals for your cable company, offering some sort of discount on a combination of Internet, cable, and (sometimes) digital phone service.

Broadband Satellite

If you can't get DSL or cable Internet in your area, you have another option—connecting to the Internet via satellite. Any household or business with a clear line of sight to the southern sky can receive digital data signals from a geosynchronous satellite at 700Kbps.

The largest provider of satellite Internet access is HughesNet. (Hughes also developed and markets the popular DIRECTV digital satellite system.) The HughesNet system (www.hughesnet.com) enables you to receive Internet signals via a small dish that you mount outside your house or on your roof. Fees range from $60 to $100 per month, depending on the plan.

Before You Connect

When you sign up with an ISP, both you and the ISP have to provide certain information to each other. You provide your name, address, and credit card number; your ISP provides a variety of semitechnical information, including

- Your username and password
- Your email address
- Your email account name and password
- The names of the ISP's incoming and outgoing mail servers (which you'll need to set up your email program)
- The phone number to dial into (if you're using a dial-up connection)

tip

For most ISPs, your username, email account name, and the first half of your email address will all be the same. It's also likely that you will be assigned a single password for both your initial login and email access.

You'll need this information when you configure Windows for your new Internet connection—which we'll discuss next.

Setting Up a New Connection

Naturally, you need to configure your computer to work with your ISP. How you do this depends on which operating system you're using.

Connecting in Windows Vista

In Windows Vista, how you set up a new Internet connection depends on the type of connection you have. If you're connecting to a broadband connection via your home network, you don't have to do anything more than connect your computer to the network; Vista does the rest.

On the other hand, if you're connecting to a dial-up connection or a broadband connection that requires a username and password, you have a little work to do. Follow these steps:

1. Click the Start button; then select Control Panel.

2. From the Control Panel, select Network and Internet, and then select Connect to a Network.

3. When the next window appears, select Set Up a Connection or Network.

4. Select Connect to the Internet, and click Next.

5. You're now asked how you want to connect. Select either Broadband or Dial-Up.

6. If you selected Broadband, enter the username and password supplied by your ISP.

7. If you selected Dial-Up, follow the onscreen instructions to select which modem you're using and enter your ISP's dial-up phone number, your username, and your password.

That's it. Vista does a good job of configuring your Internet connection automatically, without a lot of input on your part.

Connecting in Windows XP

The configuration process isn't as simple in Windows XP. After you connect your computer to the broadband modem (or connect your PC's dial-up modem to your telephone line), you follow these steps:

1. Click the Start button; then select Connect To, Show All Connections.

2. When the Network Connections window opens, select Create a New Connection from the Network Tasks panel.

3. When the New Connection Wizard dialog box appears, click the Next button.

4. When the Network Connection Type screen appears, check the Connect to the Internet option and then click the Next button.

note

If the Show All Connections option doesn't appear on your Start menu, open My Computer, select Network Places, and then select View Network Connections.

tip

If you've already set up a home network with its own Internet connection, select Set Up a Home or Small Office Network and follow the instructions from there.

5. When the Getting Ready screen appears, check the Set Up My Connection Manually option and then click Next.

6. When the Internet Connection screen appears, select which type of connection you have—dial-up broadband with username and password, or always-on broadband—then click Next.

7. If prompted, enter the name of your Internet service provider and then click Next.

8. If you have a dial-up ISP, enter the provider's dial-up phone number and then click Next.

9. If prompted, enter your username and password (as provided by your ISP); then click Next.

10. Click the Finish button to complete the process.

Whew—that's a lot of work! Still, after you get it set up, you're good to go and ready to start exploring the Internet.

> **tip**
>
> If your ISP provided you with an installation CD, check the Use the CD I Got From an ISP option, and follow the onscreen instructions from there.

> **tip**
>
> If you haven't yet signed up for Internet service, select Choose From a List of Internet Service Providers and follow the instructions from there. You can subscribe to Microsoft's own MSN service, or select from a list of other available ISPs.

Sharing an Internet Connection

If you have more than one PC in your home, you can connect them to share a single Internet connection. This is particularly useful if you have a high-speed broadband connection.

You share an Internet connection by connecting your broadband modem to your home network. It doesn't matter whether you have a wired or a wireless network; the connection is similar in both instances. All you have to do is run an Ethernet cable from your broadband modem to your network hub or router and then Windows will do the rest, connecting your modem to the network so that all your computers can access the connection.

> **note**
>
> If you selected the always-on broadband connection option, you won't be prompted for any information about your ISP, username, or password.

To work through all the details of this type of connection, turn to Chapter 9, "Setting Up a Home Network." It's really quite easy!

Connecting to a Public WiFi Hotspot

If you have a notebook PC, you also have the option to connect to the Internet when you're out and about. Many coffeehouses, restaurants, libraries, and hotels offer wireless WiFi Internet service, either free or for an hourly or daily fee. Assuming that your notebook has a built-in WiFi adapter (and it probably does), connecting to a public WiFi hotspot is a snap.

When you're near a WiFi hotspot, your PC should automatically pick up the WiFi signal. Make sure that your WiFi adapter is turned on (some notebooks have a switch for this, either on the front or on the side of the unit), and then look for a wireless connection icon in Windows' system tray or notification area. Click this icon (or select Start, Connect To), and Windows displays a list of available wireless networks near you. Select the network you want to connect to; then click the Connect button.

After Windows connects to the selected hotspot, you can log on to the wireless network. This is typically done by opening Internet Explorer or a similar web browser. If the hotspot has free public access, you'll be able to surf normally. If the hotspot requires a password, payment, or other logon procedure, it will intercept the request for your normal home page and instead display its own login page. Enter the appropriate information, and you'll be surfing in no time!

note

A wireless access point is called a *hotspot*. Hotspots can be either public (accessible to all—sometimes via password) or private.

note

At present, the Starbucks chain offers WiFi service via T-Mobile, at $9.99/day or $29.99/month. The Caribou Coffee chain gives you one free hour of access per day and then requires a coffee purchase to get additional hours of access. (They give you a card with a login password.)

THE ABSOLUTE MINIMUM

When you're configuring your new PC system to connect to the Internet, remember these important points:

- You connect to the Internet through an Internet service provider; you need to set up an account with an ISP before you can connect.

- You can sign up for either dial-up (slower and less expensive) or broadband (faster and more expensive) service.

- There are three different types of broadband service—DSL, cable, and satellite.

- After you have an account with an ISP, you need to configure Windows for your new account.

- If you have more than one computer at home, you can share your Internet connection by connecting your broadband modem to your home network.

- If you have a notebook PC, you can connect to the Internet wirelessly at any public WiFi hotspot, such as those offered by Starbucks, Caribou Coffee, and similar establishments.

20

SENDING AND RECEIVING EMAIL

Email is a modern way to communicate with friends, family, and colleagues. An email message is like a regular letter, except that it's composed electronically and delivered almost immediately via the Internet.

You can use several programs to send and receive email messages. If you're in a corporate environment, or running Microsoft Office, you can use Microsoft Outlook for your email. (Outlook is also a scheduler and personal information manager.) If you're connecting from home, the simpler Windows Mail (in Windows Vista) or Outlook Express (in Windows XP) might be a better choice; these programs are easier to learn and use than their bigger brother, Outlook.

Because Windows Mail is included free with all Windows Vista PCs, that's the one we'll cover in this chapter. Know, however, that it's almost identical to the older Outlook Express, so if you're a Windows XP user, most of what you see here is directly applicable to the program you're using. In fact, most of what's here also works with Microsoft Outlook; all of these email programs look and act similarly.

Setting Up Your Email Account

Back in Chapter 19, "Connecting to the Internet—At Home and on the Road," you learned how to configure your computer for your particular Internet service provider. When you did your main configuration, you should have entered information about your email account.

If you later change email providers, or add a new email account, you'll have to access your email settings separately. To configure Windows Mail for a new email account, you'll need to know the following information:

- The email address assigned by your ISP, in the format *name@domain.com*.
- The type of email server you'll be using; it's probably a POP3 server. (It could also be an HTTP or IMAP server, but POP3 is more common.)
- The name or address of the incoming email and outgoing email servers.
- The account name and password you use to connect to the email servers.

After you have this information (which should be supplied by your ISP), you can enter it manually into Windows Mail by following these steps:

1. From within Windows Mail, select Tools, Accounts to display the Internet Accounts dialog box.
2. When the Internet Accounts dialog box appears, click Add.
3. When prompted, choose to add an E-mail Account and then click Next.
4. When the next dialog box appears, enter your name and then click Next.
5. When the next dialog box appears, enter the email address assigned by your ISP; then click Next.
6. When the next dialog box appears, select the type of email server you're using (typically POP3), the incoming email server name or address, and the outgoing email server name or address. Click Next.

tip

To avoid entering your password every time you check your email, select the Remember Password option in the Internet Mail Logon dialog box.

7. When the next dialog box appears, enter your email username and password and then click Next.

8. When the final dialog box appears, click Finish.

You're now ready to send and receive email.

Understanding the Windows Mail Window

Before we start working with email, let's take a look at the Windows Mail window. As you can see in Figure 20.1, the basic Windows Mail window is divided into three panes. The pane on the left is called the folder list, and it's where you access your Inbox and other message folders. The top pane on the right is the message pane, and it lists all the messages stored in the selected folder. Below that is the preview pane, and it displays the contents of the selected message.

Folder list   Message pane   Preview pane

FIGURE 20.1
Use Windows
Mail to send and
receive email.

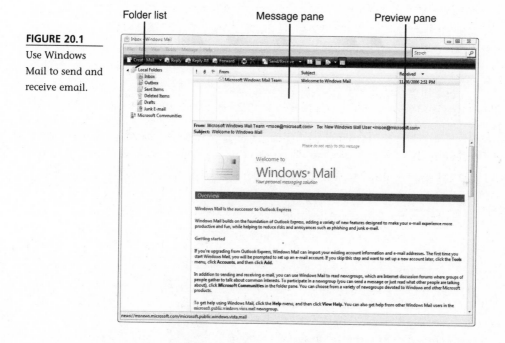

The way it all works is that you select a location in the Folder List (typically your inbox), select a message header in the Message pane, and view the contents of that message in the Preview pane.

Managing Your Email

Using Windows Mail is easy—and composing a new email message isn't much different from writing a memo in Microsoft Word. You just have to know which buttons to push!

Composing a Message

It's easy to create a new email message. Just follow these steps:

1. Click the Create Mail button on the Windows Mail toolbar; this launches a New Message window, similar to the one shown in Figure 20.2.

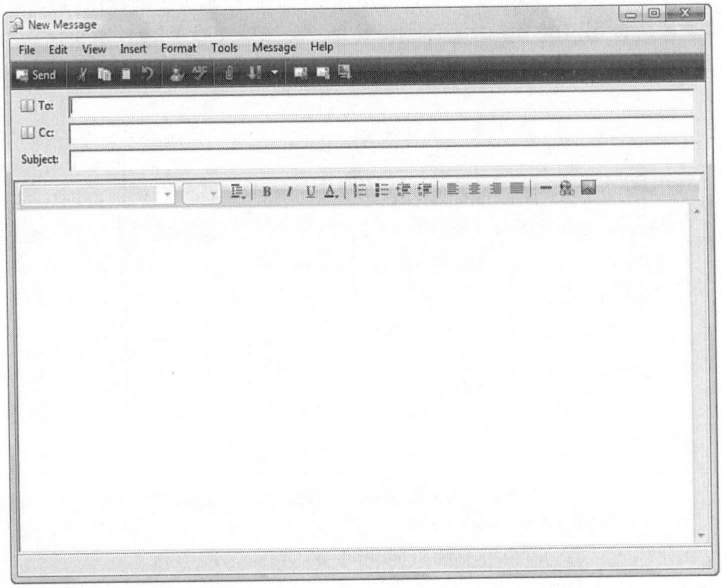

FIGURE 20.2

Use the New Message window to compose a new email message.

2. Enter the email address of the recipient(s) in the To field and then enter the address of anyone you want to receive a carbon copy in the Cc box. You can enter multiple addresses, as long as you separate multiple addresses with a semicolon (;), like this: `mmiller@molehill-group.com;gjetson@sprockets.com`.

3. Move your cursor to the main message area and type your message.

4. When your message is complete, send it to the Outbox by clicking the Send button.

tip

You can test your email account by sending a message to yourself; just enter your own email address in the To field.

Now you need to send the message from your Outbox over the Internet to the intended recipient (you!). You do this by clicking the Send/Receive button on the Windows Mail toolbar. Assuming your computer is connected to the Internet, your message will now be sent.

Reading New Messages

When you receive new email messages, they're stored in the Windows Mail Inbox. To display all new messages, select the Inbox icon from the Folders list. All waiting messages now appear in the Message pane.

To read a specific message, select its header in the Message pane. The contents of that message are displayed in the Preview pane.

Replying to a Message

To reply to an email message, follow these steps:

tip

You also can double-click a message header to display the message in a separate window.

1. Select the message header in the Message pane.

2. Click the Reply button on the Windows Mail toolbar; this opens a Re: window, which is just like a New Message window except with the text from the original message "quoted" in the text area and the email address of the recipient (the person who sent the original message) pre-entered in the To field.

3. Enter your reply text in the message window.

4. Click the Send button to send your reply back to the original sender.

Sending Files Via Email

The easiest way to share a file with another user is via email, as an *attachment*.

Attaching a File to an Email Message

To send a file via email, you attach that file to a standard email message. When the message is sent, the file travels along with it; when the message is received, the file is right there, waiting to be opened.

To attach a file to an outgoing email message, follow these steps:

1. Start with a new message and then click the Attach button in the message's toolbar; this displays the Insert Attachment dialog box.

2. Click the Browse button to locate and select the file you want to send.

3. Click Attach.

The attached file is now listed in a new Attach: field below the Subject: field in the message window. When you click the Send button, the email message and its attached file are sent together to your Outbox.

Opening an Email Attachment

When you receive a message that contains a file attachment, you'll see a paper clip icon in the message header and a paper clip button in the preview pane header. You can choose to view (open) the attached file or save it to your hard disk.

To view or open an attachment, click the paper clip button in the preview pane header, and then click the attachment's filename. (At this point you may be prompted by a security message; make sure you know where the attachment came from before you proceed.) This opens the attachment in its associated application. If you're asked whether you want to save or view the attachment, select view.

To save an attachment to your hard disk, click the paper clip button in the preview pane header, and then select Save Attachments. When the Save Attachments dialog box appears, select a location for the file and click the Save button.

Protecting Against Spam, Phishing Scams, and Viruses

Although Windows Mail may look a lot like its predecessor, Outlook Express, it's much improved under the hood. Some of the most important improvements have to do with security—in particular, the capability to block spam, phishing scams, and email viruses.

note

Learn more about spam, phishing, and viruses in Chapter 12, "Protecting Your PC from Viruses, Spam, and Other Online Nuisances."

Spam Blocking

If you're like most users, you get more than your fair share of junk email messages—also known as *spam*. These spam messages can fill up your inbox and are a major annoyance.

To help stop the flood of spam email messages, Windows Mail includes a powerful Junk Mail Filter. This new filter uses Bayesian filtering, which analyzes the probability of any given word being included in spam messages and then applies that analysis to all incoming messages. Emails that include high-probability spam words are automatically routed to the Junk E-mail folder.

You can open the Junk E-mail folder to view your spam messages, or just delete the messages without review. In either case, you don't have to deal with them clogging your inbox!

Phishing Filter

Also new in Windows Vista is the inclusion of anti-phishing technology. Microsoft's Phishing Filter helps protect you from identity theft by warning you of the fake email messages common to phishing scams.

Phishing is a technique used by online scam artists to steal your identity by tricking you into disclosing valuable personal information, such as passwords, credit card numbers, and other financial data. A phishing scam typically starts with a phony email message that appears to be from a legitimate source, such as your bank, eBay, or PayPal.

When you click the link in the phishing email, you're taken to a fake website masquerading as the real site, complete with logos and official-looking text. You're encouraged to enter your personal information into the forms on the web page; when you do so, your information is sent to the scammer, and you become a victim of identity theft. When your data falls into the hands of criminals, it can be used to hack into your online accounts, make unauthorized charges on your credit card, and maybe even drain your bank account.

Microsoft's Phishing Filter compares all the links in your Windows Mail email messages to an online list of known phishing websites. If the link matches a fraudulent site, Windows Mail blocks the links in the email and displays a warning message at the top of the message. When you see this type of message, just delete the email—and never, *never* click through any of the links!

Virus Protection

Computer viruses are files that can attack your system and damage your programs and documents. Most viruses are spread when someone sends you an email message with an unexpected file attachment—and then you open the file. It's just too easy to receive an email message with a file attached, click the file to open it, and then launch the virus file. Boom! Your computer is infected.

Viruses can be found in many types of files. The most common file types for viruses are .EXE, .VBS, .PIF, and .COM. Viruses can also be embedded in Word (.DOC) or Excel (.XLS) files. You *can't* catch a virus from a picture file, so viewing a .JPG, .GIF, .TIF, and .BMP file is completely safe.

The best way to avoid catching a virus via email is to *not open any files attached to incoming email messages.* Period.

That includes messages where you know the sender, because some viruses are capable of taking over an email program and "spoofing" other users' addresses. An email message might look like it's coming from a friend, but it's really coming from another machine and includes a virus. (Pretty tricky, eh?)

By default, Windows Mail is configured to automatically reject files that might contain viruses. You can verify this setting (or turn it off, if you want to receive a file), by opening the Options dialog box, selecting the Security tab, and checking both options in the Virus Protection section.

caution

Remember, you activate a virus only when you open a file attached to an email message. You can't activate the virus just by viewing the message itself.

Using Address Book to Manage Your Contacts

Windows includes a contact manager application, called *Windows Contacts*, that you can use to store information about your friends, family, and business associates. (In older versions of Windows, this was called the Address Book.) You can then import this contact information into Windows Mail (to send email), Windows Calendar (to remind you of birthdays), and Microsoft Word (to personalize letters and address envelopes and labels).

To add a new contact to your Windows Contacts, click the New button on the Windows Contacts toolbar and then select New Contact. Enter all the information you know (you don't have to fill in *all* the blanks) and click OK. (You can also add a contact directly from Windows Mail by selecting File, New, Contact.)

note

The Windows Contacts database is identical to the Address Book included with Microsoft Works, as you learned in Chapter 14, "The Suite Spot: Working with Microsoft Works and Microsoft Office."

You can also add contacts from any email messages you receive. Just right-click the sender's name in the email message and select Add to Contacts. This creates a new contact for that person; you can then go to Windows Contacts and add more detailed information later—as described next.

To send email to one of your contacts, all you have to do is click the To button in your new Windows Mail message. This displays the Select Recipients dialog box, shown in Figure 20.3. Select the contact(s) you want and click either the To, Cc, or Bcc buttons. Click OK when you're finished adding names.

note

A Cc (carbon copy) message is one sent to someone other than the main recipient. A Bcc (blind carbon copy) is just like a Cc, except the Bcc recipient is hidden from the other recipients. The Bcc field only appears when you select View, All Headers within an email message.

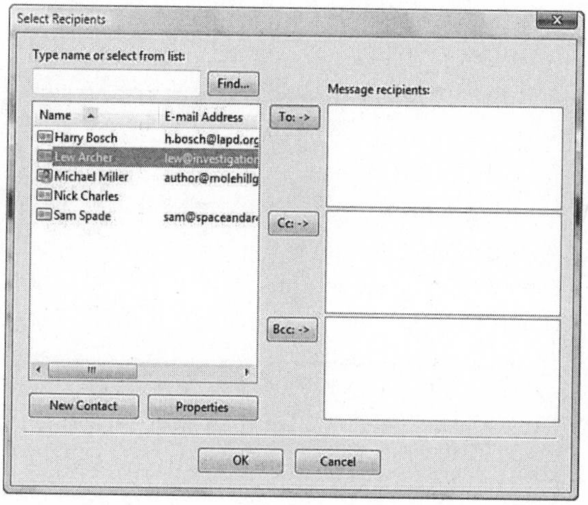

FIGURE 20.3
Sending email to contacts in Windows Contacts.

THE ABSOLUTE MINIMUM

Here are the key points to remember from this chapter:

■ Email is a fast and easy way to send electronic letters over the Internet.

■ You can send and receive email messages using the Windows Mail program, preinstalled on most new Windows Vista PCs.

■ Sending a new message is as easy as clicking the Create Mail button; reading a message is as easy as selecting it in the Message pane (and viewing it in the Preview pane).

■ Windows Mail includes new junk email and phishing filters, to protect you from spam and fraudulent email messages.

■ Don't open any unexpected files attached to incoming email messages—they might contain computer viruses!

■ You can store frequently used email addresses in the Windows Contacts utility.

21

SURFING THE WEB WITH INTERNET EXPLORER

After you're signed up with an ISP and connected to the Internet, it's time to get surfing. The World Wide Web is a particular part of the Internet with all sorts of cool content and useful services, and you surf the Web with a piece of software called a *web browser*.

The most popular web browser today is Microsoft's Internet Explorer, and you probably have a copy of it already installed on your new PC. This chapter shows you how to use Internet Explorer and then takes you on a quick trip around the Web—just enough to get your online feet wet!

Understanding the Web

Before you can surf the Web, you need to understand a little bit about how it works.

Information on the World Wide Web is presented in *pages*. A web page is similar to a page in a book, made up of text and graphics. A web page differs from a book page, however, in that it can include other elements, such as audio and video, and links to other web pages.

It's this linking to other web pages that makes the Web such a dynamic way to present information. A *link* on a web page can point to another web page on the same site or to another site. Most links are included as part of a web page's text and are called *hypertext links*, or just *hyperlinks*. (If a link is part of a graphic, it's called a *graphic link*.) These links are usually in a different color from the rest of the text and often are underlined; when you click a link, you're taken directly to the linked page.

Web pages reside at a *website*. A website is nothing more than a collection of web pages (each in its own individual computer file) residing on a host computer. The host computer is connected full-time to the Internet so that you can access the site—and its web pages—anytime you access the Internet. The main page at a website usually is called a *home page*, and it often serves as an opening screen that provides a brief overview and menu of everything you can find at that site. The address of a web page is called a *URL*, which stands for uniform resource locator. Most URLs start with http://, add a www., continue with the name of the site, and end with a .com.

> **tip**
>
> You can normally leave off the http:// when you enter an address into your web browser. In most cases, you can even leave off the www. and just start with the domain part of the address.

Using Internet Explorer 7

The web browser included in Windows is Internet Explorer (IE). In Windows Vista, the version of IE is Internet Explorer 7. This version is also available for Windows XP, although you may need to upgrade from a previous version to get IE7.

> **note**
>
> To upgrade Windows XP to Internet Explorer 7, go to http://www.microsoft.com/windows/ie/. The download is free.

Internet Explorer 7 is easy to use. To launch IE, follow these steps:

1. Click the Start button to display the Start menu.

2. Select Internet Explorer (at the upper-left part of the menu).

Figure 21.1 shows the various parts of the IE program, and Table 21.1 tells you what each of the buttons on the toolbar does.

note

You can use any web browser to surf the Web. The instructions here work equally as well with Mozilla Firefox or AOL Explorer—or with previous versions of Internet Explorer.

Address box   Tabs   Toolbar

FIGURE 21.1

Microsoft's Internet Explorer 7 web browser.

Table 21.1   Internet Explorer Toolbar Buttons

Button	Operation
Back	Return to the previously viewed page
Forward	View the next page
Stop	Stop loading the current page
Refresh	Reload the current page
Favorites	Go to your favorite web pages
Add to Favorites	Add the current page to your Favorites list
Quick Tabs	View all tabbed pages on a single page
New Tab	Open a new tab to view a new web page
Home	Return to your designated start page
Feeds	View the latest headlines from RSS news feeds
Print	Print the current page
Page	Perform various page-related operations (cut, copy, zoom, send via email, and so on)
Tools	Configure IE's settings

Basic Web Surfing

Internet Explorer enables you to quickly and easily browse the World Wide Web—just by clicking your mouse. Here's a step-by-step tour of IE's basic functions:

1. When you first launch Internet Explorer, it loads your predefined home page.

2. Enter a new web address in the Address box, and press Enter. Internet Explorer loads the new page.

3. Click any link on the current web page. Internet Explorer loads the new page.

tip

To change Internet Explorer's home page, drag a page's icon from Internet Explorer's Address box onto the Home button on the toolbar.

4. To return to the previous page, click the Back button (or press the Backspace key on your keyboard). If you've backed up several pages and want to return to the page you were on last, click the Forward button.

5. To return to your start page, click the Home button.

Using Tabbed Browsing

In previous versions, Internet Explorer utilized a single-document interface—that is, each browser window could contain only a single web page. IE7, in contrast, has a multidocument interface, with multiple web pages displayed in a single browser window via the use of tabs.

The use of tabs within a single browser window lets you keep multiple web pages open simultaneously. This is great when you want to keep previous pages open for reference or want to run web-based applications in the background.

To open a web page on a new tab, just click the next (empty) tab and enter a URL. You can also choose to open a link within a page in a new tab, by right-clicking the link and selecting Open in New Tab.

You switch between tabs by clicking a tab with your mouse or by pressing Ctrl+Tab on your keyboard. You can also reorder your tabs by dragging and dropping them into a new position.

You can view the contents of all open tabs with IE's Quick Tabs feature. When you click the Quick Tab icon or press Ctrl+Q, all open web pages are displayed as thumbnails in a single window, as shown in Figure 21.2. Click any thumbnail to open that tab in the full window.

FIGURE 21.2

Viewing multiple pages via the Quick Tabs feature.

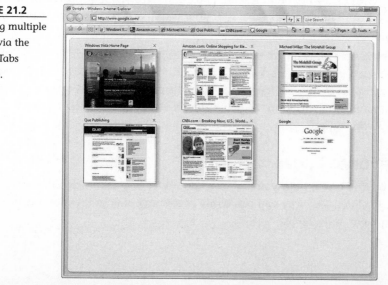

Advanced Operations

Internet Explorer 7 can do much more than simple browsing. Let's take a quick look at some of the more advanced operations in Internet Explorer that can make your online life a lot easier.

Searching from the Browser

If you search the Web a lot, and I know you do, you spend a lot of time going to your favorite search site. In Internet Explorer 7 you don't have to keep going back to that site; you can do all your searching from within the browser window.

That's because Internet Explorer 7 adds an Instant Search box to the main toolbar, to the right of the Address box. This lets you perform web searches without having to first navigate to a separate search site.

Learn more about web searching in Chapter 22, "Searching the Web."

To conduct a search from within IE7, just enter your query into the Search box and press the Enter key on your keyboard. Your query is sent via IE over the Internet to the selected search provider. The search site receives the query, searches its own previously compiled index of web pages, and returns a page of search results, which is displayed in the Internet Explorer window. It's that easy.

By default, IE routes your search to Microsoft's Windows Live Search site. If you prefer to use another search engine, such as Google, you can change this default. Just click the down arrow next to the Search box and select Change Search Defaults; when the next dialog box appears, select the search engine you want and click the Set Default button.

If the search site you want isn't listed in the Change Search Defaults list, select Find More Providers from the pull-down list, instead. When the Add Search Providers web page appears, as shown in Figure 21.3, click the search engine you want to use. You can then return to the Change Search Defaults dialog box to select this new search engine as your default.

Saving Your Favorite Pages

When you find a web page you like, you can add it to a list of Favorites within Internet Explorer. This way you can easily access any of your favorite sites just by selecting them from the list.

FIGURE 21.3

Choosing a new
search provider
in Internet
Explorer 7.

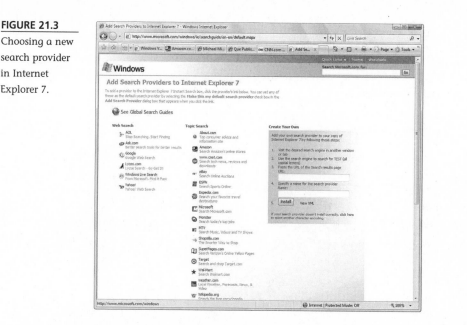

To add a page to your Favorites list, follow these steps:

1. Go to the web page you want to add to your Favorites list.
2. Click the Add to Favorites button and select Add to Favorites from the pop-up menu.
3. When the Add a Favorite dialog box appears, confirm the page's name and select the folder where you want to place this link.
4. Click OK.

To view a page in your Favorites list, follow these steps:

1. Click the Favorites Center button. A new pane appears in the browser window, as shown in Figure 21.4.
2. Click the Favorites button in this new pane.
3. Click any folder in the Favorites pane to display the contents of that folder.
4. Click a favorite page, and that page is displayed in the browser window.

Revisiting History

Internet Explorer has three ways of keeping track of web pages you've visited, so you can easily revisit them without having to re-enter the web page address.

To revisit the last page you visited, click the Back button on the toolbar. You can continue clicking Back to go the last previous page.

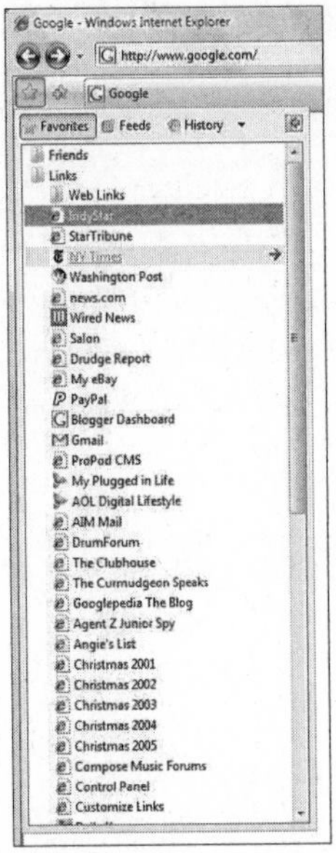

FIGURE 21.4

Click the
Favorites button
to display the
Favorites pane.

To revisit one of the last half-dozen or so pages
viewed in your current session, click the down
arrow next to the Forward button. This drops
down a menu containing the last ten pages
you've visited. Highlight any page on this
menu to jump directly to that page.

To revisit pages you've viewed in the past several
days, you use IE's History pane. Just follow
these steps:

1. Click the Favorites Center button to display the Favorites pane.

2. In the new pane, click the History button.

3. Click a specific page to display that page in the right pane.

tip

To sort the sites in the
History pane by date, site,
most visited, or order visited
today, click the down arrow
next to the History button in
the Favorites pane and
make a new selection.

Printing

Printing a web page is easy—just click the Print button. If you want to see a preview
of the page before it prints, click the down arrow next to the Print button and select
Print Preview.

Viewing RSS News Feeds

Another new feature in Internet Explorer 7 is the capability to view the latest content from blogs, news sites, and other similar web pages. This is done via *Real Simple*

Syndication (RSS), a technology used to syndicate, or distribute, frequently updated content.

Previously, you had to use a separate news reader program to view these RSS news feeds. With Internet Explorer 7, however, you can easily subscribe to and read RSS feeds directly in the web browser.

To subscribe to the feed for a given website, navigate to the site and then click the Feeds button on the Internet Explorer 7 toolbar. This displays an RSS-friendly version of the current page, such as the one shown in Figure 21.5; click Subscribe to This Feed to add the subscription. This feed is then added to your list of RSS subscriptions.

FIGURE 21.5

An RSS-friendly web page; click to subscribe.

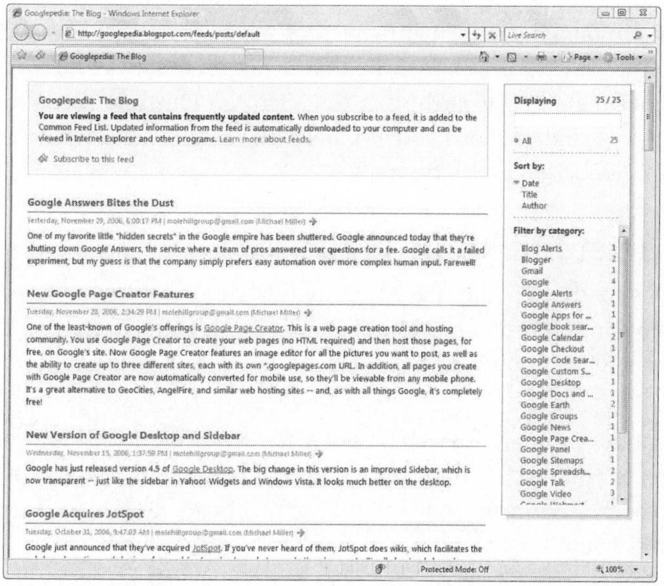

To view the latest news and headlines from your subscribed feeds, follow these steps:

1. Click the Favorites Center button to display the Favorites pane.
2. In the new pane, click the Feeds button.
3. Click a specific feed to display the latest posts from that feed in the browser window.
4. You can now click a specific feed headline to read the full article or posting.

Internet Security with IE7

Also new in Internet Explorer 7 are several security-related features. Compared to previous versions of the browser, IE7 is much more immune to a variety of security-related issues.

Protecting Against Phishing Scams

You learned about phishing scams back in Chapter 12, "Protecting Your PC from Viruses, Spam, and Other Online Nuisances." To protect you from phishing scams, IE7 incorporates Microsoft's Phishing Filter. This filter automatically connects to an online service that contains a huge database of suspicious websites and alerts you if you attempt to go to one of these sites.

If you attempt to click a link to a known phishing site, the Microsoft Phishing Filter blocks access to the site, changes the Address Bar to red, navigates to a neutral page, and displays a warning message. In other words, if the site is fraudulent, IE7 won't let you go there.

In addition, the Phishing Filter helps protect you from sites that might be fake. If you attempt to click a link to a site that is not on the list of known fraudulent sites but behaves similarly to such sites, the Microsoft Phishing Filter changes the Address Bar to yellow and cautions you of potentially suspicious content. Unless you're sure the site is good, don't click through.

Protecting Against Malicious Websites

Another way that IE7 improves security is to run in *Protected Mode*. This mode prevents malicious websites or programs from modifying system files and settings without your explicit approval, thus protecting you from viruses, spyware, and computer attacks.

You see, hackers often use web browsers to deliver malicious software (called *malware*) to your system and cause damage to your PC. This is typically done by executing code within a web page that then takes over your browser and accesses critical parts of your system.

To block these web-based attacks, IE7's Protected Mode isolates suspicious programs from other applications and the operating system, thus preventing any destructive program from taking over your browser and initiating an attack. Any program or code downloaded from the Internet is isolated in its own browser window, which insulates the Windows operating system from the potentially malicious code.

It's security that operates completely in the background. You may not be aware that it's there, but IE7's Protected Mode operation is always working to keep you safe.

note

Protected mode is only available with the Windows Vista version of IE7, not the XP version.

Blocking Pop-up Ads

If you've surfed the Web for any time at all, you've noticed those annoying pop-up windows that appear when you visit some websites. Not so with Internet Explorer 7, which incorporates a Pop-up Blocker. This feature, which is enabled by default, blocks the automatic opening of unwanted pop-up windows.

When a site tries to open a pop-up window that is blocked by Internet Explorer, a notification appears in the Information Bar of the browser window. If you click the notification, you can choose to temporarily or permanently allow pop-ups from this site. Otherwise, say bye-bye to unwanted pop-ups!

THE ABSOLUTE MINIMUM

Here are the key things to remember about surfing the Web:

■ You surf the Web with a program called a web browser; Internet Explorer is probably the browser installed on your new PC.

■ The latest version of IE, Internet Explorer 7, is available for both Windows Vista and Windows XP.

■ You can go to a particular web page by entering the page's address in the Address box and then pressing Enter; click a hyperlink on a web page to jump to the linked page.

■ New to IE7 is tabbed browsing, where new web pages can be opened in additional tabs; click a tab to switch to that web page.

■ IE7 lets you search the Web from within the browser, thanks to the Instant Search box at the top of the window.

■ IE7 also includes an RSS feed reader, pop-up blocking, and a phishing filter.

22

SEARCHING THE WEB

Now that you know how to surf the Web, how do you find the precise information you're looking for? Fortunately, there are numerous sites that help you search the Web for the specific information you want. Not surprisingly, these are among the most popular sites on the Internet.

This chapter is all about searching the Web. You'll learn the best places to search, and the best ways to search. I'll even help you cheat a little by listing some of the most popular sites for different types of information.

So pull up a chair, launch your web browser, and loosen up those fingers—it's time to start searching!

How to Search the Web

Most Internet search sites are actually *search engines*. They employ special software programs (called *spiders* or *crawlers*) to roam the Web automatically, feeding what they find back to a massive bank of computers. These computers then build giant *indexes* of the Web, hundreds of millions of pages strong.

When you perform a search at a search engine site, your query is sent to the search engine's index. (You never actually search the Web itself, you only search the index that was created by the spiders crawling the Web.) The search engine then creates a list of pages in its index that match, to one degree or another, the query you entered.

Constructing a Query

Almost every search site on the Web contains two basic components—a *search box* and a *search button*. You enter your query—one or more *keywords* that describe what you're looking for—into the search box, and then click the Search button (or press the Enter key) to start the search. The search site then returns a list of web pages that match your query; click any link to go directly to the page in question.

How you construct your query determines how relevant the results will be that you receive. It's important to focus on the keywords you use, because the search sites look for these words when they process your query. Your keywords are compared to the web pages the search site knows about; the more keywords found on a web page, the better the match.

Choose keywords that best describe the information you're looking for—using as many keywords as you need. Don't be afraid of using too many keywords; in fact, using too *few* keywords is a common fault of many novice searchers. The more words you use, the better idea the search engine has of what you're looking for.

Using Wildcards

But what if you're not quite sure which word to use? For example, would the best results come from looking for *auto*, *automobile*, or *automotive*? Many search sites let you use *wildcards* to "stand in" for parts of a word that you're not quite sure about.

In most instances, the asterisk character (*) is used as a wildcard to match any character or group of characters, from its particular position in the word to the end of that word. So, in the previous example, entering `auto*` would return

caution

One notable site that *doesn't* let you use the wildcard character is Google. Instead, Google uses word stemming technology, which automatically searches for all forms of a word—plural, past tense, and so on—without any direction on your part.

all three words—auto, automobile, *and* automotive (as well as automatic, autocratic, and any other word that starts with "auto").

Searching for an Exact Phrase

Normally, a multiple-word query searches for web pages that include all the words in the query, in any order. There is a way, however, to search for an exact phrase. All you have to do is enclose the phrase in quotation marks.

For example, to search for Monty Python, *don't* enter **Monty Python**. Instead, enter **"Monty Python"**—surrounded by quotation marks. Putting the phrase between quotation marks returns results about the comedy troupe, while entering the words individually returns pages about snakes and guys named Monty.

Where to Search

Now that you know how to search, *where* should you search? There's one obvious choice, and a lot of alternatives.

Google—The Most Popular Search Site on the Web

The best (and most popular) search engine today is Google (www.google.com). Google is easy to use and extremely fast and returns highly relevant results. That's because it indexes more pages than any other site—billions and billions of pages, if you're counting.

Most users search Google several times a week, if not several times a day. The Google home page, shown in Figure 22.1, is a marvel of simplicity and elegant web page design. All you have to do to start a search is to enter one or more keywords into the search box and then click the Google Search button. This returns a list of results ranked in order of relevance, such as the one shown in Figure 22.2. Click a results link to view that page.

Google also offers a variety of advanced search options to help you fine-tune your search. These options are found on the Advanced Search page, which you get to by clicking the Advanced Search link on Google's home page. To narrow your search results, all you have to do is make the appropriate selections from the options present.

Another neat thing about Google is all the specialty searches it offers. Table 22.1 details some of these "hidden" search features.

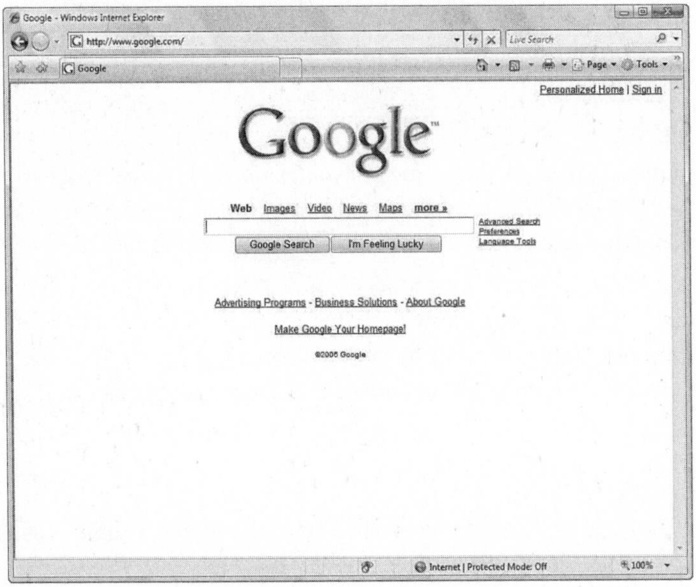

FIGURE 22.1

Searching the
Web at Google.

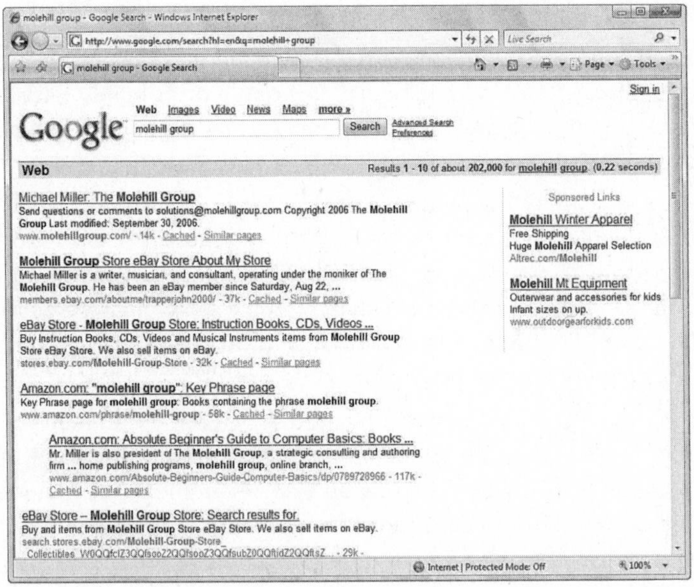

FIGURE 22.2

The results of a
Google search.

Table 22.1   Google Search Options

Search	URL	Description
Froogle	froogle.google.com	Comparison shopping
Google Apple Macintosh Search	www.google.com/mac	Searches for technical information on Apple's website
Google Blog Search	blogsearch.google.com	Searches blogs and blog postings
Google Book Search	books.google.com	Searches the full text of thousands of fiction and nonfiction books
Google Catalogs	catalogs.google.com	Displays print catalogs from major catalog retailers
Google Directory	directory.google.com	Editor-selected search results
Google Groups	groups.google.com	Searches Usenet newsgroups
Google Image Search	images.google.com	Searches for pictures
Google Local	local.google.com	Searches for local businesses
Google Maps	maps.google.com	Displays maps and driving directions—as well as cool satellite photos
Google Microsoft Search	www.google.com/microsoft	Searches for technical information on Microsoft's website
Google News	news.google.com	Searches the latest news headlines—as well as historical new archives dating back two centuries
Google Scholar	scholar.google.com	Searches various scholarly papers
Google U.S. Government Search	www.google.com/ig/usgov	Searches U.S. government sites
Google University Search	www.google.com/options/universities.html	Searches college and university websites

Google also owns a number of related websites that might be of interest. Of particular interest are Blogger (www.blogger.com), home to tens of thousands of personal weblogs, and YouTube (www.youtube.com), the Web's premiere site for posting and viewing videos.

Other Search Sites

Although Google is far and away the most popular search engine, many other search engines provide excellent (and sometimes different) results. These search engines include

- AllTheWeb (www.alltheweb.com)
- AltaVista (www.altavista.com)
- Ask.com (www.ask.com)
- ChaCha (www.chacha.com)
- HotBot (www.hotbot.com)
- LookSmart (search.looksmart.com)
- Open Directory (www.dmoz.org)
- Windows Live Search (www.live.com)
- Yahoo! (www.yahoo.com)

Searching for People and Businesses

As good as Google and other search sites are for finding specific web pages, they're not always that great for finding people. (Although, to be fair, Google is getting much better at this.) When there's a person (or an address or a phone number) you want to find, you need to use a site that specializes in people searches.

People listings on the web go by the common name of *white pages directories*, the same as traditional white pages phone books. These directories typically enable you to enter all or part of a person's name and then search for his address and phone number. Many of these sites also let you search for personal email addresses and business addresses and phone numbers.

tip

You can also use Google to display stock quotes (enter the stock ticker), answers to mathematical calculations (enter the equation), and measurement conversions (enter what you want to convert). Google can also track USPS, UPS, and FedEx packages (enter the tracking number), as well as the progress of airline flights (enter the airline and flight number).

tip

A number of search engines also let you search multiple search engines and directories from a single page—which is called a *metasearch*. The top metasearchers include Dogpile (www.dogpile.com), Mamma (www.mamma.com), MetaCrawler (www.metacrawler.com), and Search.com (www.search.com).

The best of these directories include

- AnyWho (www.anywho.com)
- InfoSpace (www.infospace.com)
- Switchboard (www.switchboard.com)
- WhitePages.com (www.whitepages.com)

In addition, all of these white pages directories also serve as yellow pages directories for looking up businesses. They're one-stop search sites for any individual or business you want to look up!

THE ABSOLUTE MINIMUM

Here are the key points to remember from this chapter:

- When you need to search for specific information on the Internet, you can use one of the Web's many search engines and directories.
- The most popular Internet search engine is Google, which indexes billions of individual web pages.
- Other popular search engines and directories include Yahoo!, Windows Live Search, AltaVista, and Ask.com.
- It's better to search for people (and their phone numbers and addresses) at specific people-search sites, such as InfoSpace and Switchboard.

23

Shopping Online

Many users have discovered that the Internet is a great place to buy things—all kinds of things. All manner of online merchants make it easy to buy books, CDs, and other merchandise with the click of a mouse.

In spite of the popularity of online retailing, many users are still a little hesitant to do their shopping online. Although there certainly is some amount of online fraud (just as there's plenty of fraud in the real world), in general the Internet is a fairly safe place to shop—if you follow the rules, and take a few simple precautions.

Read on, then, to find out the best places to shop online—and how to shop safely.

How to Shop Online

If you've never shopped online before, you're probably wondering just what to expect. Shopping over the Web is actually easy; all you need is your computer and a credit card—and a fast connection to the Internet!

Online shopping is pretty much the same, no matter which retailer you shop at. You proceed through a multiple-step process that goes like this:

1. **Find a product**, either by browsing or searching through the retailer's site.

2. **Examine the product** by viewing the photos and information on a product listing page.

3. **Order the product** by clicking a "buy it now" button on the product listing page that puts the item in your online shopping cart.

4. **Check out** by entering your payment and shipping information.

5. **Confirm the order** and wait for the merchant to ship your merchandise.

Let's look at each of these steps separately.

Step 1: Find a Product

The first step in online shopping is the actual shopping. That means finding the site where you want to shop, and then either browsing through different product categories or using the site's search feature to find a specific product.

Browsing product categories online is similar to browsing through the departments of a retail store. You typically click a link to access a major product category, and then click further links to view subcategories within the main category. For example, the main category might be Clothing; the subcategories might be Men's, Women's, and Children's clothing. If you click the Men's link, you might see a list of further subcategories: outerwear, shirts, pants, and the like. Just keep clicking until you reach the type of item that you're looking for.

Searching for products is often a faster way to find what you're looking for if you have something specific in mind. For example, if you're looking for a men's silk jacket, you can enter the words **men's silk jacket** into the site's Search box, and get a list of specific items that match those criteria. The only problem with searching is that you might not know exactly what it is you're looking for; if this describes your situation, you're probably better off browsing. But if you *do* know what you want—and you don't want to deal with lots of irrelevant items—then searching is the faster option.

tip

When searching for items at an online retailer, you can use the same general search guidelines I discussed in Chapter 22, "Searching the Web."

Step 2: Examine the Product

Whether you browse or search, you'll probably end up looking at a list of different products on a web page. These listings typically feature one-line descriptions of each item—in most cases, not near enough information for you to make an informed purchase.

The thing to do now is to click the link for the item you're particularly interested in. This should display a dedicated product page, complete with picture and full description of the item. This is where you can read more about the item you selected. Some product pages include different views of the item, pictures of the item in different colors, links to additional information, and maybe even a list of optional accessories that go along with the item.

If you like what you see, you can proceed to the ordering stage. If you want to look at other items, just click your browser's Back button to return to the larger product listing.

Step 3: Order the Product

Somewhere on each product description page should be a button labeled Purchase or Buy Now or something similar. This is how you make the actual purchase: by clicking the Buy Now button. You don't order the product just by looking at the product description; you have to manually click that Purchase button to place your order.

When you click the Purchase or Buy Now button, that particular item is added to your *shopping cart*. That's right, the online retailer provides you with a virtual shopping cart that functions just like a real-world shopping cart. That is, each item you choose to purchase is added to your virtual shopping cart.

After you've ordered a product and placed it in your shopping cart, you can choose to shop for other products on that site or proceed to the site's checkout. It's important to note that when you place an item in your shopping cart, you haven't actually completed the purchase yet. You can keep shopping (and adding more items to your shopping cart) as long as you want.

You can even decide to abandon your shopping cart and not purchase anything at this time. All you have to do is leave the website, and you won't be charged for anything. It's the equivalent of leaving your shopping cart at a real-world retailer, and walking out the front door; you don't actually buy anything until you walk through the checkout line.

Step 4: Check Out

To finalize your purchase, you have to visit the store's checkout. This is like the checkout line at a traditional retail store; you take your virtual shopping cart through the checkout, get your purchases totaled, and then pay for what you're buying.

The checkout at an online retailer typically consists of one or more web pages with forms you have to fill out. If you've visited the retailer before, the site might remember some of your personal information from your previous visit. Otherwise, you'll have to enter your name, address, and phone number, as well as the address you want to ship the merchandise to (if that's different from your billing address). You'll also have to pay for the merchandise, typically by entering a credit card number.

The checkout provides one last opportunity for you to change your order. You can delete items you decide not to buy, or change quantities on any item. At some merchants, you can even opt to have your items gift-wrapped and sent to someone as a gift. All these options should be somewhere in the checkout.

You might also have the option of selecting different types of shipping for your order. Many merchants offer both regular and expedited shipping—the latter for an additional charge.

Another option at some retailers is to group all items together for reduced shipping cost, or to ship items individually as they become available. Grouping items together is attractive cost-wise, but you can get burned if one of the items is out-of-stock or not yet available; you could end up waiting weeks or months for those items that could have been shipped immediately.

tip

The better online retailers will tell you either on the product description page or during the checkout process whether or not an item is in stock. Look for this information to help you decide how to group your items for shipment.

Step 5: Confirm the Order

After you've entered all the appropriate information, you're asked to place your order. This typically means clicking a button that says Place Your Order or something similar. (I told you it's easy!) You might even see a second screen asking you whether you *really* want to place your order, just in case you had second thoughts.

After your order has been placed, you'll see a confirmation screen, typically displaying your order number. Write down this number or print out this page; you'll refer to this number in case you ever need to contact customer service. Most online merchants will also send you a confirmation message via email, containing this same information.

And that's all there is to it. You shop, examine the product, place an order, proceed to checkout, and then confirm your purchase. It's that easy!

How to Find the Best Prices Online

Now that you know *how* to shop, *where* should you spend your money online? Just a few short years ago, if you wanted to find the best bargains on the Web, you had to manually visit the sites of dozens of different online retailers—a very time-consuming process. Not so today, as there are numerous sites that exist to automatically do this price comparison for you. Go to a price comparison site, find the product you want, and have the site return a list of merchants offering that product, along with current prices. Choose the merchant that offers what you want, and you're ready to buy!

> **note**
>
> Want to find the best bargains online? Then check out my companion book, *Bargain Hunter's Secrets to Online Shopping* (Que, 2004), available in bookstores everywhere.

Price Comparison Sites

The best of these price comparison sites offer more than just pricing information. These full-service sites let you sort and filter their search results in a number of different ways, and often include customer reviews of both the products and the available merchants. Some even let you perform side-by-side comparisons of multiple products, which is great if you haven't yet made up your mind as to what you want to buy.

The most popular (and useful) of these price comparison sites include

- BizRate (www.bizrate.com)
- Froogle (froogle.google.com)
- mySimon (www.mysimon.com)
- NexTag (www.nextag.com)
- PriceGrabber.com (www.pricegrabber.com)
- Shopping.com (www.shopping.com)
- Yahoo! Shopping (shopping.yahoo.com)

Comparing Prices at Shopping.com

All of these comparison shopping sites are good, but my favorite is Shopping.com (shown in Figure 23.1). What I really like about Shopping.com is that it gives you more than just simple price comparisons; you also get customer reviews of both products and merchants, to help you make better purchase decisions.

FIGURE 23.1

Comparing products and prices at Shopping.com.

Like all the other price comparison sites, Shopping.com enables you to either search for specific products or browse through major product categories. Whether you search or browse, you eventually end up at a product listing page like the one shown in Figure 23.2. From here you can filter the results by price, product type, brand, or other product attributes. You can sort the results by best matches (default), price, or product rating. (The product ratings are provided by the customers at Epinions.com, Shopping.com's companion site.) You can also display the products as a grid rather than a list by clicking the View as a Grid link.

When you're in the process of choosing a particular product, Shopping.com makes it easy to perform side-by-side product comparisons. Just check the Select to Compare box next to the items you're looking at, and then click the Compare Selected Items button. The result is a chart with the features of each product displayed in tabular format.

To learn more about a particular product, click the Compare Prices button. This displays a product page where you can read detailed product information (by clicking the See Product Details link) or customer reviews (by clicking the Consumer Reviews link).

Below the product picture is a listing of all stores carrying this product. You can sort this list by store

tip

To see the total price (which includes shipping and taxes), enter your ZIP code into the Enter ZIP box, and then click the Calculate button. Obviously, total price is more important than base price because some merchants like to stick it to you when it comes to shipping and handling charges.

name, store rating (when available, from Epinions.com customers), or price. When you're ready to buy, click the Buy It button to go directly to the merchant's product page.

FIGURE 23.2

The results of a product search at Shopping.com.

How to Shop Safely

Shopping online is every bit as safe as shopping at a traditional bricks and mortar retailer. The big online retailers are just as reputable as traditional retailers, offering safe payment, fast shipping, and responsive service.

How do you know that you're shopping at a reputable online retailer? Simple—look for the following features:

- Payment by major credit card. (Not being able to accept credit cards is the sign of either a very small or fly-by-night merchant.)

- A *secure server* that encrypts your credit card information—and keeps online thieves from stealing your credit card numbers. (You'll know that you're using a secure site when the little lock icon appears in the lower-right corner of your web browser.)

- Good contact information—email address, street address, phone number, fax number, and so on. (You want to be able to physically contact the retailer if something goes wrong.)

- A stated returns policy and satisfaction guarantee. (You want to be assured that you'll be taken care of if you don't like whatever you ordered.)

■ A stated privacy policy that protects your personal information. (You don't want the online retailer sharing your email address and purchasing information with other merchants—and potential spammers.)

■ Information *before you finalize your order* that tells you whether the item is in stock and how long it will take to ship. (More feedback is better.)

How to Book Travel Reservations Online

One specific type of online shopping deserves special coverage. I'm talking about shopping for travel reservations—plane tickets, hotel rooms, rental cars, and more. Fortunately, many websites are designed to help you book the perfect trip, including the following:

■ Expedia (www.expedia.com)

■ Hotwire (www.hotwire.com)

■ Orbitz (www.orbitz.com)

■ Priceline (www.priceline.com)

■ TravelNow.com (www.travelnow.com)

■ Travelocity (www.travelocity.com)

These online travel sites all offer similar content and services, including the ability to book airline tickets, hotel rooms, and rental cars all in one place. Most of these sites (such as Expedia, shown in Figure 23.3) let you search for the lowest rates or for flights and lodging that match your specific requirements.

tip

Credit card purchases are protected by the Fair Credit Billing Act, which gives you the right to dispute certain charges and limits your liability for unauthorized transactions to $50. In addition, some card issuers offer a supplemental guarantee that says you're not responsible for *any* unauthorized charges made online. (Make sure that you read your card's statement of terms to determine the company's exact liability policy.)

tip

When you make reservations online, look for a site that employs real people behind-the-scenes—and offers a 24/7 800 number to contact those people if something goes wrong. Talking to a real person over the phone can be a lifeline if you're stranded somewhere without a reservation.

FIGURE 23.3

Shopping for airline and hotel reservations at Expedia.

THE ABSOLUTE MINIMUM

Here are the key points to remember from this chapter:

- You can find just about any type of item you want to buy for sale somewhere on the Internet.

- Shopping online is a lot like shopping in a traditional store; you find the product you want, go through the checkout system, and make your payment.

- To find the lowest price online, use a price comparison site, such as Shopping.com or Froogle.

- Internet shopping is very safe, especially if you buy from a major merchant that offers a secure server and a good returns policy.

- The Internet is also a great place to make your travel reservations by using an online travel site such as Expedia or Orbitz.

24

BUYING AND SELLING IN EBAY ONLINE AUCTIONS

Some of the best bargains on the Web come from other consumers, just like you, selling items via eBay. eBay is the Web's largest online marketplace, facilitating transactions between the people and businesses who have things to sell and the customers who want to buy those things.

Most transactions on eBay are in the form of *online auctions*. An online auction is, quite simply, a web-based version of a traditional auction. You find an item you'd like to own and then place a bid on the item. Other users also place bids, and at the end of the auction—typically a seven-day period—the highest bidder wins.

Not every transaction on eBay is an auction transaction, however. eBay also serves up a fair number of fixed-price sales through its Buy It Now feature and through merchants who run their own eBay Stores. With more than 36 million items listed for sale on any given day, you're bound to find something you want to buy; eBay has it all, from rare collectibles and vintage sports memorabilia to trendy clothing and the latest electronics equipment.

Who Sells on eBay?

eBay started out as a pure online auction site. eBay's job was to host the auction listings and facilitate the transactions between buyers and sellers. (Note that eBay doesn't actually sell anything itself, nor does it hold any inventory; all the transactions are between individual buyers and sellers, with eBay functioning solely as the middleman.)

In the beginning, eBay sellers were almost exclusively individuals—people like you and me with unwanted items they wanted to sell. In this way, eBay functioned like a giant garage sale or yard sale. An individual had something to sell, he listed it on eBay, and another individual decided to buy it. The second individual paid the first individual, who then shipped the item to the buyer. It was pretty simple.

Today, however, eBay is more than just person-to-person transactions. Many of eBay's original sellers have gotten quite big, listing hundreds of auctions every week and turning their eBay sales into real businesses. In addition, many existing businesses have turned to eBay as a way to make additional sales. So when you buy on eBay today, you may be buying from an individual selling just a few items, an individual running a small business out of her home, or a large business selling eBay items on the side.

Whomever you buy from, the process for the buyer is the same—as are the protections. The eBay marketplace is a level one, where all buyers and sellers follow the same rules and regulations. And the process for bidding and buying is the same no matter who you're buying from; just remember, you're buying from an independent seller, not from eBay itself.

How Does an eBay Auction Work?

If you've never used eBay before, you might be a little anxious about what might be involved. Never fear; participating in an online auction is a piece of cake, something hundreds of millions of other users have done before you. That means you don't have to reinvent any wheels; the procedures you follow are well-established and well-documented.

An eBay auction is an Internet-based version of a traditional auction—you know, the type where a fast-talking auctioneer stands in the front of the room, trying to coax potential buyers into bidding *just a little bit more* for the piece of merchandise up for bid. The only difference is that there's no fast-talking auctioneer online (the bidding process is executed by special auction software on the auction site), and your fellow bidders aren't in the same room with you—in fact, they might be located anywhere in the world. Anyone can be a bidder, as long as he or she has Internet access.

note

There is no cost to register with eBay, although if you want to sell items, you'll have to provide your credit card and checking account numbers. (eBay uses this information to help weed out potential scammers, and to provide a billing option for the seller's eBay fees.)

Here's how the auction process works, in general terms:

1. You begin (as either a buyer or a seller) by registering with eBay. You can do this by clicking the Register link on eBay's home page, shown in Figure 24.1.

FIGURE 24.1
Where all the auction action starts—eBay's home page.

2. The seller creates an ad for an item and lists the item on the auction site. (eBay charges anywhere from $0.20 to $4.80 to list an item.) In the item listing, the seller specifies the length of the auction (1, 3, 5, 7, or 10 days) and the minimum bid he or she will accept for that item.

3. A potential buyer searching for a particular type of item (or just browsing through all the merchandise listed in a specific category) reads the item listing and decides to make a bid. The bidder specifies the maximum amount he or she will pay; this amount has to be equal to or greater than the seller's minimum bid, or higher than any other existing bids.

4. eBay's built-in bidding software automatically places a bid for the bidder that bests the current bid by a specified amount—but doesn't reveal the bidder's maximum bid. For example, the current bid on an item might be $25. A bidder is willing to pay up to $40 for the item, and enters a maximum bid of $40. eBay's "proxy" software places a bid for the new bidder in the amount of $26—higher than the current bid, but less than the specified maximum bid. If there are no other bids, this bidder will win the auction with a $26 bid. Other potential buyers, however, can place additional bids; unless their maximum bids are more than the current bidder's $40 maximum, they are informed (by email) that they have been outbid—and the first bidder's current bid is automatically raised to match the new bids (up to the specified maximum bid price).

5. At the conclusion of an auction, eBay informs the high bidder of his or her winning bid. The seller is responsible for contacting the high bidder and arranging payment. When the seller receives the buyer's payment (by check, money order, or credit card), the seller then ships the merchandise directly to the buyer.

6. Concurrent with the close of the auction, eBay bills the seller for a small percentage (starting at 5.25%) of the final bid price. This selling fee is directly billed to the seller's credit card.

eBay Bidding, Step-by-Step

Bidding in an online auction is kind of like shopping at an online retailer—except that you don't flat-out make a purchase. Instead, you make a bid—and you only get to purchase the item at the end of the auction if your bid was the highest bid made.

Here's how it works:

1. You look for items using eBay's search function (via the Search box on eBay's home page) or by browsing through the product categories.

note

Learn even more about eBay auctions in my companion book, *Absolute Beginner's Guide to eBay, 4th Edition* (Que, 2006), available where you purchased this title.

2. When you find an item you're interested in, take a moment to examine all the details. A typical item listing (like the one shown in Figure 24.2) includes a photo of the item, a brief product description, shipping and payment information, and instructions on how to place a bid.

FIGURE 24.2

An eBay item listing—ready to bid?

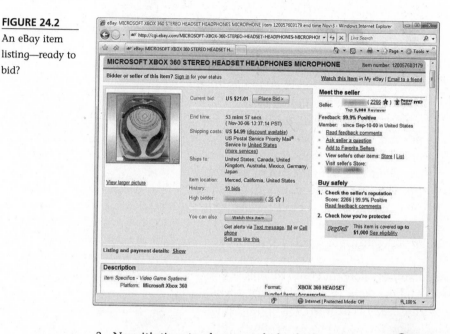

3. Now it's time to place your bid, which you do by clicking the Place Bid button. Remember, you're not buying the item at this point; you're just telling eBay how much you're willing to pay. Your bid must be at or above the current bid amount. My recommendation is to determine the maximum amount you'd be willing to pay for that item, and bid that amount—regardless of what the current bid level is.

4. eBay uses automatic proxy bidding software to automatically handle the bidding process from here. You bid the maximum amount you're willing to pay, and eBay's proxy software enters the minimum bid necessary—without revealing your maximum bid amount. Your bid will be automatically raised (to no more than your maximum amount) when other users bid.

> **note**
>
> Some auctions have a *reserve price*. The high bid must be above this price (which is hidden) to actually win the auction. If bids don't reach the reserve, the seller is not obligated to sell the item.

5. The auction proceeds. Most auctions run for seven days, although sellers have the option of running 1-, 3-, 5-, 7-, and 10-day auctions.

6. If you're the high bidder at the end of the auction, eBay informs you (via email) that you're the winner.

7. You can pay immediately (with a credit card, via the PayPal service) by clicking the Pay Now button in this end-of-auction notice. Otherwise, send the seller the appropriate payment via personal check, money order, or cashier's check. Your payment should include both the cost of the item (the winning bid amount) and a reasonable shipping/handling charge, as determined by the seller.

8. The seller ships the item to you.

It's important to note that even though you've been using the services of the eBay site, the ultimate transaction is between you and the individual seller. You don't pay eBay; eBay is just the middleman.

> **note**
>
> PayPal is a service (owned by eBay) that lets sellers accept credit card payments in their auctions. PayPal functions as a middleman; the buyer pays PayPal (via credit card) and then PayPal deposits the funds in the seller's bank account. Because the majority of buyers prefer to pay by credit card, using PayPal to accept credit card payments is a necessity!

Buy It Quick with Buy It Now

Tired of waiting around for the end of an auction, only to find out you didn't have the winning bid? Well, there's a way to actually *buy* some items you see for auction without going through the bidding process. All you have to do is look for those auctions that have a Buy It Now (BIN) option.

> **tip**
>
> To increase your chances of winning an auction, use a technique called *sniping*. When you snipe, you hold your bid until the very last seconds of the auction. If you bid high enough and late enough, other bidders won't have time to respond to your bid—and your high bid will win!

Buy It Now is an option that some (but not all) sellers add to their auctions. With Buy It Now, the item is sold (and the auction ended) if the very first bidder places a bid for a specified price. (For this reason, some refer to Buy It Now auctions as "fixed-price" auctions—even though they're slightly different from eBay's *real* fixed-priced listings.)

Buying an item with Buy It Now is really simple. If you see an item identified with a Buy It Now price (as shown in Figure 24.3), just enter a bid at that price. You'll immediately be notified that you've won the auction (and instructed to pay—typically via PayPal), and the auction will be officially closed.

NIB Apple iPod 8GB Black Nano MP3 Player (5.5 gen)

Seller of this item? Sign in for your status

Starting bid: US $215.00   [Place Bid >]

Buy It Now price: US $249.00   [Buy It Now >]

No payments for up to 6 months ? Apply

End time: **4 hours 5 mins** (Nov-30-06 17:01:22 PST)
Shipping costs: **US $15.00**
Standard Flat Rate Shipping Service
Service to United States
Ships to: United States
Item location: Buffalo Grove, Illinois, United States
History: 0 bids

View larger picture

Other eBay sellers choose to skip the auction process entirely and sell their items at a fixed price. These listings also display the Buy It Now button but without a bidding option. Fixed-priced listings are common in eBay Stores, where larger sellers offer a constant supply of fixed-priced merchandise for sale all year round.

More Than Auctions: eBay Express, eBay Stores, and Half.com

eBay offers more than just online auctions. In addition to the traditional online auction marketplace, eBay offers three other marketplaces that focus on selling fixed-priced items: eBay Express, eBay Stores, and Half.com

eBay Stores

> **tip**
>
> Even if a seller offers the Buy It Now option, you don't have to bid at the Buy It Now price. You can bid at a lower price and hope that you win the auction, which then proceeds normally. (The Buy It Now option disappears when the first bid is made—or, in a reserve price auction, when the reserve price is met.)

In addition to those fixed-price items offered as part of the traditional eBay auction listings, you can also find fixed-price items for sale in eBay Stores. An eBay Store is an online storefront where eBay merchants can sell their goods without putting them up for auction—and keep them for sale indefinitely, without the typical auction expiration.

You can browse through thousands of different eBay merchants at the eBay Stores page (stores.ebay.com), shown in Figure 24.4. eBay Stores merchants are organized by the same categories as the eBay auction site—Antiques, Art, Books, and so on. You can also search for a specific store or a store selling a certain type of item, or view an alphabetical list of all stores.

Buying an item from an eBay Store is a little like buying from any other online merchant, and a little like winning an item in an eBay auction. On the one hand, you're buying from an actual merchant at a fixed price, and you can always pay by credit card (typically via PayPal). On the other hand, you have all the niceties you have on eBay, including the ability to check the merchant's feedback rating.

After you locate an item you want, you're taken to the "virtual storefront" of the eBay Store selling the item. When you're in a specific store, you can purchase the item you were looking at or shop for additional items. Your checkout is handled from within the store.

eBay Express

The newest part of the eBay marketplace is eBay Express (express.ebay.com). As you can see in Figure 24.5, eBay Express offers a streamlined shopping and checkout experience for fixed-priced items.

eBay Express consolidates nonauction listings from both the main eBay site and eBay Stores. That is, you can use eBay Express to find all the fixed-priced items offered by eBay sellers without having to search the site, browse the Stores, or wait for an auction process to end.

FIGURE 24.5

Shopping for fixed-priced items at eBay Express.

All items offered on eBay Express can be paid for with a credit card, typically using PayPal. Even better, you can purchase multiple items from multiple sellers and have all your purchases consolidated into a single shopping cart and checkout system. Buy multiple items, make a single payment—not a bad deal.

Half.com

eBay Stores and eBay Express aren't the only places you can find fixed-price merchandise in the eBay universe. eBay also runs a site called Half.com, which offers new and used merchandise for sale from a variety of merchants.

As you can see in Figure 24.6, the Half.com home page (half.ebay.com) looks a little like Amazon.com's home page. That's by design; Half.com was originally conceived as an Amazon competitor. Today, Half.com offers merchandise from large and small retailers and from individuals, too. The site specializes in CDs, DVDs, video games, books, and textbooks.

When you make a purchase at Half.com, you're buying directly from the individual seller, just as you do in an eBay auction. The big difference, of course, is that it's not an auction; you're buying an item (new or used) at a fixed price. The other difference is that you don't pay the seller separately; all your Half.com purchases end up in the same shopping cart, just like at Amazon.com. You check out once for all your purchases and make just one payment (to Half.com). Half.com then pays the individual sellers, who ship you your merchandise separately. It's fairly painless.

FIGURE 24.6

eBay's Half.com site.

Protecting Yourself Against Fraudulent Sellers

When you're bidding for and buying items on eBay, you're pretty much in "buyer beware" territory. You agree to buy an item, almost sight unseen, from someone whom you know practically nothing about. You send that person a check and hope and pray that you get something shipped back in return—and that the thing that's shipped is the thing you thought you were buying, in good condition. If you don't like what you got—or if you received nothing at all—the seller has your money. And what recourse do you have?

Checking Feedback

The first line of defense against frauds and cheats is to intelligently choose the people you deal with. On eBay, the best way to do this is via the Feedback system.

Next to every seller's name is a number and percentage, which represents that seller's Feedback rating. You should always check a seller's Feedback rating before you bid. If the number is high with an overwhelmingly positive percentage, you can feel safer than if the seller has a lot of negative feedback. For even better protection, click the seller's name in the item listing to view his Member Profile, where

tip

If you're new to eBay, you can build up your feedback fast by purchasing a few low-cost items—preferably using the Buy It Now feature, so you get the transaction over quickly. It's good to have a feedback rating of 20 or better before you start selling!

you can read individual feedback comments. Be smart and avoid those sellers who have a history of delivering less than what was promised.

Getting Help After a Bad Transaction

What do you do if you follow all this advice and still end up receiving unacceptable merchandise—or no merchandise at all? Fortunately, eBay offers a Purchase Protection Program for any auction transaction gone bad. This Purchase Protection Program is the final step in a long process with an equally long name—the Item Not Received or Significantly Not as Described Process.

You can initiate the process 10 days after the end of an auction by going to eBay's Security & Resolution Center (pages.ebay.com/securitycenter/), checking the Item Not Received option, and then clicking the Report Problem button. eBay will contact the seller on your behalf, and if the problem isn't resolved within 30 days, you can then file a claim under eBay's Purchase Protection Program.

The Purchase Protection Program insures you for up to $200 on all items with a final value greater than $25. (There's also a $25 deductible on each claim.) To get your money back under this program, you have to go through the Item Not Received or Significantly Not Described Process, and then (after 30 days have passed with no resolution) close your dispute and select "end communication with the seller." You'll then be presented with a link to the proper claim form, which you fill out as instructed. Sometime in the next 45 days you will be contacted by the eBay claims administrator; if your claim is approved, you'll be sent a check for the disputed amount (less the $25 deductible, of course).

Fortunately, the vast majority of eBay sellers are extremely honest—so you'll probably never have to take advantage of this program. Most transactions are good transactions!

eBay Selling, Step-by-Step

Have some old stuff in your garage or attic that you want to get rid of? Consider selling it on eBay. Selling on eBay is a little more involved than bidding—but can generate big bucks if you do it right. Here's how it works:

1. If you haven't registered for an eBay seller account yet, do so now. You'll need to provide eBay with your credit card and checking account number, for verification and billing purposes.

> **note**
>
> eBay makes its money by charging sellers two types of fees. (Buyers don't pay any fees to eBay.) *Insertion fees* are based on the minimum bid or reserve price of the item listed. *Final value fees* are charged when you sell an item, based on the item's final selling price. Fees are typically charged directly to the seller's credit card account.

2. Before you list your first item, you need to do a little homework. That means determining what you're going to sell and for how much, as well as how you're going to describe the item. You'll need to prepare the information you need to write a full item description, as well as take a few digital photos of the item to include with the listing.

3. Homework out of the way, it's time to create the auction listing itself. Start by clicking the Sell button on eBay's home page. As you can see in Figure 24.7, eBay displays a series of forms for you to complete; the information you enter into these forms is used to create your item listing. You'll need to select a category for your item; enter a title and description; determine how long you want your auction to run and what kind of payments you'll accept; insert a photo of the item, if you have one; and enter the amount of the desired minimum (starting) bid.

FIGURE 24.7

Creating a new eBay item listing.

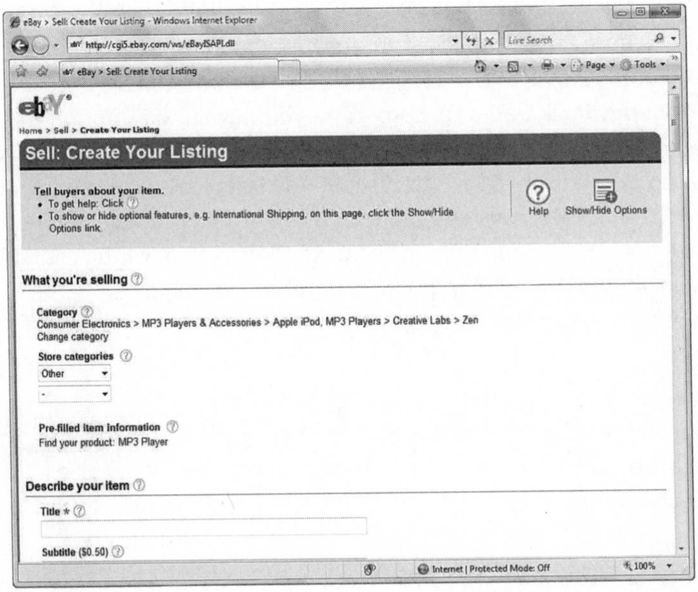

4. After you enter all the information, eBay creates and displays a preliminary version of your auction listing. If you like what you see, click OK to start the auction.

5. Sit back and wait for the auction to progress.

6. When the auction is over, eBay notifies you (via email) of the high bid and provides the email address of the winning bidder.

7. Many winning bidders will pay via credit card (using the PayPal service) as soon as the auction is over, by clicking the Pay Now link in the end-of-auction notice they receive. If the high bidder doesn't pay immediately, email him an invoice containing the final bid price and the shipping/handling charges.

8. After you've been paid, pack the item and ship it out.

> **tip**
>
> You can monitor the progress of all your current auctions with the My eBay page. Just click the My eBay link at the top of eBay's home page.

That's it—you've just completed a successful eBay auction!

THE ABSOLUTE MINIMUM

Here are the key points to remember from this chapter:

- An eBay auction is a lot like a real-world auction; a seller lists an item for sale, interested people bid increasing amounts on the item, and the highest bid wins.

- To bid on an item, enter the highest price you're willing to pay and let eBay's proxy bidding software do the rest.

- Many items feature the Buy It Now option, which lets you purchase the item immediately for a fixed price, without waiting for the entire auction process to end.

- eBay also offers fixed-priced items for sale via eBay Stores, eBay Express, and Half.com.

- To protect against fraudulent sellers, check the seller's feedback rating before you bid; if a transaction goes bad, eBay has processes in place to protect you.

- To sell an item, make sure you have all the information you need to write a detailed item description—as well as a few digital photos of the item.

25

EXPLORING BLOGS AND PODCASTS

If you've been on the Internet for any length of time, you've probably heard something about *blogs*. A blog (short for "web log") is a kind of online journal that its author updates frequently with new musings and information.

Hundreds of thousands of blogs are on the Internet, from the intensely personal to the most gregariously public; some blogs are so influential that they actually make the news from time to time. What you might not know is that anyone can create a blog. It's easy and can be fun.

Whether you want to create your own blog or read someone else's, blogs are an essential part of the Internet today. Read on to learn more!

Welcome to the Blogosphere

When it comes to blogs, you have to get used to a whole new vocabulary. A *blog*, of course, is a journal that's hosted on the Web and visible to other web users. *Blogging* is the activity of updating a blog; someone who keeps a blog is a *blogger*; and the entire universe of blogs is the *blogosphere*. Got that?

Some people view their blogs as a kind of personal-yet-public scrapbook—an online diary to record their thoughts for posterity. Even if no one else ever looks at it, it's still valuable to the author as a repository of thoughts and information he can turn to later.

Other bloggers are more focused. Some blogs are devoted to hobbies, sports teams, local events, particular industries, and so on. Some people blog for a cause, political or otherwise. (In fact, many people get their first exposure to the blogosphere via the network of left-wing and right-wing political blogs—especially during an election year!)

In a way, the most serious bloggers are like columnists in the traditional media. They write with a passion, a point of view, and a personal sensibility that makes their blogs interesting to read. Even bloggers who don't inject personal comments still offer a viewpoint based on what they choose to include and link to in their blogs. The blogosphere is an interesting world, and it's revolutionizing journalism (and journals) for the new online reality.

Of course, a blog can be more—or less—than personal comments and observations. A big part of blogging is about interlinking to other blogs and to news and information on the Web. Look at any blog, and you're likely to see a list of related blogs (sometimes titled, "friends of …"). Bloggers like to link to other blogs that they enjoy—as well as to news stories, photos, audio files, you name it.

In fact, many blogs are nothing more than links to interesting blog entries—there isn't always a lot of original content there. The blogger finds something interesting and then uses his blog to draw attention to that other posting. In this way, bloggers are a lot like radio disc jockeys, "spinning" links and snippets just as a DJ spins songs.

That said, serious bloggers not only sort through the blogosphere to find the most interesting articles,

note

For what it's worth, I personally contribute to three different blogs—two of which are hosted by Blogger. Googlepedia: The Blog (googlepedia.blogspot.com) is the place to find new information about Google and updates to my *Googlepedia* book. The Curmudgeon Speaks (curmudgeonspeaks.blogspot.com) is my personal blog, full of all manner of rants and raves. And AOL's My Plugged In Life (digital-lifestyle.aol.com/my-plugged-in-life) is a celebration of all things related to the digital lifestyle.

they also provide some background and organization to these postings, and in many cases add their own commentary. The best blogs have a definite point of view, no matter what content they're linking to.

Reading—And Commenting On— Blogs

What does a blog look like? As you can see in Figure 25.1, a typical blog is a collection of individual *posts*, or articles. The posts are arranged in reverse chronological order, with the newest posts at the top. Older posts are relegated to the blog archives, which are generally accessible via a link in the sidebar column.

At the end of each post is generally a link to comments on that post. Depending on the blog, readers may be able to post their own personal comments about any given post. Click the comments link to read all the comments to date or to post your own comment.

note

A blog's sidebar column is also where you'll find links to other items of interest, as determined by the blog's host. You might find links to the blogger's favorite books or videos, or to related websites, for example.

FIGURE 25.1

A typical blog— the author's Googlepedia blog.

Most blogs are all text, but blogs can also display photos, audio files, and even videos. It's all up to the blogger, and how involved he wants his blog to be. (Some blogs even have multiple hosts, with posts coming from a number of different authors.)

Searching for Blogs

The Web has literally hundreds of thousands of blogs, covering just about any topic you can think of. How do you find blogs of interest to you?

To find a particular blog, check out the following blog directories:

- Blog Search Engine (www.blogsearchengine.com)
- Feedster (www.feedster.com)
- Globe of Blogs (www.globeofblogs.com)
- Google Blog Search (blogsearch.google.com)
- Weblogs.com (www.weblogs.com)

tip

Also look for blogs associated with the websites you regularly visit. For example, the *New York Times* hosts a variety of blogs that accompany its regular features and columns. (See www.nytimes.com/ref/topnews/blog-index.html for a complete listing.)

Tracking Your Blogs with Feed Reader Software

Many blogs let you subscribe to a *feed* of their posts. This is an updated list of all new posts; a feed subscription uses Real Simple Syndication (RSS) technology to notify you of all new posts made to that blog.

You typically subscribe to a blog's RSS feed directly from the blog itself. Look for a "subscribe" or "feed" or "RSS" button. (An alternative form of syndication, Atom feeds, is sometimes offered; it works the same way as RSS.) Click the button to display the feed page and then copy this page's URL into your feed reader program.

Ah, but what's a feed reader? That's a software program that monitors and displays all the RSS feeds you've subscribed to. Some of the more popular feed readers include FeedDemon (www.feeddemon.com) and Feedreader (www.feedreader.com); you can also monitor your RSS subscriptions with a web-based feed aggregator site, such as Bloglines (www.bloglines.com), Google Reader (reader.google.com), or NewsGator (www.newsgator.com).

Even better, you can use Internet Explorer 7 to monitor all your RSS subscriptions. As discussed in Chapter 21, "Surfing the Web with Internet Explorer," this latest version of the popular web browser includes an integrated feed reader. When you go to a blog's RSS page, IE7 displays a boxed message at the top of the page. Click the Subscribe to This Feed link, and IE7 will track all new posts made to this blog. You can view all your blog feeds by going to IE7's Favorites Center and clicking the Feeds button.

Creating Your Own Blog

Bloggers typically update their blogs on a regular basis—weekly, daily, or even hourly, depending on the blogger. The process of updating a blog is facilitated by the blogging software used. Hosting a blog requires little or no technical expertise on the part of the blogger; all the heavy lifting is handled by the blogging software or the site that hosts the blog.

If you want to create your own personal blog, look for a blog hosting community. These websites offer easy-to-use software tools to build and maintain your blog, and do all the hosting for you—often for free.

Some of the most popular blog hosting communities include

- BlogEasy (www.blogeasy.com)
- Blogger (www.blogger.com)
- blogthing (www.blogthing.com)
- eBloggy (www.ebloggy.com)
- tBlog (www.tblog.com)
- TypePad (www.typepad.com)
- WordPress (www.wordpress.com)

Of these communities, Blogger (which is owned by Google) and TypePad are probably the biggest. As you can see in Figure 25.2, these sites make it easy to create your own blog—it's really a matter of clicking a few buttons and filling out a few forms. And after your blog is created, you can update it as frequently as you want, again by clicking a link or two. (Figure 25.3 shows how easy it is to create a new blog entry with Blogger.) After you get started blogging your daily thoughts, you'll never want to stop!

tip

The MySpace community also functions as a blog host, as you'll learn in Chapter 26, "Social Networking with MySpace." In addition, many traditional website hosting communities offer blogging features. Learn more in Chapter 27, "Creating Your Own Web Page."

FIGURE 25.2

Use Blogger to host your personal blog.

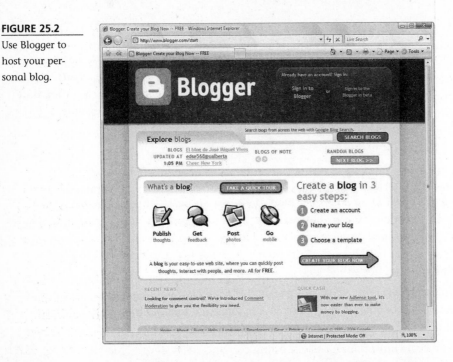

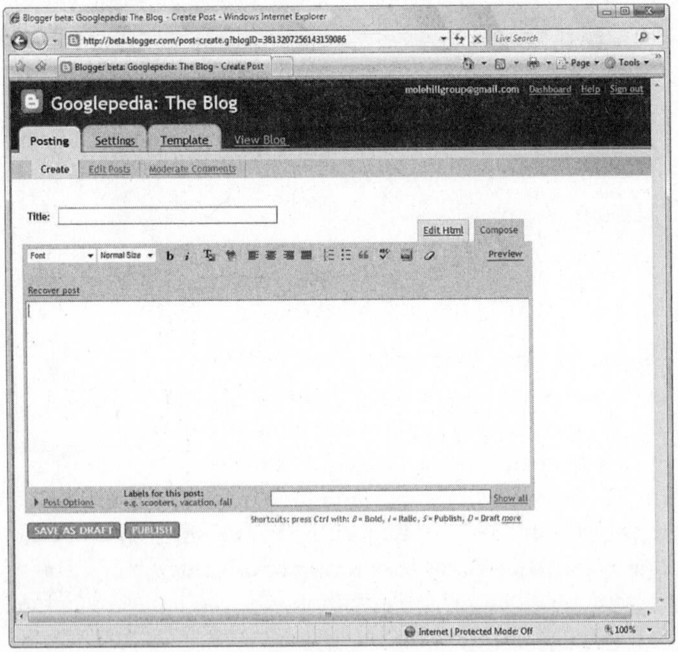

FIGURE 25.3

Creating a new blog entry with Blogger.

Blogs on the Radio: Listening to Podcasts

A text-based blog isn't the only way to express yourself online. If you have an iPod or other portable MP3 player, you can listen to audio blogs called *podcasts*. A podcast is essentially a homegrown radio program, distributed over the Internet, that you can download and play on any portable audio player—iPods included.

How Podcasts Work

Anyone with a microphone and a computer can create her own podcasts. That's because a podcast is nothing more than an MP3 file posted to the Internet. Most podcasters deliver their content via an RSS feed, which enables users to easily find future podcasts by subscribing to the podcaster's feed. The podcasts are then downloaded to the listener's portable audio player and listened to at the listener's convenience.

What kinds of podcasts are out there? It's an interesting world, full of all sorts of basement and garage productions. Probably the most common form of podcast is the amateur radio show, where the podcaster assembles a mixture of personally selected music and commentary. But there are also professional podcasts by real radio stations and broadcasters, interviews and exposés, and true audio blogs that consist of running commentary and ravings. The variety is staggering, and the quality level ranges from embarrassingly amateurish to surprisingly professional.

Finding Podcasts

Want to jump into the wild, wonderful world of podcasts? Then you need to browse through a podcast directory and see what's there for the listening. Some of the most popular podcast directories include

- Digital Podcast (www.digitalpodcast.com)
- Podcast Alley (www.podcastalley.com)
- Podcast Bunker (www.podcastbunker.com)
- Podcast Directory (www.podcastdirectory.com)
- Podcast.net (www.podcast.net)
- Podcasting News Directory (www.podcastingnews.com/forum/links.php)
- Podcasting Station (www.podcasting-station.com)
- PodcastPickle.com (www.podcastpickle.com)
- PodCastZoom (www.podcastzoom.com)
- Podfeed.net (www.podfeed.net)
- Syndic8 Podcast Directory (www.syndic8.com/podcasts/)
- Yahoo! Podcasts (podcasts.yahoo.com)

Podcasts on the iPod

If you're an iPod owner, you've probably noticed the Podcasts item on your iPod's menu. This lets you dial up all your stored podcasts and then play them back in any order.

You download podcasts to your iPod via the iTunes Podcast Directory. Just click iTunes Store in the Source pane of the iTunes software and then click the Podcasts link. As you can see in Figure 25.4, you can browse or search through the available podcasts, download the ones you like, and subscribe to the ones you want to hear again. Most of the podcasts here are relatively professional, including programs from ABC News, ESPN, and podcast guru Adam Curry. Best of all, all the podcasts from iTunes are free.

FIGURE 25.4
Browsing for podcasts in the iTunes Podcast Directory.

When you subscribe to a podcast, iTunes automatically checks for updates and downloads new episodes to your computer. Your downloaded podcasts are accessible by clicking the Podcasts link in the iTunes Source pane. Naturally, the new podcasts are transferred to your iPod when it's next connected and synced. It's a quick and easy way to check out the whole podcast phenomenon—as long as you're an iPod owner, that is.

Creating Your Own Podcasts

If you think podcasts are cool, why not create your own? It's surprisingly easy to do. Here's what you need:

- A microphone (any type will do)
- A PC (no special technical requirements)

- Audio recording software, such as MixCast Live (www.mixcastlive.com) or ePodcast Creator (www.industrialaudiosoftware.com)
- Headphones (optional, but nice)
- Internet connection, so you can post your podcasts to the Web
- A podcast hosting service or RSS syndicator

Making a podcast recording doesn't have to be any more complex than setting the volume levels, clicking the Record button in the recording software, and then talking into the microphone. Naturally, you can stop and restart the recording as necessary; you can even go back and rerecord any section that you don't like. Most recording programs also let you edit your recordings by snipping out unwanted sections and moving sections around as necessary.

Your original recording should be saved in high-quality WAV format, and you should stay in the WAV format throughout the editing process. After your podcast is in its final form, you then export the file into MP3 format. If the podcast is voice-only, a relatively low bitrate (32 or 64kbps) is fine. If the podcast has a lot of music, consider a higher bitrate, up to 128kbps. Make sure you add the appropriate metatags for all the podcast info, and it's ready for distribution.

After you save your podcast in MP3 format, you have to upload the MP3 file to a server. If you have your own personal website, you can use that server to store your podcasts. You'll need a fair amount of storage space; audio files can get large, depending on the recording quality and length. For example, a 30-minute podcast saved at 64kbps in mono will be about 8MB in size. Use a higher bitrate, and the file size goes up accordingly.

If you don't have your own server, consider using an audio blog hosting service, such as Audio Blog (www.audioblog.com), Liberated Syndication (www.libsyn.com), Ourmedia.org (www.ourmedia.org), and Podbus.com (www.podbus.com). You'll pay $5–$10 per month for file storage, and most of these sites will also help you with the RSS syndication of your podcasts.

Which leads to the final step of the process, the RSS syndication. This is best accomplished via an audio blog hosting service, or via blogging software. Most blogging software and services can generate an RSS feed, or you can use FeedBurner (www.feedburner.com) to do the work for you (for free). If you use FeedBurner, you'll have to create a link on your website to the FeedBurner file so that people can find the feed.

And that's that. All you have to do now is wait for users to find your podcasts and subscribe to your feed!

THE ABSOLUTE MINIMUM

Here are the key points to remember from this chapter:

- A blog is a private or public journal on the Internet, consisting of numerous individual posts.

- Most blogs let readers comment on the blog posts.

- You can use a blog-hosting community, such as Blogger, to create and host your own blog.

- A blog in audio format is called a podcast.

- One of the best ways to find and download podcasts is via the iTunes Podcast Directory.

26

SOCIAL NETWORKING WITH MYSPACE

Forget the malt shop. Forget the movies. Forget the mall. Today's teenagers do their hanging out online, at the social networking site called MySpace.

MySpace is collection of millions of individual web pages, posted and updated by users, that combine to create an interactive social network. Users' profile pages contain blog postings, photos, music, videos, and links to lots and lots of online friends.

And it's not just teenagers, either. MySpace is a place where users of any age can network with one another, sharing their likes and dislikes, opinions and advice. It's a website unlike any you've seen before—and it's one of the hottest places on the Web, period.

What Is MySpace?

MySpace (www.myspace.com), shown in Figure 26.1, is a social networking site. That means it's a site where users connect with one another online via links, photos, email, and so on.

FIGURE 26.1
The MySpace
home page.

MySpace is totally free to use, although you do need to sign up for an account to access many of the site's features. (You don't need an account to browse other users' profiles, however.)

Welcome to Social Networking

Each MySpace user has her own profile page. The profile page contains information about the user, likes and dislikes, photos, links to music and videos, and—most important—links to "friends."

It's the friends that make MySpace the social network. When you find someone you know—or someone who shares similar interests—you can add them to your list of friends. For teenagers, anyway, the more friends you have, the more popular you are. It's all about the friends.

MySpace's History

Interestingly, MySpace started (in 2003) as a site for twenty-somethings into the Los Angeles indie music scene. Other musicians soon glommed onto the site, and that attracted a larger (and younger) audience. Today, users as young as 14 spend an inordinate amount of time on MySpace, making their profile pages as cool as possible and browsing the site for new friends.

And you can still find plenty of musicians on MySpace—along with artists, movie stars, comedians, and many wanna-be celebrities. Many bands and performers use MySpace as their home base to launch new CDs and support their latest tours.

Who's on MySpace?

So who's on MySpace? It's not just teenagers. MySpace is home to all sorts of users, including

- Business colleagues who use the site for networking
- Friends who want to talk online
- Singles who want to meet and match up with other singles
- Classmates who need study partners and homework advice
- Hobbyists looking for others who share their interests
- People looking for long-lost friends
- Musicians, actors, and celebrities connecting with their fans
- And, of course, teenagers

The average MySpace user is in the 14–24 age range. The site sports more than 100 million accounts and gets close to a quarter-million visitors everyday—which makes it one of the top five sites on the Web, up there with Google and eBay.

What Do People Do on MySpace?

MySpace is all about hanging out—virtually. Typical users spend a fair amount of time cruising through the profiles, looking for people they know or who share similar interests. They play music and watch videos posted on other profile pages. They see who's online, and they send instant messages, bulletins (short messages), and emails to each other.

note

Originally, MySpace was limited to users 18 and older. That's changed, however, and the minimum age limit is now 14.

In addition, users spend time updating their own profile pages—their face to the online world. They redecorate their pages by changing templates, changing color schemes, adding new backgrounds and images, even adding pictures of themselves and their friends. Few MySpace pages are static.

Friending on MySpace

On MySpace, the process of finding new friends is called *friending*, and some specific rules are involved—especially if you're a teenager.

First, it's important to be connected to all your real-world friends and acquaintances. Second, you want to be connected to people whom you might not personally know, but whom you've heard of and respect. Third, although it's important to have a lot of friends, the coolness of your friends matters more. In other words, it's better to have ten high-profile friends than a hundred nobodies.

Know, however, that when you add someone as friend, that doesn't imply they're a friend in the traditional use of the word. It doesn't even mean that you know that person, or want to know that person—only that you've added him or her to your friends list.

After a time, linking from one friend to a friend of that friend to a friend of a friend of a friend leads to a kind of "six degrees of separation" thing. It's fun to see how many friends it takes to connect you to various people (Kevin Bacon included). And you get to find new friends by seeing who your friends are friends with.

Browsing MySpace Profiles

Anyone can browse MySpace and search for specific profiles. Here's how it works.

Browsing the Profiles

One of the most popular activities on MySpace is browsing the profiles. This is how you find new friends.

Browsing starts when you click the Browse link on the MySpace menu bar. This displays the Browse Users page, shown in Figure 26.2, where you set your browse criteria. The Basic tab on this page lets you filter your browsing by the following criteria:

- Gender
- Age range
- Relationship (single, married, divorced, in a relationship)
- Location
- Here for (dating, networking, relationships, or friends)

You can also choose to show only those profiles that have photos.

For more sophisticated browsing, click the Advanced tab. This adds more browsing options, including ethnicity, body type, height, and lifestyle (smoker, drinker, sexual orientation, education, religion, income, children). You can choose to sort results by recently updated, last login, new to MySpace, or physical distance from your location.

FIGURE 26.2

Browsing for new friends on MySpace.

Searching for Users

If you know who you're looking for, you can search the MySpace profiles for a specific user. All you have to do is click the web link above the search box at the top of the page, enter the user's actual name or profile name, and then click the Search button. MySpace returns a list of matching profiles; make sure you click the Next button if the profile you want doesn't show up in the first page of results.

Viewing a Profile

Figure 26.3 shows a typical MySpace profile. Because users can personalize their profile pages, few MySpace profiles look the same. Still, all MySpace profiles have common elements, including

- **Blurbs**—Tells visitors a little about the user. This section contains two parts: About Me and Who I'd Like to Meet.

- **Interests**—Lists favorite music, movies, television shows, books, and so on.

- **Details**—Gives more information about the person, including marital status, location, astrological sign, and so on.

- **Contact Info**—Contains links to send email and instant messages, and to add this person to your friends list.

- **Blog**—That's right, MySpace functions as a blog hosting site. Users can create their own personal blogs and link to blog postings from their profile pages.

■ **Images**—Lets users post pictures on their profile page. Lots of them, if they want. One default image is shown on the main page; additional photos are accessed via the Pics link.

■ **Videos**—Lets users upload videos to their profile pages. Click the Videos link to view.

■ **Calendar**—For users who post their schedules online.

■ **Friend Space**—Lists all friends. This section includes a list of the user's total friends, a list of the user's top eight friends (as determined by the user), and a link to view all of the user's friends.

■ **Comments**—Displays comments made by the user's friends for the user and all other visitors to read.

FIGURE 26.3

A typical MySpace profile.

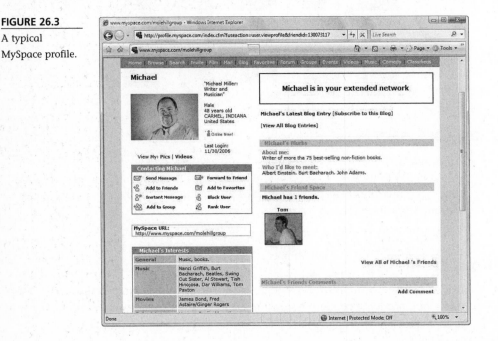

As mentioned previously, profile pages are fully customizable. In fact, if the user is conversant with HTML, CSS, and JavaScript, some fancy customization is possible. Otherwise, users can choose their own themes, backgrounds, colors, and content modules. This is why no two MySpace pages look the same!

Creating Your Own MySpace Profile

To create your own MySpace profile, you first have to sign up to MySpace. You do this from the MySpace home page by clicking the Sign Up! button.

Signing up is simple (and free). All you have to provide is your name, email address, country and postal code, birthday, and desired password.

After you've signed up, you're prompted to upload a photo of yourself. The photo can be in JPG or GIF format, must be smaller than 600KB, and shouldn't contain any nudity.

Next, you're encouraged to invite your friends to view your MySpace page. Enter their email addresses, if you want, and then click the Invite button.

MySpace now dumps you into your own personal account page. This is your home page on the MySpace site because it lists any email or bulletins you've received as well as all your friends. It also includes the URLs for your profile and blog pages.

To personalize your profile, start by clicking the Pick Your MySpace Name/URL link. This lets you choose your MySpace display name—the name that others will know you by. Choose this name carefully; once chosen, you can't change it. Ever.

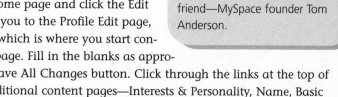

Every new MySpace user starts with one friend—MySpace founder Tom Anderson.

Next, return to your home page and click the Edit Profile link. This takes you to the Profile Edit page, shown in Figure 26.4, which is where you start constructing your profile page. Fill in the blanks as appropriate; then click the Save All Changes button. Click through the links at the top of the pages to tab to additional content pages—Interests & Personality, Name, Basic Info, Background & Lifestyle, Schools, Companies, Networking, and Song & Video on Profile.

This adds content to your profile page. To change the look of your profile, you'll need to insert HTML codes into the About Me section on the Profile Edit page. This is a bit more involved than we have space for here. Instead, I direct you to some of the many pages devoted to customizing MySpace profile pages, which include

- Customize Your MySpace (www.customizeyourspace.com)
- NuclearCentury.com MySpace layouts (www.myspace.nuclearcentury.com)
- Pimp-My-Profile.com (www.pimp-my-profile.com)
- Pimp MySpace (www.pimpmyspace.org)
- SpaceMisc.com (www.spacemisc.com)

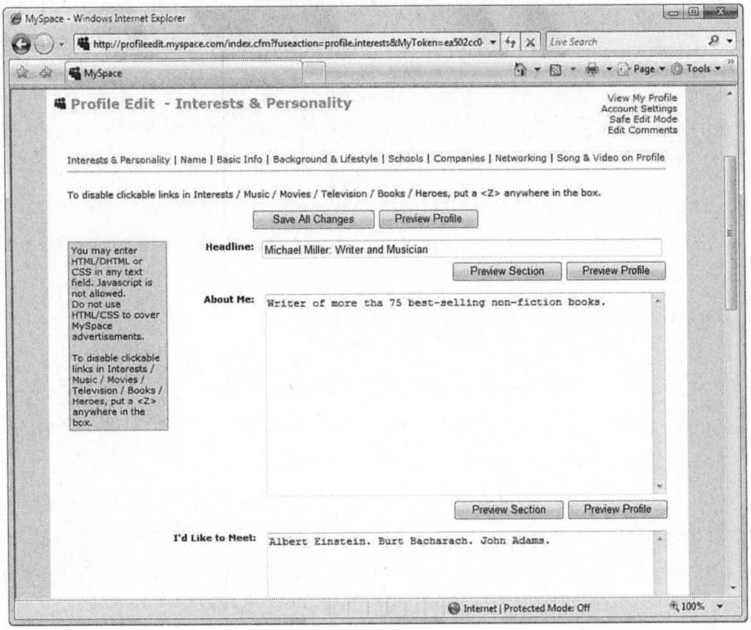

FIGURE 26.4

Adding content to your MySpace profile.

MySpace for Parents

Given that MySpace is such a huge thing to teenagers, it should also be of much interest to parents. You need to know what your kids are doing online.

First of all, note that MySpace tries to police itself, to some degree. Users with ages set to 14 or 15 years automatically have private profiles—that is, they're not browsable by the mass MySpace public. Users aged 16 or older have the option to restrict profile access to people on their friends list, although most teens don't exercise this option. (Of course, MySpace doesn't actually verify ages, so a younger child can claim to be older to get more access.)

It's important that you visit your kids' MySpace pages on a regular basis. Not all teens are wise about what they put online. It's not unusual to find provocative pictures posted on MySpace profiles; you might not want your children exposing themselves in this fashion, however.

You also need to warn your kids that not everyone on MySpace is truly a "friend." They should

tip

Although MySpace is the largest social networking site on the Web, it's not the only one. Other popular sites include Bebo (www.bebo.com), Facebook (www.facebook.com), Friendster (www.friendster.com), Hi5 (www.hi5.com), LinkedIN (www.linkedin.com), Orkut (www.orkut.com), Tagged (www.tagged.com), and Yahoo! 360 (360.yahoo.com).

be circumspect about the information they make public and about whom they personally communicate with. It's also worth noting again that kids shouldn't arrange to meet in person strangers who they're "friends" with online; it's not unheard of for unsavory adults to use MySpace as a stalking ground.

In other words, teach your kids to be careful. Hanging out at MySpace is normally no more dangerous than hanging out at the mall, but even malls aren't completely safe. Caution and common sense are always called for.

THE ABSOLUTE MINIMUM

Here are the key points to remember from this chapter:

- MySpace is a social networking site that caters to teenagers wanting to hang out online.

- MySpace users create their own profile pages, complete with personal info, photos, lists of friends, blog entries, and so forth.

- You can browse for users who share your interests, or search for specific users by name.

- MySpace accepts users as young as 14 years old; parents need to police their children's MySpace profile pages.

27

CREATING YOUR OWN WEB PAGE

In the previous chapters you learned two ways to establish a personal presence on the Web—by creating your own blog (via Blogger or a similar service) and by creating a profile page on the MySpace social networking site. But what do you do if you want a more robust web presence, a real web page or website that anyone can access?

The solution, quite simply, is to just do it. Anyone can create her own page or site on the Web. All you need is a web page editing program (to create your pages) and a web hosting community (to host your pages). And, to no surprise, many hosting sites offer both these features.

Read on to learn how to create your own pages on the Web.

Building a Web Page at a Home Page Community

If you want a one-stop solution to creating and hosting your own web pages, turn to one of the major *home page communities* on the Web. These sites not only help you create your own web pages, they even host your pages on the Web. And, in many cases, this basic hosting service is free!

Visiting the Communities

The most popular of these home page communities include

- Angelfire (angelfire.lycos.com)
- Google Page Creator (pages.google.com)
- Microsoft Office Live (office.microsoft.com/en-us/officelive/)
- Tripod (www.tripod.lycos.com)
- Yahoo! GeoCities (geocities.yahoo.com)

Many Internet service providers also offer free personal home pages to their subscribers; check with your ISP to see what services are available.

> **tip**
>
> Many of these sites also offer tools for building and hosting your own personal blog. Learn more about blogs in Chapter 25, "Exploring Blogs and Podcasts."

Creating a Home Page with Google Page Creator

One of the newest, and easiest to use, home page communities is hosted by Google. Google Page Creator not only lets you create your own personal web pages but also hosts the pages you create—for free.

To use Google Page Creator, you need to first sign up for a Gmail account, which is free. Just click the sign-up link on the initial Google Page Creator page.

After you've signed in, you're taken directly to the Page Manager page shown in Figure 27.1. This is your home base for all Page Creator activities; it's where you start when you want to create your own web page.

To create your first web page, follow these steps:

1. From the Page Manager, click the Create a New Page link.
2. The link changes to a text box; enter a title for your page and then click the Create and Edit button.
3. The Edit Page page appears. As you can see in Figure 27.2, the title for your new page is already in place, with the rest of the page ready for editing. Start by clicking the Change Look link.

FIGURE 27.1

Google Page Creator—your own web page, no technical expertise required.

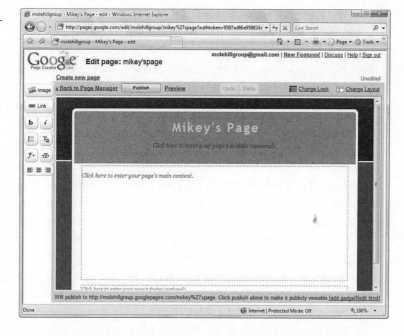

FIGURE 27.2

Your newly created web page—ready for editing.

4. Google displays a variety of different page designs, as shown in Figure 27.3. After you find a design you like, click it to apply it to your page. (Alternatively, you can click the Preview link below any thumbnail to view a larger example of that page design.)

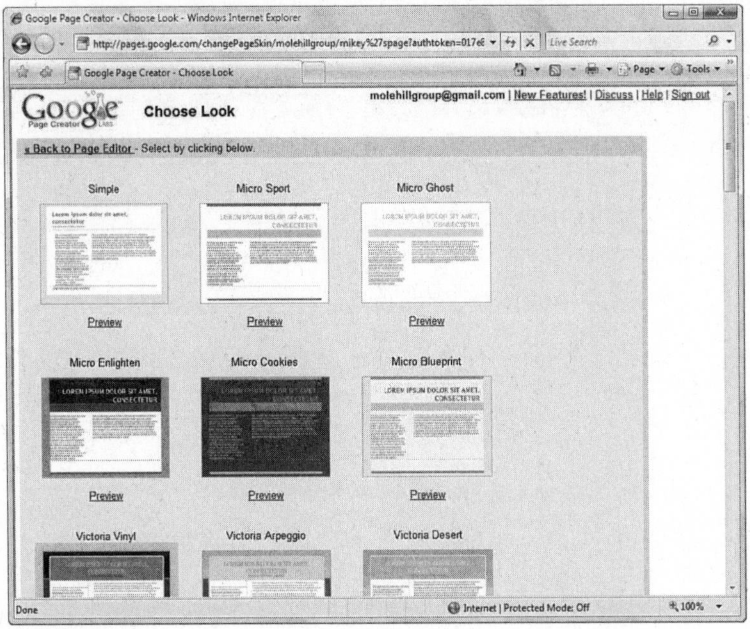

FIGURE 27.3

Choosing a
design for your
web page.

5. The Edit Page page changes to reflect the page design you selected. Now it's time to edit your page layout, which you do by clicking the Change Layout link.

6. The Choose Layout page, shown in Figure 27.4, displays four different types of page layouts—one column, two column left, two column right, and three column designs. Click the layout you want to use for your web page.

7. The Edit Page page changes to reflect the layout you selected. It's time to begin entering content on your web page. Start by clicking the subtitle section and then enter a subtitle for your page.

8. Click the other sections of your page to enter main and sidebar content.

9. To add an image to your page, position your cursor where you want the image to appear and then click the Image button. When the Add an Image dialog box appears, you can choose to upload an image from your PC or link to an image hosted on another website.

10. To insert a link to another web page, highlight the text from which you want to link and then click the Link button. You can link to another page you have on the Google site (Your Pages), a file you upload from your PC (Your Files), or another page on the Web (Web Address). You can also choose to insert an email link so that users can click to send you an email (Email Address).

FIGURE 27.4

Choosing a lay-
out for your web
page.

Choosing a layout for your web page.

11. Apply any desired formatting to your text, using the formatting controls in the left column.

12. When you're finished creating your page, click the Publish button. This publishes your page on the Web and displays the URL for that page at the bottom of the Edit Page page. Click the URL to see your completed page.

note

At any time, you can see how your in-progress page looks by clicking the Preview link at the top of the Edit Page page.

After your page is published, you can notify your friends of your new page. Just return to the Page Manager page, check the page you just created, pull down the More Actions list, and select Tell Your Friends. This opens a new Gmail message window on your desktop; add your friends' addresses to the To: list; then click the Send button. They'll receive your email message, complete with a link to your new web page.

Using Page-Building Software

The web page you create at a web hosting community is a relatively simple one. If you want to create more sophisticated pages—or multiple pages, in a complete website—you need a more powerful tool. Fortunately, there are numerous software programs available you can use to build really fancy web pages.

The two most popular web page editing programs are Adobe Dreamweaver (www.adobe.com/products/dreamweaver/) and Microsoft Expression Web Designer (www.microsoft.com/products/expression/). Both of these programs let you design everything from simple personal pages to sophisticated e-commerce websites; you can construct pages using a WYSIWYG interface, or enter raw HTML code.

note

All web pages are based on a special programming code, called *Hypertext Markup Language (HTML)*. Fortunately, most web page editing programs and services enable you to create web pages without hand-coding the pages in HTML—although you can still edit the raw HTML code, if you want.

Uploading Your Pages to a Web Host

If you build your own web pages with a program such as Dreamweaver or Expressions Web Designer, you still have to find a site on the Web to host your pages. Yahoo! GeoCities and the other home page communities offer separate page hosting services (usually for a fee), geared toward personal web pages. If you need a host for a complete website (or for small business purposes), you should probably examine a service that specializes in more sophisticated website hosting.

note

Microsoft Expression Web Designer is the replacement for Microsoft's venerable FrontPage HTML editing program.

A website hosting service will manage all aspects of your website. For a monthly fee, you'll receive a fixed amount of space on their servers, your own website address (and your own personal domain, if you want to pay for it), and a variety of site management tools. Pricing for these services typically starts at $10 or so a month, and goes up from there.

The best way to look for a website host is to access a directory of hosting services. Most of these directories let you search for hosts by various parameters, including monthly cost, disk space provided, programming and platforms supported, and extra features offered. Among the best of these host search sites are the following:

- HostIndex.com (www.hostindex.com)
- HostSearch (www.hostsearch.com)
- TopHosts.com (www.tophosts.com)

THE ABSOLUTE MINIMUM

Here are the key points to remember from this chapter:

- Web pages are built using the HTML programming language—although you don't have to know how to program to create a simple web page.
- To create a personal web page, check out one of the large page building communities, such as Yahoo! GeoCities or Google Page Creator.
- To create a more sophisticated web page or website, use a dedicated page-building program, such as Adobe Dreamweaver or Microsoft Expression Web Designer.

28

EXPLORING OTHER COOL AND USEFUL WEBSITES

Throughout this section of the book we've looked at many different kinds of websites—search engines, online auctions, price comparison sites, even blogs and social networking sites. But there's even more on the Web than that—much more.

That's where this chapter comes in. Without further ado, this chapter presents some of the most popular sites on the Web—and some of my personal favorites.

News, Sports, and Weather

The Internet is a great place to find both news headlines and in-depth analysis. Most news-related websites are updated in real-time, so you're always getting the latest news—on your computer screen, when you want it.

News Sites

Some of the biggest, most popular news sites on the Web are run by the major broadcast and cable news networks, or by the major national newspapers. You can turn to these sites to get the latest headlines, and—in many cases—live audio and video feeds.

The major news sites on the Web include

- **ABC News** (abcnews.go.com)
- **BBC News** (news.bbc.co.uk)
- **CBS News** (www.cbsnews.com)
- **CNN** (www.cnn.com)
- **Fox News** (www.foxnews.com)
- **MSNBC** (www.msnbc.com)
- *New York Times* (www.nytimes.com)
- *USA Today* (www.usatoday.com)

tip

If all you want is a quick overview of the latest headlines, check out Google News (news.google.com). This site offers the top headlines from a variety of news sources; click any headline to read the complete story.

Sports Sites

The Web is also a great resource for sports fans of all shapes and sizes. Whether you're a fan or a participant, at least one site somewhere on the Web focuses on your particular sport.

The best sports sites resemble the best news sites—they're actually portals to all sorts of content and services, including up-to-the-minute scores, post-game recaps, in-depth reporting, and much more. If you're looking for sports information online, one of these portals is the place to start:

- **CBS SportsLine** (www.sportsline.com)
- **ESPN.com** (espn.go.com)
- **FOXSports** (msn.foxsports.com)
- **NBC Sports** (www.nbcsports.com)
- **SI.com—Sports Illustrated** (sportsillustrated.cnn.com)
- **SportingNews.com** (www.sportingnews.com)

tip

If you follow a particular sports team, check out that team's local newspaper on the Web. Chances are you'll find a lot of in-depth coverage there that you won't find at these other sites.

Weather Sites

Then there's the issue of weather. Although you can't do much about the weather, you can find a lot of weather-related information on the Web.

First, know that most of the major news portals and local websites offer some variety of weather-related services. The Web also offers many dedicated weather sites, all of which provide local and national forecasts, weather radar, satellite maps, and more.

Here are the most popular weather sites on the Web:

- **AccuWeather.com** (www.accuweather.com)
- **Intellicast.com** (www.intellicast.com)
- **Weather Underground** (www.wunderground.com)
- **Weather.com** (www.weather.com)

Financial Information

The Internet is a great place to find up-to-the-minute information about stocks and other securities. Several sites and services specialize in providing real-time (or slightly delayed) stock quotes—free!

Here's a short list of the best financial sites on the Web—both free and for a fee:

- **CNN/Money** (money.cnn.com)
- **Hoovers Online** (www.hoovers.com)
- **Marketwatch** (www.marketwatch.com)
- **Motley Fool** (www.fool.com)
- **MSN Money** (moneycentral.msn.com)
- **Yahoo! Finance** (finance.yahoo.com)

Medical Information

When you're looking for useful health-related information, you don't have to wait for your next doctor's appointment. A number of websites offer detailed information about illnesses, diseases, and medicines. Many of these sites focus on preventive medicine and wellness, and almost all help you match symptoms with likely illnesses and treatments. Indeed, some of these sites provide access to the same medical databases used by most physicians—without waiting for an appointment!

caution

As useful as these health sites are, they should not and cannot serve as substitutes for a trained medical opinion.

The top medical sites on the Web include

- ■ **KidsHealth** (www.kidshealth.org)
- ■ **MDChoice** (www.mdchoice.com)
- ■ **MedicineNet** (www.medicinenet.com)
- ■ **National Library of Medicine** (www.nlm.nih.gov)
- ■ **WebMD** (www.webmd.com)

> **tip**
>
> You can also use the Web to search for a new or specialist physician in your area. Two of the best physician search sites are AMA DoctorFinder (http://webapps.ama-assn.org/doctorfinder/) and DoctorDirectory.com (www.doctordirectory.com).

Photos, Clip Art, and Other Images

Next up, let's look at some sites where you can view and download photos, graphics, clip art, and other artwork. Some of these sites let you view for free; others charge to download their image files.

- ■ **Alta Vista Image Search** (www.altavista.com/image/)
- ■ **Classroom Clipart** (www.classroomclipart.com)
- ■ **Clip Art Center** (www.clip-art-center.com)
- ■ **Clip Art Review** (www.webplaces.com/html/clipart.htm)
- ■ **Clipart.com** (www.clipart.com)
- ■ **Corbis** (pro.corbis.com)
- ■ **Ditto.com** (www.ditto.com)
- ■ **Freefoto.com** (www.freefoto.com)
- ■ **Getty Images** (www.getty-images.com)
- ■ **GoGraph.com** (www.gograph.com)
- ■ **Google Image Search** (images.google.com)
- ■ **MediaBuilder** (www.mediabuilder.com)
- ■ **Photos.com** (www.photos.com)
- ■ **Smithsonian Photographic Services** (photo2.si.edu)
- ■ **WebSEEk** (www.ctr.columbia.edu/webseek/)

Maps and Travel Guides

If you're going on a trip, the Web is a great source of travel information. From maps and driving directions to full-fledged travel guides, these sites will help you find your way:

- AAA Travel Services (www.aaa.com)
- AOL CityGuide (cityguide.aol.com)
- Concierge.com (www.concierge.com)
- Fodors (www.fodors.com)
- Frommer's Travel Guides (www.frommers.com)
- Google Maps (maps.google.com)
- GORP.com Adventure Travel and Outdoor Recreation (gorp.away.com)
- Lonely Planet (www.lonelyplanet.com)
- MapQuest (www.mapquest.com)
- Rand McNally (www.randmcnally.com)
- Rough Guides (www.roughguides.com)
- TripAdvisor (www.tripadvisor.com)
- VirtualTourist.com (www.virtualtourist.com)
- Windows Live Maps (maps.live.com)
- Yahoo! Maps (maps.yahoo.com)

Classifieds and Local Shopping

As you learned in Chapter 24, "Buying and Selling in eBay Online Auctions," eBay is a great place to find items for sale from other individuals (and to sell your own stuff, of course). But eBay's not so great for finding larger and difficult-to-ship items, or for locating items and services in your own home town. For that, turn to this collection of local websites:

- Craigslist (www.craigslist.com)
- Google Base (base.google.com)
- LiveDeal (www.livedeal.com)
- Oodle Online Classifieds (www.oodle.com)
- Yahoo! Classifieds (classifieds.yahoo.com)

Job Hunting

Looking to change jobs? Then check out these jobs and careers sites. Most let you post your resume online and search for open positions locally or nationwide.

- America's Job Bank (www.ajb.dni.us)
- Career.com (www.career.com)
- CareerBuilder (www.careerbuilder.com)

- CareerWeb (www.careerweb.com)
- jobfind.com (www.jobfind.com)
- JobWeb (www.jobweb.com)
- Monster (www.monster.com)
- NationJob Network (www.nationjob.com)
- NowHiring.com (www.nowhiring.com)
- Yahoo! Hot Jobs (hotjobs.yahoo.com)

Religion

The Web is a treasure trove of information about all the world's major religions. You can find everything from searchable Bible databases to full-featured spiritual portals. Try these websites:

- Bible Search (www.biblesearch.com)
- BibleGateway.com (www.biblegateway.com)
- BuddhaNet (www.buddhanet.net)
- Crosswalk.com (www.crosswalk.com)
- eSpirituality.com (www.espirituality.com)
- Gospelcom.net (www.gospelcom.net)
- Hindu Universe (www.hindunet.org)
- Islam 101 (www.islam101.com)
- Islam Page (www.islamworld.net)
- Net Ministries (www.netministries.org)
- ReligionsUSA.com (www.religionsusa.com)
- Religious Resources (www.religiousresources.org)
- Religious Texts (www.hti.umich.edu/relig/)
- Religious Tolerance (www.religioustolerance.org)
- World of Religions (www.religionworld.org)

Entertainment

The Web is a fount of information about all things entertainment-related, from the latest movie reviews to the inside scoop on upcoming films and TV shows. Here's just a sampling of the entertainment sites online:

- Ain't It Cool News (www.aintitcool.com)
- All-Movie Guide (www.allmovie.com)

- **All-Music Guide** (www.allmusic.com)
- **Dark Horizons** (www.darkhorizons.com)
- **E! Online** (www.eonline.com)
- **Entertainment Weekly** (www.ew.com)
- **Film.com** (www.film.com)
- **Internet Movie Database** (www.imdb.com)
- **People.com** (people.aol.com)
- **Rotten Tomatoes** (www.rottentomatoes.com)
- **TV Guide Online** (www.tvguide.com)

Education and Reference

Whether you need to look up a relevant fact or get some help with your homework, the Web is the place to look! The following are a few education and reference sites:

- **Awesome Library** (www.awesomelibrary.org)
- **DiscoverySchool.com** (school.discovery.com)
- **Fact Monster** (www.factmonster.com)
- **Homework Center** (www.factmonster.com/homework/)
- **HomeworkSpot** (www.homeworkspot.com)
- **Infoplease Homework Center** (www.infoplease.com/homework/)
- **Internet Public Library** (www.ipl.org)
- **Kid Info Homework Resource** (www.kidinfo.com)
- **KidsClick** (www.kidsclick.org)
- **LibDex Library Index** (www.libdex.com)
- **Library of Congress** (www.loc.gov)
- **MadSci Network** (www.madsci.org)
- **Refdesk.com** (www.refdesk.com)
- **Word Central** (www.wordcentral.com)

Games

All work and no play would make for a boring Internet. So when you're finished doing your homework, turn to one of these game sites to have a little fun:

- **All Game Guide** (www.allgame.com)
- **All Games Free** (www.allgamesfree.com)

- ArcadeTown.com (www.arcadetown.com)
- BoxerJam.com (www.boxerjam.com)
- Games Kids Play (www.gameskidsplay.net)
- Games.com (www.games.com)
- GameSpot (www.gamespot.com)
- GameSpy (www.gamespy.com)
- Gamesville (www.gamesville.lycos.com)
- GameZone (www.gamezone.com)
- GameZone's KidZone! (www.gzkidzone.com)
- Internet Chess Club (www.chessclub.com)
- Internet Park Word Games (www.internet-park.com)
- iWin.com (www.iwin.com)
- MSN Gaming Zone (zone.msn.com)
- PlayLater.com (www.playlater.com)
- Pogo.com (www.pogo.com)
- Xbox Live (www.xbox.com/live/)

Sites for Kids

If you're a parent looking for fun and safe sites for your kids to visit, look no further—here's a quick list of some of the most popular kids sites on the Web:

- ChildFun Family Website (www.childfun.com)
- FamilyFun.com (familyfun.go.com)
- Funology.com (www.funology.com)
- Grossology (www.grossology.org)
- Kaboose (www.kaboose.com)
- KiddoNet (www.kiddonet.com)
- Kids' Space (www.kids-space.org)
- KidsCom (www.kidscom.com)
- MaMaMedia (www.mamamedia.com)
- World Kids Network (www.worldkids.net)
- Yahooligans! (www.yahooligans.com)
- Yuckiest Site on the Internet (www.yucky.com)

Sites for Seniors

Just as the Web has plenty of sites for younger surfers, it also has sites for those on the other end of the age spectrum. Here are just a few of the online sites dedicated to seniors:

- **AARP** (www.aarp.org)
- **AgeNet Eldercare Network** (www.agenet.com)
- **Senior Women Web** (www.seniorwomen.com)
- **Senior.com** (www.senior.com)
- **SeniorNet** (www.seniornet.com)
- **SeniorSite.com** (www.seniorsite.com)
- **ThirdAge** (www.thirdage.com)
- **Today's Seniors** (www.todaysseniors.com)

THE ABSOLUTE MINIMUM

Here are the key points to remember from this chapter:

- The latest news, sports, and weather information can be found at numerous news-related websites.
- Both financial and medical information is in abundance online.
- The Web is home to tons of free (and not-so-free) images and clip art you can download to your PC.
- If you're planning a vacation, go online for maps, driving directions, and travel guides.
- Buy and sell items locally via Craigslist and similar local classified advertising sites.
- The Web is also a good resource if you're looking to change jobs.
- You can also find numerous websites that specialize in other types of information about religion, entertainment, and so on.
- Kids can find all sorts of useful information to help them in their homework—or relax with a fun online game.

29

Sending and Receiving Instant Messages

People like to talk—even when they're online.

When you want to hold a private one-on-one talk, you use an application called *instant messaging*. When you instant message, or IM, someone, you send a short text-based message directly to that person. It's a way of keeping in touch when you're online—and everybody's doing it!

Understanding Instant Messaging

Instant messaging lets you communicate one on one, in real-time, with your friends, family, and colleagues. It's faster than email and less chaotic than chat rooms. It's just you and another user—and your instant messaging software.

There are several big players in the instant messaging market today, including

- AOL Instant Messenger (www.aim.com)
- Google Talk (www.google.com/talk/)
- ICQ (www.icq.com)
- Windows Live Messenger (messenger.live.com)
- Yahoo! Messenger (messenger.yahoo.com)

note

Windows Live Messenger was formerly known as both MSN Messenger and Windows Messenger.

Unfortunately, many of these products don't work well (or at all) with each other; if you're using Yahoo! Messenger, for example, you won't be able to communicate with someone running AOL Instant Messenger. That means you'll want to use the IM program that all your friends are using—so find that out before you download any software. (That said, the Windows Live Messenger and Yahoo! Messenger networks do talk to each other, but this is definitely an exception to the rule.)

Using AOL Instant Messenger

The most popular instant messaging program today is AOL Instant Messenger, or AIM, with Yahoo! Messenger a close second. AIM is especially popular among the teen and preteen crowd, although people of all ages can and do use it. We'll use AIM for the examples in this chapter, but know that all instant messaging programs work in pretty much the same fashion.

caution

Instant messaging only works if both parties are online at the same time; you can't send an instant message to someone who isn't available. That said, some IM programs save your messages until the recipient returns online, and then sends them.

Downloading the AIM Software

To use AIM, you first have to download the AIM client software. AIM is free to both download and use on a daily basis.

Go to the AIM website (www.aim.com) and click the Downloads menu. Several different versions of AIM are available; the most current version, as of this writing, is AIM 6.0. (Be on the lookout for newer versions, however.) Select the version you want to download; when the next page appears, click the Install Now link. This downloads the AIM software and installs it on your PC.

Launching AIM and Signing In

After you have AIM installed, you launch the program by either clicking the AIM icon that the program installs on your desktop or selecting Start, All Programs, AIM, AIM. The program opens with the main window displayed, as shown in Figure 29.1.

If you're a new user, you'll need to choose a screen name before you can start using the program. You do this by clicking the Get a Screen Name link in the AIM window. Follow the onscreen instructions to choose a screen name and password for your account.

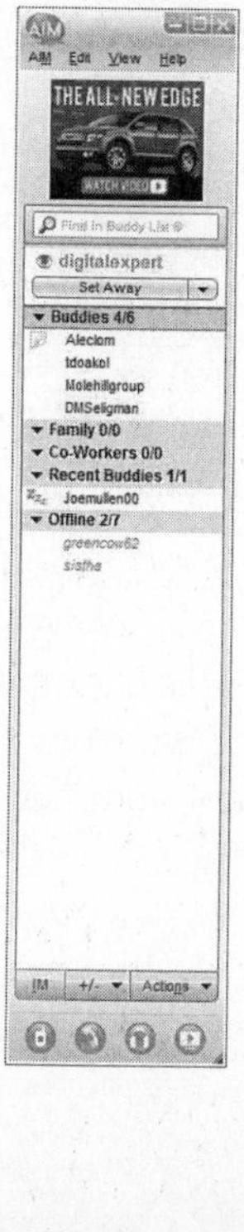

note

One of the other versions you can download is AIM Pro, which offers videoconferencing, online meetings, desktop and file sharing, and other features designed for corporate users. Most of these features are overkill for home users, however; I recommend you stick with the basic version of AIM.

FIGURE 29.1
The main AIM window, complete with online and offline Buddies.

After you have your screen name and password, you have to sign into the AIM service before you can start messaging. When you launch the AIM software, enter your screen name and password, and then click the Sign In button. This connects you to the service and notifies any of your friends that you're online and ready to chat.

Adding New Buddies

The people you chat with via AIM are called your *buddies*. To send an instant message to another user, that person has to be on your Buddy List.

When you first launch AIM, you're prompted to import buddies from your existing Hotmail, Outlook, Outlook Express, and Yahoo! contacts. Do this if you have friends and contacts who you know use the AIM service.

After this initial import, you can manually add users to your AIM Buddy List. To add a new Buddy, click the Buddy List Setup button at the bottom of the AIM window and select Add Buddy. When the New Buddy window appears, as shown in Figure 29.2, enter the person's screen name and then click the Save button. This person is now added to your Buddy List.

FIGURE 29.2
Adding a new Buddy to your Buddy List.

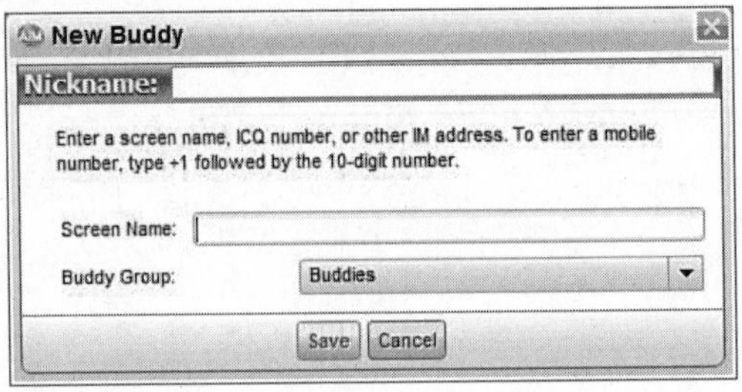

After you've added people to your Buddy List, they show up in the main AIM window. Buddies who are online and ready to chat are displayed on the top of the list; Buddies who aren't currently online appear at the bottom of the list, in the Offline section.

Sending a Message

To send an instant message to one of your Buddies, double-click that person's name in your Buddy List. This opens a separate IM window, like the one shown in Figure 29.3. Enter your message in the lower part of the window and then click the Send button (or press Enter).

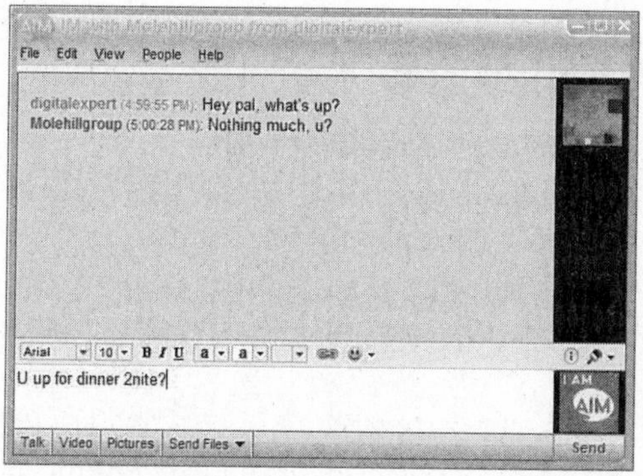

FIGURE 29.3

Send and receive
instant messages
via the IM
window.

FIGURE 29.3

Send and receive
instant messages
via the IM
window.

Your message appears in the top part of the window, as does the reply from your
Buddy. Continue talking like this, one message
after another. Your entire conversation is displayed in the top part of the window, and you
can scroll up to reread earlier messages.

Receiving a Message

When you're logged onto the AIM service and
someone else sends you an instant message,
AIM lets out a little bleeping sound and then
displays an alert in the lower-right corner of
your screen. To reply to the message, click the
alert; this opens a new IM window for your
chat.

tip

You can use AIM to send
pictures and other files to
other users; just click the
Pictures or Send Files buttons
at the bottom of any IM window. AIM can also be used
for voice and video mes-
saging, if you have a microphone
and/or webcam connected to your
PC. Click the Talk or Video buttons
in any AIM window to initiate a
voice or video chat.

THE ABSOLUTE MINIMUM

Here are the key points to remember from this chapter:

- Whereas email is great for longer, more formal messages, instant messaging is better for short one-on-one conversation.

- There are many different instant messaging networks, including AOL Instant Messenger (AIM), Google Talk, ICQ, Windows Live Messenger, and Yahoo! Messenger.

- To message another user, you both must be online at the same time, using the same instant messaging software.

- The people you message with become part of your friends or Buddy List; double-click a name on this list to start a live chat session.

PART VI

Exploring the Digital Lifestyle

30

USING YOUR PC WITH A DIGITAL CAMERA

Chances are, you've already traded in your old film camera for a new digital camera. If you want to edit or print your digital photos, you'll need to connect that digital camera to your PC—which is relatively easy to do.

There are several different ways to get your photos into your computer—you can transfer digital files directly from your camera's memory card, download pictures from your camera via a USB connection, or even scan existing photo prints. We'll discuss them all in this chapter.

Transferring Pictures Via USB

Connecting a digital camera or scanner to your PC is easy. Most digital cameras today come with a USB connector, so you can connect your camera directly to your PC using a USB cable. With this type of setup, Windows recognizes your camera or scanner as soon as you plug it in and installs the appropriate drivers automatically.

When you connect a USB cable between your camera and your PC, one of several things is likely to happen:

note

Some digital cameras connect via FireWire instead of USB. The process is the same.

- If you're using Windows Vista, it should recognize when your camera is connected and automatically download the pictures in your camera, while displaying a dialog box that notifies you of what it's doing.

- If you're using Windows XP, connecting your camera may open the Removable Disk dialog box. Select Copy Pictures to a Folder on My Computer Using Microsoft Scanner and Camera Wizard, and you'll launch the Scanner and Camera Wizard. Use this wizard to select which photos you want to download and where.

- If you've installed a proprietary picture management program that comes with your digital camera, it may launch and ask to download the pictures from your camera. Follow the onscreen instructions to proceed.

- If you've installed a third-party photo editing program, such as Adobe Photoshop Elements, it may launch and ask to download the pictures from your camera. Follow the onscreen instructions to proceed.

- If nothing happens when you connect your camera, click the Start menu, and select Computer (My Computer in Windows XP). The Computer Explorer opens, and there should be a new icon for your digital camera. Double-click this icon to view the current contents of your camera and to copy files from your camera to a location on your PC's hard drive.

note

After you've saved a digital picture file to your hard disk, you can then use picture-editing software to edit and otherwise manipulate the picture. Learn more in Chapter 31, "Organizing and Editing Your Digital Photos."

Transferring Pictures from a Memory Card

Copying digital pictures via USB cable is nice—if your camera supports this method. For many users, an easier approach is to use a memory card reader. A memory card reader is a low-cost external peripheral that connects to a USB port on your PC. You then insert the memory card from your digital camera into the memory card reader, and your PC recognizes the card as if it were another hard disk.

You can then use Computer Explorer or My Computer to copy files from the memory card to your computer. Just open the Explorer and click the drive icon for the memory card. This displays the card's contents, typically in a subfolder labeled DCIM. You can then move, copy, and delete the photos stored on the card, as you would with any other type of file in Windows.

tip

Many color photo printers include memory card slots that let you print directly from your camera's memory card, bypassing your computer entirely.

Scanning a Picture

If your photos are of the old-fashioned print variety, you can still turn them into digital files, using a flatbed scanner. What happens when you start a scan depends on what version of Windows you're using.

In Windows Vista, the scanning starts automatically when you press the Scan button on your scanner. The resulting file is saved to your hard disk and displayed in Windows Photo Gallery.

In Windows XP, pressing your scanner's Scan button launches the Scanner and Camera Wizard. From here you can select the Picture Type (color or grayscale, depending on the photo) or click the Options button to change the resolution of the scan. You can also preview what the scan will look like and crop the picture if needed. Click the Next button to specify a location for the scanned file; then click Next again to make the scan. The photo is then scanned and saved to your hard disk.

That's all there is to it. Your print photo is saved as a digital file for future use.

Storing Your Photos in Windows

Where are all your photos stored after they've been scanned or downloaded from your digital camera? By default, Windows Vista stores all your pictures in the Pictures folder, shown in Figure 30.1; Windows XP stores your pictures in the similar My Pictures folder. This folder includes a number of features specific to the management of picture files. In Windows Vista, you find these features on the main toolbar; they include

- **Preview** in a photo editing program
- View as a **Slide Show**
- **Print** your photos at various sizes
- **E-mail** selected photos
- **Share** your photos with other users
- **Burn** selected photos to CD

FIGURE 30.1

Use the Pictures folder to store and organize your digital pictures.

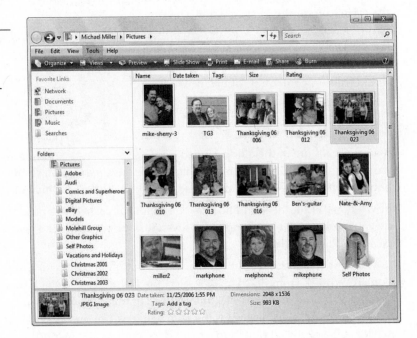

From here you can also perform all the normal file-related tasks, such as copying, moving, or even deleting your photos. If you want to edit your photos, however, you have to use a different program—a photo editing program, which we'll discuss in Chapter 31.

THE ABSOLUTE MINIMUM

Here are the key points to remember from this chapter:

- You can connect a digital camera to your PC via USB or use a memory card reader to transfer files from the camera's media card.

- Some cameras, when connected, launch proprietary picture transfer software; in other cases, Windows automatically downloads your pictures as soon as you connect your camera.

- When you scan a photo print, your photo is converted to a digital file that is saved on your hard disk.

- By default, Windows stores your digital pictures in the Pictures or My Pictures folder.

31

ORGANIZING AND EDITING YOUR DIGITAL PHOTOS

After you've transferred a digital photo from your camera to your PC, a lot of options are available to you. A digital picture file is just like any computer file, which means that you can copy it, move it, delete it, or whatever. You can also use special picture editing software to manipulate your photos—to touch up bad spots and red eye, crop the edges, and apply all sorts of special effects.

After you've touched up all your photos, you can choose to create digital photo albums, use them in all manner of picture-related projects and documents, or print them out—either on your own four-color printer, or at a traditional photo processor. The combination of digital photography and personal computing is definitely the way to go—and it's a lot more versatile than traditional film-based photography!

Choosing a Photo Editing Program

To manage and edit your photos, you need a full-featured photo organization and editing program. This type of program lets you organize and catalog all the digital photos on your system, edit your photos (to remove red eye, crop out unwanted elements, adjust color and brightness, and so forth), and create full-sized prints or multiple-photo contact sheets on your PC's printer.

When it comes to picking a photo editing program, you have a lot of choices. You can choose a low-priced, consumer-oriented program or a high-priced program targeted at professional photographers. And if your PC is running Windows Vista, you have a good photo editing program, Windows Photo Gallery, already installed.

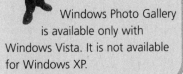

note Windows Photo Gallery is available only with Windows Vista. It is not available for Windows XP.

Aside from Windows Photo Gallery, the most popular low-priced photo editing programs include the following:

- Adobe Photoshop Elements (www.adobe.com), $89.99
- IrfanView (www.irfanview.com), free
- Microsoft Digital Image Suite (www.microsoft.com/products/imaging/), $49.95
- Paint Shop Pro Photo (www.corel.com), $99.99
- Picasa (www.picasa.com), free
- Roxio PhotoSuite (www.roxio.com), $29.99

All of these programs perform many of the same functions. You'll be able to organize your photos; tag your photos with useful data; resize your photos larger or smaller; adjust your photos' brightness, contrast, color, and tint; crop your photos to focus on the main part of the picture; make your photos sharper or softer; and, in some cases, add various types of special effects.

note Don't confuse the low-cost Photoshop Elements with the higher-priced Photoshop CS2 program, which is used by more serious and professional photographers.

Editing Your Photos with Windows Photo Gallery

Not all the pictures you take are perfect. Sometimes an image is a little out of focus or off center, or maybe your subject caught the glare of a flash for a "red eye" effect. The nice thing about digital pictures is that you can easily edit them to correct for these and other flaws.

If your PC is running Windows Vista, you have the capable Windows Photo Gallery installed. You can use Windows Photo Gallery to edit your photos and to organize them on your hard disk.

Let's look at how you use Windows Photo Gallery to perform some of these tasks.

Organizing Your Photos

In Windows Vista, you launch Windows Photo Gallery by clicking the Start button and selecting All Programs, Windows Photo Gallery. As you can see in Figure 31.1, the Photo Gallery window is initially divided into three panes. The left pane is used for navigation—selecting which folders and photos to view. The middle pane displays thumbnails of all the photos in the currently selected folder. And the right pane displays information about the currently selected photo.

FIGURE 31.1

Organizing photos in Windows Photo Gallery.

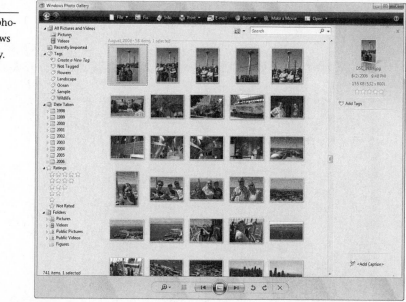

The navigation pane is especially useful because it lets you find your photos in a number of different ways:

■ To view all your photos, organized by year (and within each year, in chronological order), click Pictures under All Pictures and Videos.

- To view your most recent photos, click Recently Imported.

- To view photos by a particular characteristic, click a tag in the Tags section. (Of course, you first have to assign tags to your photos…)

- To view pictures taken in a given year, click the year in the Date Taken section.

- To view your favorite photos, click a star rating in the Ratings section. (Assuming you've assigned star ratings to your photos, of course…)

- To view photos in a particular folder, click the folder (or subfolder) in the Folders section.

To view a photo full size, all you have to do is double-click the photo. This shows the photo full frame, as shown in Figure 31.2, without the other thumbnails or the navigation pane. (Information about the photo still appears in the right-hand pane.) You can move to the next or previous photo by using the navigation controls at the bottom of the Photo Gallery window. Return to your other photos by clicking the Back To Gallery button at the top left of the window.

tip

You can also search for a particular folder by using the Search box at the top of the window.

FIGURE 31.2
Viewing a full-sized photo.

Editing a Photo

Windows Photo Gallery is more than just a photo manager or viewer. It also lets you touch up your digital photos, with easy-to-use photo editing controls.

To fix a photo, all you have to do is select it in the Photo Gallery and then click the Fix button. This displays the photo in the full window, with a series of editing controls in the right-hand pane, as shown in Figure 31.3. Here's what you can do:

- To do a quick touch up of brightness and color, click Auto Adjust.

- To increase or decrease brightness and contrast, click Adjust Exposure. This displays Brightness and Contrast sliders; move the sliders to adjust these parameters.

FIGURE 31.3

Touching up a photo in Windows Photo Gallery.

- To adjust the color levels, click Adjust Color. This displays three color sliders—Color Temperature (left to make the picture cooler, or more blue; right to make the picture warmer, or more red), Tint, and Saturation.

- To crop out unwanted areas at the edges of the picture, click Crop Picture. This displays a rectangular area within your picture, as shown in Figure 31.4; use your mouse to drag the edges of this rectangle to reframe your picture; then click Apply.

- To remove the red eye effect, click Fix Red Eye; then click and drag the cursor to draw a rectangle around each eye you want to fix.

tip

You can crop to exact print dimensions by clicking the Proportion button and then choosing a print size.

FIGURE 31.4

Cropping a photo.

After you've made a fix, click the check mark in that editing control section. If you want to reject a fix, click the Undo button at the bottom of the pane and select which fix you want to undo; you can undo any or all fixes you've made to a particular photo.

Emailing a Resized Photo

Here's something else neat about Windows Photo Gallery. You can email photos from within the Gallery and have the application automatically resize your photos for smoother emailing.

All you have to do is select one or more photos from within Windows Photo Gallery. Then click the E-mail button at the top of the window. Photo Gallery displays an Attach Files dialog box, as shown in Figure 31.5. Click the Picture Size button and select the desired size—Smaller, Small, Medium, Large, or Original Size. The file size, in kilobytes, is shown beneath this button; you probably want to keep the files you send less than 250KB apiece.

tip

To select multiple photos, hold down the Ctrl key as you click the different photos.

FIGURE 31.5

Resizing a photo for email.

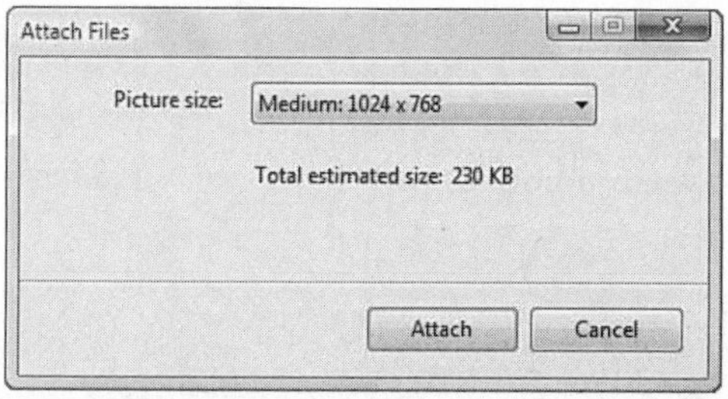

After you've selected a size, click the Attach button. This opens a new email message, with the selected photo(s) already attached. Enter the recipient's email address(es), add some text of your own, and then click the Send button. The message will be sent, along with the photos you selected.

Printing Your Photos

After you've touched up (or otherwise manipulated) your photos, it's time to print them—a task that's really easy in Windows.

Choosing the Right Printer and Paper

If you have a color printer, you can make good-quality prints of your image files. Even a low-priced color inkjet can make surprisingly good prints, although the better your printer, the better the results.

Some manufacturers sell printers specifically designed for photographic prints. These printers use special photo print paper and output prints that are almost indistinguishable from those you get from a professional photo processor. If you take a lot of digital photos, one of these printers might be a good investment.

The quality of your prints is also affected by the type of paper you use. Printing on standard laser or inkjet paper is okay for making proofs, but you'll want to use a thicker, waxier paper for those prints you want to keep. Check with your printer's manufacturer to see what type of paper it recommends for the best quality photo prints.

Making the Print

Any photo-editing program lets you print your pictures from within the program. You can also print directly from Windows Vista, using the print functions built into Windows Photo Gallery.

In Windows Vista, you can start the print process from the Pictures Explorer or from the Windows Photo Gallery application; what happens next is the same, no matter how you start.

Begin by selecting the photo(s) to print; then click the Print button at the top of the window. This displays the Print Pictures window, shown in Figure 31.6. Here's where the fun begins.

tip

In Windows Photo Gallery, you have the additional option of sending your photos to an online photo service for printing. Just click the Print button and select Order Prints.

FIGURE 31.6

Printing a photo in Windows Vista.

Start by using the buttons at the top of the window to select which printer to use, as well as the printer's paper size, print quality, and paper type. Then use the selections on the right side of the window to select how many pictures per page to print. The options here depend on the size of your original photo and the size paper you're using. In most instances, you can choose from a full-page photo, two 4- by 6-inch photos, two 5- by 7- inch photos, one 8- by 10- inch photo, four 3.5- by 5-inch photos, nine wallet-sized photos, or 35 photos on a contact sheet. (This last option is useful if you selected more than one photo to print.)

Finally, select how many copies you want to print; then click the Print button. Your photos are sent to your printer, and the printing begins.

Printing Photos Professionally

If you don't have your own photo-quality printer, you can use a professional photo-processing service to print your photos. You can create prints from your digital photos in two primary ways:

- Copy your image files to CD or memory card and deliver the CD or card by hand to your local photo finisher.

- Go to the website of an online photo-finishing service and transfer your image files over the Internet.

The first option is convenient for many people, especially because numerous drug stores, supermarkets, and discount stores (including Wal-Mart) offer onsite photo printing services. Often the printing service is via a self-serve kiosk; just insert your CD or memory card, follow the onscreen instructions, and come back a half-hour later for your finished prints.

The second option is also convenient, if you don't mind waiting a few days for your prints to arrive. You never have to leave your house; you upload your photo files from your computer over the Internet and then receive your prints in your postal mailbox. These web-based services are often lower-priced than local print services, too—although don't forget to factor in the mailing costs.

Learn more about using online photo sites in Chapter 32, "Sharing Your Digital Photos Online."

THE ABSOLUTE MINIMUM

Here are the key points to remember from this chapter:

- You can use a photo-editing program, such as Adobe Photoshop Elements, to touch up or edit your photos.

- Windows Vista includes a built-in photo editing program, called Windows Photo Gallery, that you can use to organize and edit your digital photos.

- Some of the most popular "touch ups" include removing red eye, adjusting brightness and contrast, changing color and tint, and cropping the edges of the photo.

- You can print your photos to any four-color printer or send them (via the Internet) to an online photo processor for printing.

32

SHARING YOUR DIGITAL PHOTOS ONLINE

In the old days, if you wanted to share your photos with friends and family, you had to have extra prints made and then hand them out or mail them off, as appropriate. This approach is not only time-consuming, it's also costly; you have to pay money for each extra print you make.

In today's age of digital photography, you can still make photo prints. (In fact, you can make the prints on your own PC, as you learned in Chapter 31, "Organizing and Editing Your Digital Photos.") But now you also can share your photos digitally, online, with anyone who has an Internet connection. Let's look at how you can do this.

Emailing Digital Photos

Perhaps the easiest way to share your digital photos is to email them. No special software or service is involved; all you have to do is attach your photos to an email message you create in your regular email program and then send that message to as many recipients as you want.

You learned how to attach files to email messages back in Chapter 20, "Sending and Receiving Email." Because a digital photo is just another type of computer file, the process is the same when you want to send a photo. Create a new message in your email program, click the attachments button, and then select those photos you want to attach. Click the Send button, and your message is sent on its way, complete with the photos you selected.

As easy as this process is, you need to be aware of one issue before you start emailing your photos far and wide—that is, the size of the photo files you email.

If you're emailing photos pretty much as they were shot with your camera, you're probably emailing some large files. This can be a problem if you or your recipients are using a slow dial-up Internet connection; the larger the attached files, the longer it takes to send or receive an email message. In addition, some ISPs have trouble handling messages that are too large; you want to avoid messages more than 1 or 2MB in size.

For this reason, you probably want to resize your photos before you email them. If your recipients will be viewing your photos only on their computer screens, you should make your photos no larger than the typical screen—no more than 1024 pixels wide or 768 pixels tall. Anything larger won't fit on a typical computer screen.

In Windows Vista, resizing can be automatic. As you learned in Chapter 31, both the Pictures Explorer and Windows Photo Gallery include an E-mail button. When you click this button, Windows displays an Attach Files dialog box. You use this dialog box to select a size for the picture you want to send; you can choose to send the photo as small as 640×480 pixels, or as large as its original size. A copy of the selected picture is then resized appropriately and attached to an email message. The original photo remains at its original size on your hard disk.

note

You can use any photo editing program, including Windows Photo Gallery, to resize your pictures. For more detailed instructions, turn to Chapter 31.

On the other hand, if your recipients will be printing the photos, you probably don't want to resize them. A photo resized to 1024×768 pixels doesn't have enough picture resolution to create a detailed print. You'll want to keep your photos at their original size if they're going to be printed; any resizing will result in fuzzy prints.

Sharing Photos at a Photo Sharing Site

If you're sharing your photos with many people, an even better solution is to post your pictures on a photo sharing website. These sites let you store your photos in online photo albums, which can then be viewed by any number of visitors via their web browsers—for free. These sites also offer photo printing services, and some also sell photo-related items, such as picture tee shirts, calendars, mugs, and so on. Most of these sites are free to use; they make their money by selling prints and other merchandise.

To use a photo sharing site, you start by signing up for a free account. After your account is created, choose which photos on your PC you want to share. After the photos are selected, the site automatically uploads them from your PC to the website. You then organize the photos into photo albums, each of which has its own unique URL. You can then email the URL to your friends and family; when they access the photo site, they view your photos on their computer screens. If they like what they see, they can order their own photo prints (which they pay for, not you).

The most popular of these photo sharing sites include

- **Club Photo** (www.clubphoto.com)
- **dotPhoto** (www.dotphoto.com)
- **DropShots** (www.dropshots.com)
- **Flickr** (www.flickr.com)
- **Fotki** (www.fotki.com)
- **FotoTime** (www.fototime.com)
- **Kodak EasyShare Gallery** (www.kodakgallery.com)
- **PhotoAccess** (www.photoaccess.com)
- **PhotoSite** (www.photosite.com)
- **Picturetrail** (www.picturetrail.com)
- **Shutterfly** (www.shutterfly.com)
- **Snapfish** (www.snapfish.com)
- **Webshots** (www.webshots.com)
- **Yahoo! Photos** (photos.yahoo.com)

For example, Shutterfly, shown in Figure 32.1, lets you create any number of photo albums. You create a new album and upload photos by clicking the Add Pictures tab. You can then choose to create a new photo album or upload new photos to an existing album. When the Choose Pictures window appears, as shown in Figure 32.2, select the photos to upload and then click the Add Selected Pictures button.

FIGURE 32.1
The Shutterfly photo sharing website.

FIGURE 32.2
Choosing photos to upload to Shutterfly.

After the pictures are uploaded, you can view your photo albums by clicking the View & Enhance tab. As you can see in Figure 32.3, each album is displayed separately; click an album to view the photos in that album.

FIGURE 32.3

Online photo
albums at the
Shutterfly site.

To share your photos with others, click the Share Online tab, check the albums you want to share, and then click the Share This Album link. When the next page appears, enter the email addresses of the people you want to share with, write an accompanying note, and then click the Share Now button. The people you listed will receive an email message alerting them to your new online photo album, along with a link to that album. When they click the link, their web browser is automatically directed to your online photos.

Printing Photos Online

Most of these photo sharing websites also offer photo printing services. After you've uploaded your photos, all you have to do is select the photos you want to print and then click the appropriate button. (On Shutterfly, this is accomplished from the Order Prints tab.)

You'll probably have the option of choosing different sizes of prints. For example, Shutterfly (shown in Figure 32.4) offers 4×6, 5×7, 8×10, 11×14, 16×20, and 20×30 inch prints, and also wallet-sized prints, in either matte or glossy finish. Choose the size and quantity you want for each print; then enter your payment and shipping information.

FIGURE 32.4

Ordering photo
prints from
Shutterfly.

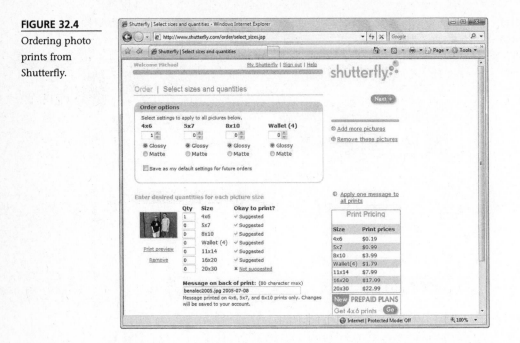

Most sites ship within a day or two of receiving your order; add shipping time, and
you should receive your prints in less than a week. Shipping is typically via the U.S.
Postal Service or similar shipping service.

THE ABSOLUTE MINIMUM

Here are the key points to remember from this chapter:

- The easiest way to share photos with friends and family is to send your photos as email attachments.

- Before you attach a photo file to an email message, resize it to a maximum of 800 pixels wide.

- Multiple people can view your photos when you create an online photo album at a photo sharing website.

- Most photo sharing sites also let you order photo prints, which are delivered via postal mail.

33

PLAYING, RIPPING, AND BURNING CDs

Your personal computer is a full-featured digital music machine. Not only can you download music from the Internet (which we'll talk about in Chapter 34, "Downloading and Playing Digital Music") but you also can use your PC to play music on CDs. Just insert a CD into your PC's CD drive, and the music starts.

In addition, assuming that you have a recordable CD drive (called a *CD burner*) in your system unit, you can make your own audio mix CDs. You can take any combination of songs on your hard disk and "burn" them onto a blank CD—and then play that CD in your home, car, or portable CD player. You can also use your PC to make copies of any CD you own and to "rip" songs from a CD to your PC's hard drive.

And the good thing is, all of this is quite easy to do. You don't have to be a geek to create your own computerized music library!

Choosing a Music Player Program

In most cases, playing a CD is as simple as inserting a disc into your computer's CD or DVD drive. This should automatically launch a music player program, which should start playing your music or movie.

Which music player program you use depends on what's installed on your PC. If you're using Windows XP or Windows Vista, you have the Windows Media Player program preinstalled and ready to go. Music player programs also come with most portable music players; for example, the popular Apple iPod comes with the iTunes music player.

Usually, it doesn't matter which music player software you use; they all perform pretty much the same functions, in pretty much the same fashion. That said, I recommend that you use iTunes if you have an iPod, or Windows Media Player if you have any other type of portable music player. Windows Media Player is also good if you don't have a portable music player; it's my favorite program for playing, ripping, and burning CDs.

This chapter looks at the two most popular player programs—Windows Media Player and iTunes—and how to use them to play, rip, and burn CDs.

Using Windows Media Player

For most users, the music player of choice is the one that comes free with Microsoft Windows. Windows Media Player (WMP) is a great little program you can use for many purposes—playing CDs and DVDs, ripping and burning CDs, listening to Internet radio broadcasts, and watching web videos. It works similarly to most other music players, so if you know how to use WMP, you should be able to figure out any other media player program.

You launch the Windows Media Player from within Windows by clicking the Start button and selecting All Programs, Windows Media Player.

Whether you're playing a CD, DVD, or digital audio file, you use the controls located at the bottom of the WMP window, shown in Figure 33.1. These are the normal transport buttons you find on a DVD player or VCR, including Play/Pause, Stop, Previous, and Next. WMP also includes buttons to turn on/off the shuffle and repeat functions, along with a volume control slider and mute button.

note

The latest and greatest version of WMP is Windows Media Player 11. WMP11 is included with Windows Vista, and a Windows XP version is available for free download from the Windows Media website (www.microsoft.com/windows/windowsmedia/).

FIGURE 33.1

Playing CDs and other audio files with Windows Media Player.

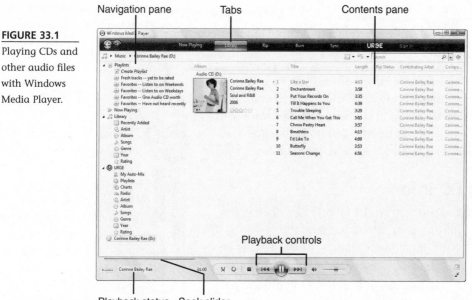

Navigation pane   Tabs   Contents pane

Playback controls

Playback status   Seek slider

To the left of the playback controls is a playback status area. This area displays the title of the currently playing track; the track's artist, album, and other metadata; the amount of time elapsed; and a small spectrum analyzer, which is kind of interesting if not totally useful.

What you see in the main part of the WMP window depends on which tab you select from the row of tabs at the top of the window. Windows Media Player assigns different functions to different tabs, and the contents of the main window vary from tab to tab. For example, to view all the contents of your media library, select the Library tab; to rip music from a CD to your PC's hard drive, select the Rip tab; and so forth.

Playing a CD

If you're using WMP as your main music player, CD playback should start automatically when you insert a CD into your computer's CD drive. If WMP doesn't start automatically in this situation, you can launch the program manually

tip

The Previous and Next buttons serve dual duty as Rewind and Fast Forward buttons. Just click and hold down the button to access the Rewind and Fast Forward functions.

tip

To view more options associated with a given function, click the down arrow beneath that particular tab.

from the Windows Start menu and then click the program's Library tab; the CD should be listed in the Navigation pane. Highlight the CD title, and you'll see the list of CD tracks in the Contents pane; click the Play button to begin playback.

To pause playback, click the Pause button (same as the Play button); click Play again to resume playback. To skip to the next track, click the Next button. To replay the last track, click the Previous button. You stop playback completely by clicking the Stop button.

Viewing CD Info

You can stay on the Library tab when you're playing your music, but that's fairly boring. It's much more interesting to switch to the Now Playing tab, as you'll soon see.

By default, the Now Playing tab displays information about the currently playing CD; this is called the Info Center view. If it's available, you get a lot of information about the album and artist from URGE, as shown in Figure 33.2. (URGE is an online music store jointly run by Microsoft and MTV.) If that information is not available (if the album is too old or obscure to be listed in URGE's database, for example), you simply see the song, artist, and album title.

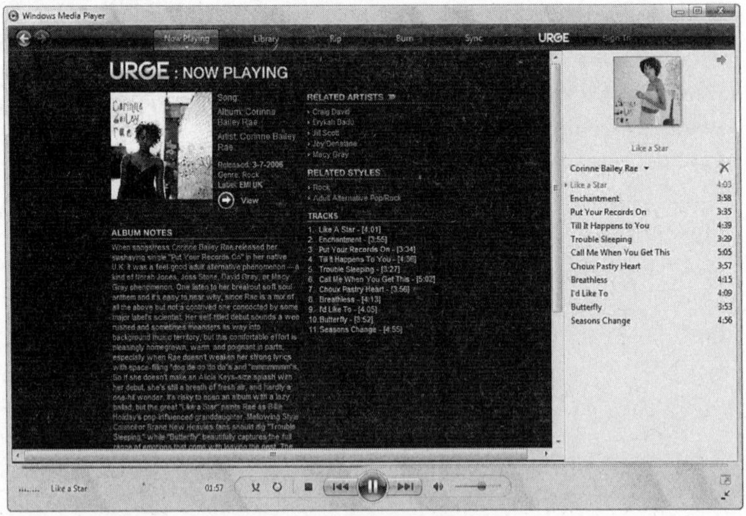

tip

To play the songs on a CD in a random order, click on the Shuffle button on the far left of the transport panel. WMP also offers a repeat function, which repeats the selected song(s) over and over. You activate this function by clicking on the Repeat button, which is next to the Shuffle button in the transport panel.

FIGURE 33.2

Detailed album information from URGE.

Ripping Songs from CD to Your PC

When you want to store your music digitally or transfer music to a portable music player, you need to copy that music from a compact disc to your computer's hard drive. This process is called *ripping*; if you have a large enough hard disk, you can rip an entire library of CDs or individual songs. Naturally, you can use Windows Media Player for the entire ripping procedure. It's easy to do.

Before you begin ripping, however, you first have to tell WMP what format you want to use for your ripped files. You also have to choose the bit rate for recording.

Let's start with the file format. Windows Media Player lets you rip audio files in a number of different formats: MP3, WMA, or WAV. For most users, the regular WMA format is good, although you might want to go with Windows Media Audio Lossless for the highest sound quality, or the MP3 format for almost-universal compatibility with all portable music players.

To select a file format, click the down arrow beneath the Rip tab, select Format, and then choose the file format you want. To set the bit rate, click the down arrow beneath the Rip tab, select Bit Rate, and then choose the bit rate you want. The available options vary by the type of file you select.

After you've set the format and bit rate, it's time to start ripping. Follow these steps:

1. Insert the CD you want to copy into your PC's CD drive.

2. Click the Rip tab in Windows Media Player.

3. As you can see in Figure 33.3, all the tracks from the CD are listed in the Rip tab. Check those tracks you want to copy.

4. Click the Start Rip button.

note

Learn more about digital music file formats in Chapter 34.

tip

When using the normal WMA format, a quality level of 128Kbps or 160Kbps is typically a good choice.

tip

Make sure you're connected to the Internet before you start ripping so that WMP can download album and track details. (If you don't connect, you won't be able to encode track names or CD cover art.)

FIGURE 33.3

Getting ready to copy selected album tracks— just click the Start Rip button.

Windows Media Player now extracts the selected tracks from the CD and converts them from their original CD Audio format to the file format you selected, sampled at the bit rate you selected. The converted files are written to your PC's hard disk and added to the Windows Media Player Library.

Burning Your Own CDs

If you can copy tracks from a CD to your hard disk, what's to stop you from going in the other direction—copying files from your hard disk to a recordable/rewritable CD?

This process of recording your own custom CDs is called *burning* a CD. And Windows Media Player 11 makes it easy to burn your own music CDs—assuming you have a CD burner drive installed in your PC, of course.

Unlike CD ripping, CD burning doesn't require you to set a lot of format options. That's because whatever format the original file is in (WMA, MP3, or WAV), when it gets copied to CD it gets encoded into the CDDA (CD Digital Audio) format. All music CDs use the CDDA format, so if you're burning an MP3 or WMA file, Windows Media Player translates it to CDDA before the copy is made.

There are no quality levels to set, either. All CDDA-format files are encoded at the same bit rate. So you really don't have any configuration to do—other than deciding which songs you want to copy.

Here's all you have to do to burn a CD:

1. Insert a blank CR-R disc into your PC's CD drive.
2. From within WMP, click the Burn tab, shown in Figure 33.4.
3. Click the Library item (or individual views) in the Navigation pane, and navigate to the items you want to burn.

4. Drag the desired tracks, albums, or playlists from the Content pane to the Burn List in the List pane.

5. Click and drag items within the Burn List to place them in the desired playback order.

6. When you're ready to burn the CD, click the Start Burn button.

FIGURE 33.4

Creating a Burn List on the Burn tab.

WMP now inspects the files you want to copy, converts them to CD-DA format, and copies them to your CD. When the entire burning process is done, WMP displays a message to that effect and ejects the newly burned CD from the disc drive.

Using Apple iTunes

Windows Media Player isn't the only music player software you can use to play, rip, and burn CDs. If you're the proud owner of an Apple iPod, you're probably already familiar with the iTunes program, which functions as a music manager/player program for the iPod.

The iTunes player functions much like Windows Media Player. The difference is that it's optimized for use with the iPod; it automatically rips music in Apple's somewhat-proprietary AAC file format.

tip

If you want to make a copy of a CD to another CD, you use a combination of ripping and burning. That is, you rip the files from the original CD to your hard disk (in WAV format) and then burn those files to a second blank CD. Alternatively, you can use a program specifically designed for CD copying, such as Easy Media Creator (www.roxio.com); this program makes copying pretty much a one-button operation.

The main iTunes window looks a lot like the main WMP window. The left-hand pane includes sections for your music and media library, a link to the online iTunes Store, and a list of all your playlists. The obligatory transport controls (Play/Pause, Rewind, Forward, and Volume) are located at the top of the window. Next to the transport controls is a panel that displays the currently playing song and artist, as well as total and elapsed time for the track.

What you see in the main part of the iTunes window depends on which view you select. (The View buttons are to the right of the track display panel.) The first button displays a text list of available songs, as shown in Figure 33.5, which can be sorted by song, artist, album, genre, and so forth. The second button displays songs grouped by album, as shown in Figure 33.6, along with a thumbnail of the CD art. The third View displays iTune's unique Cover Flow view, shown in Figure 33.7, which presents an interactive display of all the albums you have stored on your PC.

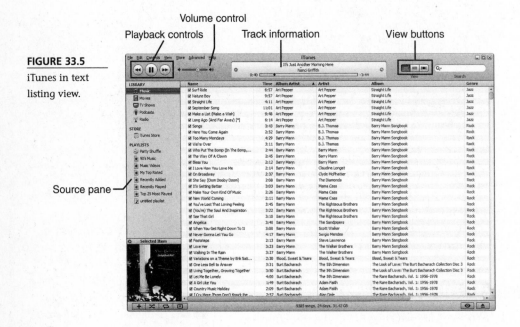

FIGURE 33.5
iTunes in text listing view.

FIGURE 33.6
iTunes in album
list view.

FIGURE 33.7
iTunes in Cover
Flow view.

Playing a CD

When you insert a CD into your PC's CD drive, that CD automatically appears in the iTunes window. To start playback, all you have to do is click the Play button. You can then use the transport controls to pause the CD, or go backward and forward through the tracks. Naturally, the volume control adjusts the playback level.

Ripping Songs from CD to Your PC

iTunes makes copying songs from CD to your PC's hard drive relatively easy. As with WMP, you first have to configure iTunes to use the desired file format and bit rate for the songs it rips.

> **tip**
>
> To play the songs on a CD in a random order, click on the Shuffle button at the bottom left of the iTunes window. iTunes also offers a repeat function, which repeats the selected song(s) over and over. You activate this function by clicking on the Repeat button, which is next to the Shuffle button.

Unlike WMP, iTunes doesn't rip songs in Microsoft's WMA format. Instead, it can rip in Apple's AAC format, as well as the MP3 and WAV formats. To choose a rip format, select Edit, Preferences to display the iTunes dialog box; then select the Importing tab, shown in Figure 33.8. Pull down the Import Using list and select the file format you want. Then pull down the Setting list and select the bit rate you want to use.

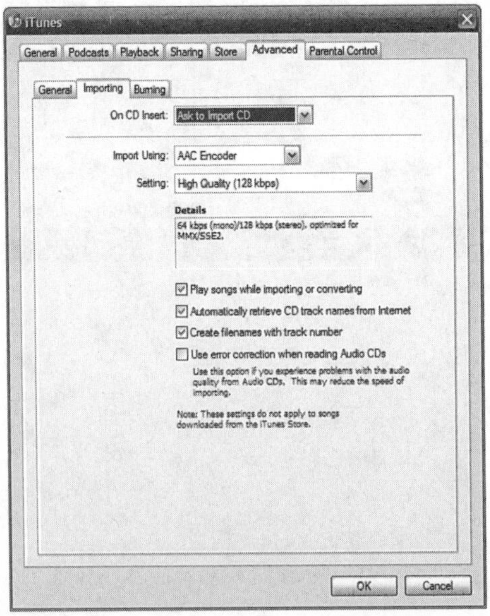

FIGURE 33.8

Configuring iTunes for ripping music.

After you've set the format and bit rate, it's time to start ripping. Follow these steps:

1. Insert the CD you want to copy into your PC's CD drive.

2. As you can see in Figure 33.9, all the tracks from the CD are now listed in the iTunes window. Check those tracks you want to copy.

3. Click the Import CD button at the bottom of the iTunes window.

tip

By default, iTunes uses the AAC Encoder at a bit rate of 128Kbps; this is a good setting for most users.

CD tracks

FIGURE 33.9

Getting ready to rip a CD using iTunes.

Import CD button

iTunes now extracts the selected tracks from the CD and converts them from their original CD Audio format to the file format you selected, sampled at the bit rate you selected. The converted files are now written to your PC's hard disk and added to the iTunes library.

Burning Your Own CDs

Burning music from your PC to a blank CD is also easy with iTunes. Here's how to do it:

1. In iTunes, create a new playlist containing all the songs you want to burn to CD. Make sure that your playlist is less than 74 minutes (for a normal CD) or 80 minutes (for an extended CD) long.

2. Insert a blank CD-R disc into your PC's CD drive.

3. Select the playlist that contains the songs you want to burn, as shown in Figure 33.10, and make sure that all the songs in the playlist are checked.

4. Click the Burn Disc button at the bottom of the iTunes window.

tip

Make sure you're connected to the Internet before you start ripping so that iTunes can download album and track details. (If you don't connect, you won't be able to encode track names or CD cover art.)

FIGURE 33.10

Burning a playlist of songs to CD.

Playlist

Burn Disc button

iTunes converts the selected files to CDDA format and copies them to your CD. When the entire burning process is done, iTunes displays a message to that effect and ejects the newly burned CD from the disc drive.

note

Learn how to create iTunes playlists in Chapter 34.

THE ABSOLUTE MINIMUM

Here are the key points to remember from this chapter:

- The process of copying songs from a CD to your hard disk is called *ripping*.
- The process of copying digital audio files from your hard disk to a blank CD is called *burning*.
- You can use either Windows Media Player (included with Windows XP and Vista) or iTunes (included with the Apple iPod) to play, rip, and burn CDs.
- For best audio quality, rip files using the WMA or AAC formats; for best compatibility with music player programs and portable music players, use the MP3 format.

34

DOWNLOADING AND PLAYING DIGITAL MUSIC

In Chapter 33, "Playing, Ripping, and Burning CDs," you learned how to play music from CDs and how to rip your CDs to digital files stored on your PC's hard drive. But CDs aren't the only route to PC-based digital music; a lot of music also is available on the Internet, ready for you to purchase and download.

The music you download from the Internet can be played back on your PC, or transferred to your iPod or other portable music player. It's a great way to beef up your music collection—with no physical CDs to buy!

Understanding Digital Audio Formats

Before we get into the mechanics of creating your own digital music library, you need to understand the various audio file formats available for your use. There are many different ways to make a digital recording, and different online music stores (and portable music players) use different file formats.

Digital audio files are of two types. *Uncompressed* files reproduce the exact file contained on a compact disc; these files are large but have excellent sound quality. *Compressed* files remove bits and pieces of the original music to create a smaller file (easier to store and download from the Internet) but with reduced audio fidelity. The most common uncompressed file format is the WAV format; the most popular compressed file formats are AAC, MP3, and WMA.

AAC files often have the extension .M4A, because Apple wraps its AAC files in a special type of file that contains digital rights management information.

Which file format should you use for your digital music? There's no easy answer to that question; each format has its plusses and minuses. That said, Table 34.1 details the pros and cons of the most popular digital music file formats.

Table 34.1 Digital Audio File Formats

Format	Pros	Cons
AAC	Compresses songs into small files	Not CD quality
	Used by Apple's iPod portable music player and iTunes Store	Not compatible with Windows Media Player and other non-Apple portable music players and online music stores
		Digital rights management can restrict playback to a set number of PCs and players
MP3	Compresses songs into small files	Not CD quality
	The most universal of all audio file formats; compatible with virtually all music player programs and portable music players	
	No digital rights management, so files can be played on any number of PCs and music players	

Table 34.1   (continued)

Format	Pros	Cons
WAV	CD quality	Large file size
WMA	Compresses songs into small files	Not CD quality
	Used by most online music stores	Not compatible with Apple's iPod
	Compatible with most music player programs and portable music players	Digital rights management can restrict playback to a set number of PCs and players

Of the compressed formats, the MP3 format is the oldest and most universal; almost every music player program and portable music player is MP3-compatible. The WMA format was developed by Microsoft and is used by most commercial online music stores; it's compatible with all music player programs except Apple's iTunes, and with all portable music players except Apple's iPod. The AAC format is Apple's proprietary format and is used by both iTunes and iPod; it's not compatible with many other music player programs and portable music players.

If you're downloading music, you probably don't have a choice of formats; you have to take the music in the format that it's in. Practically, that means if you have an iPod and use the iTunes store, you'll get your music in AAC format. If you have any other type of player (such as the Microsoft Zune or Creative Zen) and get your music from any other online music store (such as Napster, URGE, or the Zune Marketplace), you'll get your music in WMA format.

When you're copying files from your CD to your PC, however, you have your choice of format. For compatibility with all portable music players (including the iPod), use the MP3 format. If you have an iPod and only want to play your files on other iPods, you can use the better-sounding AAC format. Or if you have a non-Apple player and never want to play your music on an iPod, you can use the equally good sounding WMA format.

And here's another consideration: What if you want to play your digital music not on a PC or portable audio player, but rather on your home audio system? Neither the AAC, MP3, or WMA

note

Most music you download from online music stores is encoded with digital rights management (DRM) technology to protect from unlawful distribution, copying, and sharing. Each file you download from an official site has a license that details just how the file can be used—how many different PCs or portable music players it can be copied to, whether it can be burned to CD, and so on. If you try to use the song in a way not permitted by the license, the DRM protection keeps it from playing. Check with the individual online music store for the terms of its DRM licenses.

formats have good-enough audio quality to sound good when played through a quality home system. In this instance, you can save your files in WAV format, although that will take a lot of disc space—about 650MB per CD. A better alternative is to use a format that incorporates *lossless compression*, such as WMA Lossless (for Windows PCs) or AAC Lossless (for compatibility with the iPod). These formats reproduce the exact sound of the original, with no deterioration in audio quality, but at a smaller file size than the noncompressed WAV format. (Lossless files are larger than compressed AAC, MP3, or WMA files, however.)

Downloading from Online Music Stores

One of the great things about digital music is that you can listen to just the songs you want. You're not forced to listen to an entire album; you can download that one song you really like and ignore the rest. Even better, you can take songs you like from different artists and create your own playlists; it's like being your own DJ or record producer!

Where do you go to download your favorite songs? You have a lot of choices, but the easiest is to shop at an online music store. These are websites that offer hundreds of thousands of songs from your favorite artists, all completely legal. You pay about a buck a song and download the music files directly to your computer's hard disk.

iTunes Store

The most popular online music store today is Apple's iTunes Store. The iTunes Store (www.apple.com/itunes/store/) offers more than four million songs for just 99 cents each. All songs are in Apple's somewhat-proprietary AAC file format, which means that they won't play in most third-party music player programs, or on most non-Apple portable music players. But you can use Apple's iTunes software to play the files, and (of course) play all downloaded songs on your Apple iPod.

caution

When you're downloading music, it's best to have a high-speed broadband Internet connection. Although nothing's stopping you from downloading via a dial-up connection, the process can get a tad tedious. These are big files to download!

To use the iTunes Store, you first have to download the iTunes software. We'll examine this software later in this chapter, but don't worry—it's a fairly easy program to use. To download the software, all you have to do is click the Free Download button on the iTunes Store home page and then follow the onscreen instructions.

After the iTunes software is up and running on your computer, you access the iTunes Store by clicking the iTunes Store icon in the Source pane. As you can see in Figure 34.1, there are several different ways to find music in the iTunes Store. You can browse by genre, view new releases, or use the Power Search feature to search for specific songs or artists.

FIGURE 34.1

Shopping for digital music at the iTunes Store.

When you see the results of your searching or browsing, such as the page in Figure 34.2, click the Buy Song button to purchase a particular song. After you confirm your purchase, the song will be downloaded automatically to your PC and added to your iTunes Library. You can listen to your downloaded music in the iTunes music player, or transfer the music to your iPod.

FIGURE 34.2

Downloading songs from the iTunes Store.

URGE

If you don't have an Apple iPod, you'll want to check out some of the non-Apple online music stores that offer songs in Microsoft's WMA file format. WMA files can be played in most music player programs (including Windows Media Player) and portable music players—Apple's iPod being the notable exception.

If you're using Windows Media Player as your main music player program, you have a direct connect to the URGE online service. URGE is a partnership between Microsoft and MTV, offering music for purchase (99 cents for most songs).

> **note**
>
> The first time you make a purchase from the iTunes Store, you'll be prompted to create a new account and enter your credit card information.

You access the URGE service, shown in Figure 34.3, by clicking the URGE tab in Windows Media Player. Alternatively, you can go to specific pages on the URGE site (such as Playlists, Charts, Radio, and so on) by clicking a view under the URGE item in the Navigation page; you can also sign in directly to URGE by clicking the Sign In button at the top of the WMP window.

FIGURE 34.3

Purchasing and downloading music from the URGE music service.

In addition to the purchase of individual songs, URGE also offers an "all you can eat" subscription service, called URGE All Access to Go. Under this plan, you can download as many songs as you want for just $14.95 per month, or $149 per year. As long as you continue your subscription, the songs you download are yours to listen to on your PC and sync to your portable music player. (When you cancel your subscription, the music is no longer playable.)

Other Online Music Stores

The iTunes Store and URGE are just two of many online music stores. All offer similar pricing, although the selection tends to differ from site to site. When you're shopping for songs to download, here are some of the other big online music stores to check out:

- **BuyMusic** (www.buymusic.com)
- **eMusic** (www.emusic.com)
- **MusicGiants** (www.musicgiants.com)
- **Napster** (www.napster.com)
- **Passalong** (www.passalong.com)
- **Puretracks** (www.puretracks.com)
- **Real Rhapsody** (www.rhapsody.com)
- **Wal-Mart Music Downloads** (musicdownloads.walmart.com)

And if you received a new Microsoft Zune music player for Christmas, you'll be using the Zune Marketplace (www.zune.net). It's only for Zune users—much like the iTunes Store is only for iPods.

> **caution**
>
> You can also download music from noncommercial websites and unofficial file-trading networks—although I don't recommend it. Not only is downloading from these sources legally questionable (a lot of the music isn't commercially licensed), these sites are also breeding grounds for computer viruses and spyware. If you're going to download from an unofficial site, make sure you're running both antivirus and anti-spyware software, as discussed in Chapter 12, "Protecting Your PC from Viruses, Spam, and Other Online Nuisances."

Playing Digital Music on Your PC

After you download a bunch of digital music, what do you do with it? You can, of course, transfer the songs to a portable music player, but you can also play your music right there on your personal computer. Just make sure you have a good set of speakers or headphones connected and a music player program installed. The two most popular such programs are Windows Media Player (provided with Windows) and the iTunes player (used with the Apple iPod). We'll look at both, in brief.

> **note**
>
> Learn more about transferring digital music to a portable music player in Chapter 35, "Using Your PC with an iPod or MP3 Player."

Using Windows Media Player

No matter which version of Windows you're using, you have the Windows Media Player (WMP) program preinstalled. You can use WMP to play back all your downloaded digital music—and to keep it organized on your system.

Playing Digital Audio Files

In Windows, all the music files you download should be stored in either the Music (Windows Vista) or My Music (Windows XP) folders, typically under subfolders for artist and album. All music stored in these folders is automatically sensed by Windows Media Player and added to WMP's Library.

To play a digital audio file in WMP11, you first have to load that file into the player. You do this by clicking the Library tab (shown in Figure 34.4), navigating to the song you want to play, and then either double-clicking the song title or selecting the song and clicking the Play button.

note

This chapter covers the latest version of the program, Windows Media Player 11. WMP11 is included with Windows Vista, and a Windows XP version is available for free download from the Windows Media website (www.microsoft.com/windows/windowsmedia/).

FIGURE 34.4
Playing music from WMP's Library.

You can also play back an entire album by selecting Album from the navigation pane, navigating to the album, and then clicking the Play button. Same thing with playing back all the songs by a particular artist or in a particular genre: select either Artist or Genre in the navigation pane, navigate to the artist or genre you want, and then click the Play button.

Creating a Playlist of Your Favorite Songs

By default, the music stored in the WMP Library is organized by album and artist. Although it's fine to listen to music a complete album at a time, Windows Media Player lets you organize your music however you want by creating custom *playlists*.

A playlist is simply a list of individual songs, assembled from any album or artist in your music library. A playlist can be as short as two songs or can include every song on your PC.

To create a playlist in Windows Media Player 11, follow these steps:

1. From the Library tab, go to the navigation pane and select Create Playlist.

2. This creates an item called New Playlist. Select this item and enter a new name for the playlist.

3. The new, currently empty, playlist now appears in the List pane, as shown in Figure 34.5.

4. To add items to your playlist, select them in the Library's Content pane and drag them onto the List pane.

5. When you're finished adding items to the playlist, click the Save Playlist button.

FIGURE 34.5

A new playlist created in the List pane.

To play a playlist, go to the navigation pane in the Library tab and click the Playlist item. This displays all your playlists in the Content pane. Double-click a playlist to select it and then click the Play button to begin playback. All the tracks in your playlist will play, one at a time, in the order listed.

Using the iTunes Player

If you have an Apple iPod, you have the iTunes music player program installed on your PC. You can use the iTunes player for all your music playback needs, as you'll soon see.

Playing Digital Audio Files

Playing songs with iTunes is as easy as it is with any music player program. Make sure you have Music selected in the Library section of the Source pane and then iTunes displays all the songs you have stored on your computer. You can click the View buttons to display your music in several different ways; most people like the cool-looking Cover Flow view, which lets you "flip" through all the album covers for your digital music.

As you can see in Figure 34.6, a text list of music is displayed beneath the cover display. Click a cover to view all the songs contained in that particular album. To play

> **tip**
>
> To skip a track within a playlist, click the Next button in the WMP transport. To repeat a track you really like, select the track and then click the Turn Repeat On button. You can also play the tracks in a playlist in random order by clicking the Turn Shuffle On button.

an individual song, double-click the title in the song list—or select the song and click the Play button in the transport controls. To play an entire album, just double-click the album cover.

FIGURE 34.6

Playing music in the iTunes player.

Creating a Playlist of Your Favorite Songs

Just as WMP lets you create playlists for filtered playback, so does the iTunes player. The playlists you create are displayed in the Playlists section of the Source pane; double-click a playlist to play it.

To create a new playlist, follow these steps:

1. Select File, New Playlist (or click the + button in the bottom-left corner of the iTunes window).

2. A new "untitled playlist" item appears in the Playlists section of the Source pane. Double-click this item and enter a title for the playlist.

3. Click the Music item in the Library section of the source pane.

4. Select a song you want to add to the playlist; then use your mouse to drag that item onto the name of the playlist in the Source pane.

5. Repeat step 4 as many times as you want to add more songs to your playlist.

tip

You can sort the songs displayed in the music list by name, time, artist, album, and so forth. Just click the header at the top of the column by which you want to sort; some columns sort differently if you click them a second or third time.

Listening to Internet Radio

Downloadable music isn't the only music available on the Internet. Many real-world radio stations—as well as web-only stations—broadcast over the Internet using a technology called *streaming audio*. Streaming audio is different from downloading an audio file. When you download a file, you can't start playing that file until it is completely downloaded to your PC. With streaming audio, however, playback can start before an entire file is downloaded. This also enables live broadcasts—both of traditional radio stations and made-for-the-Web stations—to be sent from the broadcast site to your PC.

> **tip**
>
> Although you can listen to Internet radio over a traditional dial-up connection, you'll hear better quality sound over a broadband connection.

Internet radio can be listened to from within many music player programs. For example, the iTunes music player has a Radio function (shown in Figure 34.7) that facilitates finding and listening to a variety of Internet radio stations. In addition, many Internet radio sites feature built-in streaming software or direct you to sites where you can download the appropriate music player software.

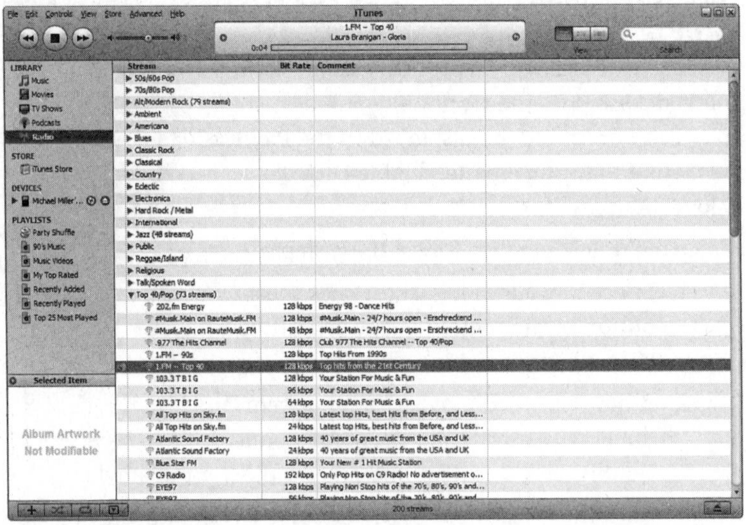

FIGURE 34.7

Listening to Internet radio with iTunes.

When you're looking for Internet radio broadcasts (of which there are thousands, daily), you need a good directory of available programming. Here's a list of sites that offer links to either traditional radio simulcasts or original Internet programming:

- **AOL Radio** (radio.aol.com)
- **LAUNCHcast** (music.yahoo.com/launchcast/)
- **Live365** (www.live365.com)
- **Radio-Locator** (www.radio-locator.com)
- **RadioMOI** (www.radiomoi.com)
- **SHOUTcast** (yp.shoutcast.com)
- **XM Radio** Online (xmro.xmradio.com)

note

Some of these sites offer original programming for a subscription fee.

THE ABSOLUTE MINIMUM

Here are the key points to remember from this chapter:

- Digital music is typically stored in one of three compressed file formats—MP3, AAC, or WMA.

- Of these formats, MP3 is the most universal; the AAC format is proprietary to Apple's iPod and iTunes; and the WMA format is used by Windows-compatible sites and players.

- You can download songs from iTunes Store, URGE, and other online music stores for 99 cents—or less—apiece.

- You can use any audio player program—such as Windows Media Player or the iTunes player—to play back digital audio files.

- If you prefer to listen to a stream of digital music, Internet radio is the way to go; hundreds of real-world and web-only radio stations are broadcasting on the Internet.

35

USING YOUR PC WITH AN iPOD OR MP3 PLAYER

One of the hottest consumer electronics gadgets today is the portable music player, sometimes called an *MP3 player*. These players are small enough to fit in the palm of your hand and, depending on the storage medium used (either micro hard drive or flash memory), can store from 512MB up to a whopping 80GB of files. That's big enough to hold tens of thousands of songs, as well as photos and (depending on the player) videos.

What's cool about these portable players is that they get their songs from your computer. The music you rip from CD or download from the Internet is transferred from your PC to the portable audio player. All you have to do is connect the MP3 player to your PC and use a music player program to transfer the songs you select.

Working with the Apple iPod

The most popular portable music player today is the Apple iPod. Apple sells several different versions of the iPod, including the standard-sized iPod, the compact iPod nano, and the ultra-small iPod shuffle—all shown in Figure 35.1. And, unlike every other product that Apple sells, the iPod is the one device that works equally well with Macintosh or Windows computers.

To use the iPod with your PC, you first have to install Apple's iTunes software, which we discussed in Chapter 34, "Downloading and Playing Digital Music." iTunes is a music player program that is fine-tuned to work with both the iPod and Apple's iTunes Store. You use the iTunes software to transfer music files to your iPod, as well as to purchase and download digital music from the iTunes Store.

note

As popular as the iPod is—and it's far and away the most popular portable audio player today—it has one drawback: It plays digital audio files only in the AAC and MP3 formats. (AAC, the format used for music downloaded from the iTunes Store, is somewhat proprietary to Apple.) It does *not* play files in Microsoft's WMA format. So you won't be able to play WMA files downloaded from Napster, URGE, and similar sites on your iPod device.

FIGURE 35.1

Apple's iPod family of portable music players. (Photo courtesy of Apple.)

Connecting an iPod to Your PC

Connecting the iPod to your PC is as simple as connecting the cable that comes with your iPod to a USB port on your computer. When the iPod is connected, your PC automatically launches the iTunes software and downloads any new songs and playlists you've added since the last time you connected.

Managing Your Music with iTunes

The key to managing the music on your iPod is mastering Apple's iTunes software. As you can see in Figure 35.2, iTunes looks like most other music player programs. You have a set of transport controls (for playing music on your PC) in the upper-left corner, a list of music files in the main window, and a list of playlists in the Source pane on the left. Select a source or playlist in the Source pane, and its contents are displayed in the main window.

> **note**
>
> Your iPod's battery is also recharged when the cable is connected to your PC.

FIGURE 35.2
Managing music files with the iTunes player.

Your master collection of songs is stored in the Music section of the Library, which is the first source in the Source pane. (iTunes creates separate libraries for Movies, TV Shows, Podcasts, and Radio.) When you first install the iTunes software, it imports all AAC, AIFF, MP3, and WAV format files in your Music or My Music folder and lists them in the Library. If you have WMA-format files that you've ripped from CDs in these folders, it asks whether you want to convert them to import into the Library. (iTunes won't convert WMA files you've purchased from an online music store, due to the files' included copyright protection.)

To transfer songs to your iPod, all you have to do is check them in the Library list. When you connect your iPod, your device automatically appears in the Source pane. Click the entry for your iPod, and you see the summary screen shown in Figure 35.3. All the checked songs in your Library are downloaded to your iPod; your device's capacity and used space are shown at the bottom of this screen.

FIGURE 35.3

Downloading tunes to your iPod.

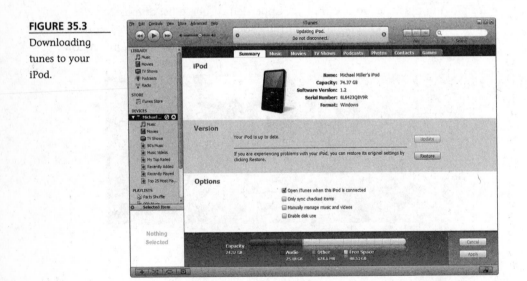

Downloading Songs from the iTunes Music Store

Back in Chapter 34 you learned how to download music from various online music sites. As discussed in that chapter, one of the most popular online music stores is Apple's iTunes Store. The entire iTunes Store is designed for users of the iPod and the iTunes software.

Connecting to the iTunes Store is as easy as clicking the iTunes Store icon in the iTunes Source pane. After you're online, you purchase songs as described in Chapter 34; all the songs you purchase are automatically added to your iTunes Library. Then, the next time you connect your iPod, the songs are automatically transferred to your portable device.

Using Windows Media Player with Other MP3 Players

If you have another brand of portable music player, such as a Creative Zen V or SanDisk Sansa, you'll use other methods to transfer music from your PC to your portable device. Some portable players have their own transfer/player software, similar to iTunes. Others appear to your PC as a new disk drive and require you to copy files using the Computer Explorer or My Computer.

Still other portable music players let you copy songs using Windows Media Player. If the player comes with a PlaysForSure label, it's fully compatible with WMP; although you can use the player's proprietary software (if it exists), you can also use WMP to manage your music library and transfer songs to the player.

With Windows Media Player 11, transferring music to a portable MP3 player is relatively painless. All you have to do is select the songs or playlists you want to copy and then connect your music player to make the transfer.

When you connect your portable music player to your PC, it appears in the right-side pane of the Sync tab, as shown in Figure 35.4. Most music players connect to your PC via USB.

note

WMP 11 should be compatible with most portable media devices on the market today, with the notable exception of the Apple iPod family. To ensure optimal compatibility, look for devices that sport the Windows Media PlaysForSure logo.

FIGURE 35.4

WMP's Sync tab, with an MP3 player connected.

If your portable music player has a large enough storage capacity, your entire music library is automatically copied to your music player as soon as you connect it to your PC. If your portable music player has less than 4GB storage capacity, or if your entire music library won't fit on the device, you can manually choose which songs to transfer to the player. Here's how to do it:

1. Connect your portable music player to your PC.

2. From within WMP, select the Sync tab.

3. Drag the songs, albums, or playlists you want to transfer from the Content pane to the Sync List in the List pane. (You can also drag and copy entire genre or artist catalogs.)

4. To copy the items in the Sync List to your portable music player, click the Start Sync button.

When the sync process begins, the WMP window changes to show the items being copied. Depending on the number of items selected, this process might take some time.

tip

WMP 11 also includes the Shuffle Sync feature, which automatically calculates the capacity of your MP3 player and fills the device with a random sampling of songs that is weighted toward the highest-rated content in your Library. To use the Shuffle Sync feature, click the down arrow beneath the Sync tab, select your device from the list, and then select Shuffle.

THE ABSOLUTE MINIMUM

Here are the key points to remember from this chapter:

- Copying digital music files from your PC to a portable music player is typically as easy as connecting the player to your PC—the transfer occurs automatically.

- You manage the files you want to copy on your PC beforehand using the appropriate music player program.

- The most popular portable music player today is the Apple iPod, which uses the iTunes software to manage all of its song transfers.

- Other portable music players use either their own propriety transfer software or Windows Media Player to move songs from your PC to the MP3 player.

36

PLAYING DVDs AND VIDEOS ON YOUR PC

Your personal computer can play back more than just music. You can also use your PC to play back full-length movies, on DVD!

DVD playback is especially useful if you have a laptop computer. Watching a movie on your laptop is a great way to pass time during a long plane flight or car ride (if you're a passenger, of course—you should never watch movies while driving!). Just charge up your laptop's battery, load up on the latest DVDs, and settle back to be entertained.

Using Windows Media Player to Play DVDs

Playing a DVD on your computer is easy—assuming that your PC has a DVD drive, of course. You can use most media player programs, such as Windows Media Player, to play back your DVDs; some DVD-specific playback programs are also available.

That said, if you're running Microsoft Windows, Windows Media Player 11 is probably the best and easiest way for most users to watch DVD movies. It's a snap to use.

Playing DVD Movies

When you insert a DVD in your PC's DVD drive, playback should start automatically. Your system should sense the presence of the DVD, launch Windows Media Player, and start playing the movie. (Or, depending on what programs are installed on your PC, you may be asked to choose a particular program to view your DVD; Windows Media Player should be one of the choices.)

As you can see in Figure 36.1, the picture from the DVD displays within WMP's Now Playing pane.

tip

You can also initiate DVD playback from within WMP by clicking the Library tab, selecting the DVD title from the navigation pane, and then clicking the Play button.

FIGURE 36.1

Watching a DVD movie with Windows Media Player.

Playing Movies Full-Screen

You can watch movies and videos within the WMP window, or you can view the program using your entire computer screen. To switch to full-screen mode, just click the View Full Screen button in the lower-right corner of the WMP window; the movie enlarges to fill your entire screen. Press Esc to return to normal viewing mode.

Navigating DVD Menus

Almost all DVDs come with their own built-in menus. These menus typically lead you to special features on the disc and allow you to select various playback options and jump to specific scenes.

To display the DVD's main menu, click the DVD button to the left of WMP's playback controls and select Root Menu. To display the DVD's special features menu, click the Title Menu option instead. You can now use your mouse to click the appropriate menu selections.

Changing DVD Audio Options

Many DVDs come with an English-language soundtrack, as well as soundtracks in other languages. Some DVDs come with different types of audio—mono, stereo, Dolby Digital 5.1 surround, and so on. Other DVDs come with commentary from the film's director or stars on a separate audio track.

You can select which audio track you listen to by clicking the DVD button and then selecting Audio and Language Tracks. This displays a list of available audio options; select the track you want to listen to and then settle back to enjoy the movie.

Displaying Subtitles and Closed Captions

Some DVDs include subtitles in other languages or closed captioning for the hearing impaired. To turn on subtitles or closed captioning, click the DVD button; select Lyrics, Captions, and Subtitles; select Options; and then select which subtitles you want to view.

Playing in Slow Motion—Or Fast Motion

Not many users know this, but WMP provides a variety of special video playback features. You can pause a still frame, advance frame by frame, or play the movie in slow or fast motion. To access these special playback features, you have to display the Play Speed Settings controls in the Enhancements panel, as shown in Figure 36.2.

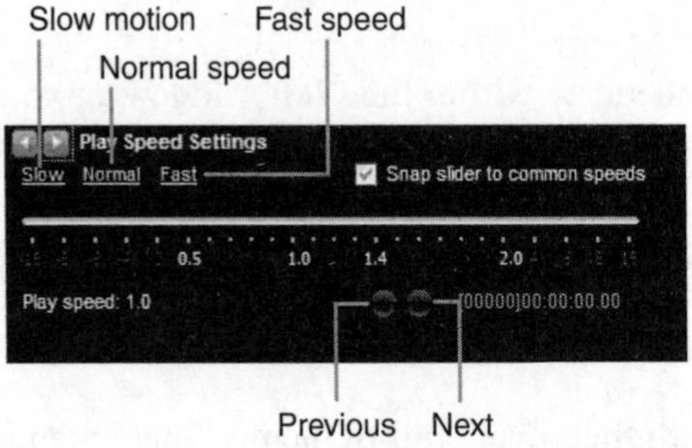

Slow motion   Fast speed

Normal speed

FIGURE 36.2

Using WMP's
Play Speed
Settings controls.

Previous   Next

To display the Enhancements panel, click the down arrow below the Now Playing tab and select Show Enhancements. Now click the blue Next and Previous buttons in the Enhancement pane until the Play Speed Settings panel appears.

The Play Speed Settings panel includes three links for variable-speed playback. For slow motion playback, click Slow; for fast-speed playback, click Fast; and to return to normal playback speed, click Normal.

You can also use the Play Speed Settings panel to move forward and backward one frame at a time. Just pause the video at a single frame and then click the Next Frame or Previous Frame buttons. Click the Play button to resume normal playback.

Playing Video Files with Windows Media Player

You can also use Windows Media Player to play back video files you've downloaded from the Internet or transferred from your home video camera. Not surprisingly, playing a video file you've stored on your PC's hard drive is similar to playing back a DVD. All you have to do is click the down arrow beneath the Library tab and then select Video. This changes the Library list in the Navigation pane to display only video files. You can choose to display recently added videos, all videos, or videos sorted by actor, genre, or rating.

Make your selection in the Navigation pane, and thumbnails of the available videos appear in the Content pane, as shown in Figure 36.3. To begin playback, double-click a video clip, or select the clip and click the Play button.

FIGURE 36.3

Selecting a video
file for playback.

Playing Recorded TV Programs with Windows Media Player

Some new PCs come with built-in TV tuners that you can use to record television programs with your PC and play them back later. And you can use Windows Media Player to play back any TV programs you've recorded.

Selecting a recorded program for playback is just like selecting a video clip. Begin by clicking the down arrow beneath the Library tab and then select Recorded TV. This changes the Library section of the Navigation pane to display all recorded programs stored on your hard disk. You can select from recently added programs, all TV programs, or programs sorted by series, genre, actors, or rating.

Make your selection in the Navigation pane, and thumbnails of the recorded programs will appear in the Content pane. To begin playback, double-click a program thumbnail—or select the program and click the Play button. That's all there is to it!

The Absolute Minimum

Here are the key points to remember from this chapter:

- To play DVDs on your PC, you use a media player program—such as Windows Media Player (WMP).

- Windows Media Player works just like a standalone DVD player; you can pause, fast forward, and rewind through any DVD movie.

- Windows Media Player can also be used to play back video files stored on your PC, as well as recorded television programs (if your PC has a TV tuner built in).

37

DOWNLOADING AND PLAYING VIDEOS FROM THE WEB

Want to re-watch last night's episode of *The Daily Show*? Or maybe a classic music video from your favorite band? How about the most recent network newscast? Or that latest "viral video" you've been hearing about?

Here's the latest hot thing on the Web—watching your favorite television programs, films, and videos online via your web browser. Assuming you have a fast enough Internet connection, you can find tens of thousands of free and paid programs to watch at dozens of different websites. And, if you have an Apple Video iPod or Sony PlayStation Portable, you can transfer the videos you find to your portable device to watch while you're on the go.

Read on to learn more.

Looking for Videos on the Web

The first trick to viewing videos on your PC is to find some videos you want to watch. This isn't difficult; many sites specialize in online videos, and many regular websites offer videos as part of their regular content.

Videos on Regular Websites

For example, the CBS News site (www.cbsnews.com) features all sorts of videos on its home page. As you can see in Figure 37.1, you can watch the previous evening's broadcast of the *CBS Evening News*, along with special web-only newscasts. All you have to do is select the video you want to watch and then click the Play button on the embedded video player; there's no separate software to launch.

note

Many sites offer their web-based videos for free. Others charge a fee to view or download their videos. At this point in time, there's no standard as to what's free and what's not, so browse around before you enter your credit card number.

Similarly, you can go to the NBC website (www.nbc.com) to view full episodes of its top prime-time shows. Missed this week's episode of *Heroes* or *The Office*? They're available online, for free—as you can see in Figure 37.2.

FIGURE 37.1

Watch news broadcasts for free at the CBS News website.

FIGURE 37.2

Prime-time
shows online at
NBC's website.

Most network TV sites have similar free video offerings. Check out ABC.com
(abc.go.com), CBS.com (www.cbs.com), Fox on Demand (www.myspace.com/fox),
and Comedy Central (www.comedycentral.com). For your favorite music videos,
both current and classic, you can't beat MTV.com (www.mtv.com) and VH1.com
(www.vh1.com). And to get your daily sports fix, check out the Motion Video link at
the ESPN website (espn.go.com).

Video-Only Websites

Then there are the websites that specialize in web-based videos. These sites offer
videos, videos, and nothing but videos—often for free.

The most popular of these online video sites include

- **AOL Video** (video.aol.com)
- **Google Video** (video.google.com)
- **Metacafe** (www.metacafe.com)
- **MSN Video** (video.msn.com)
- **Yahoo! Video** (video.yahoo.com)
- **YouTube** (www.youtube.com)

These sites offer a mix of commercial and homemade videos. For example, AOL
Video lets you purchase episodes of your favorite television shows, as well as full-
length movies. YouTube, on the other hand, offers hundreds of thousands of free
videos uploaded by its users.

Whichever service you use, you'll likely have the option of watching the videos in your web browser, no downloading necessary. Just click the Play button and settle back to watch the show.

Other sites, especially those that sell their videos, let you download the videos to your PC. Once downloaded, you can watch any video at your leisure and (in some instances) copy the video to your iPod or PSP for portable viewing.

Viewing Videos on YouTube

Unquestionably, the biggest video site on the Web is YouTube (www.youtube.com), shown in Figure 37.3. What's cool about YouTube is that all the videos are uploaded by other users, so you get a real mix of professional-quality and amateur clips.

note Initially an independent company, YouTube was acquired by Google in 2006.

FIGURE 37.3

View user-uploaded videos at YouTube.

Searching for Videos

Looking for an early performance clip of the Beatles? Or a classic toy commercial from the 1970s? Or maybe a homemade mashup of news clips with a hip hop soundtrack? Or something to do with dancing monkeys? What you're looking for is probably somewhere on YouTube; all you have to do is search for it, using the top-of-page search box. (You can also browse by category, if you want.)

The results of your search are shown on a separate page, such as the one shown in Figure 37.4. Each matching video is listed with a representative thumbnail image, the length of the video, a short description (and descriptive tags), the name of the user who uploaded the video, and a viewer rating (from zero to five stars).

FIGURE 37.4

Searching for YouTube videos.

Viewing Videos

When you find a video you like, click the image or title, and a new page appears. As you can see in Figure 37.5, this page includes an embedded video player, which starts playing the video automatically. Use the Pause and Play controls as necessary.

tip

You can also upload your own videos to YouTube for the entire Web to watch. Just click the Upload tab on the YouTube home page and follow the onscreen instructions. You'll need to create a YouTube account (it's free), and then you can upload any video you have stored on your computer.

FIGURE 37.5
Watching a video
on YouTube.

Viewing and Downloading Videos from Google Video

If you're in the market for commercial videos, you need to use a site that offers a variety of movies and television shows for viewing. One of the most popular such sites is Google Video (video.google.com), shown in Figure 37.6.

FIGURE 37.6
Commercial
videos for view-
ing or
downloading at
Google Video.

Searching for Videos

As with YouTube, you can search or browse Google Video for the shows and movies you want to watch. Google's videos are organized into several major categories—Top 100, Comedy, Music Videos, Movies, Sports, Animation, TV Shows, and More.

For example, if you want to download an episode of *CSI*, click the TV Shows link and browse until you find the show you want to watch. (Alternatively, you can use the Search box to search for an episode by name or guest star.)

Three types of playback options are available on Google Video, depending on the type of video available. These options include

- **Free**—You can download the video at no charge.

- **Purchase**—You can pay a set price to download the video. After you've downloaded it, it's yours to view as often as you want.

- **Day Pass**—You can *rent* the video for viewing within a 24-hour period. You pay a set fee and can watch the video an unlimited number of times within 24 hours. After the 24-hour period is up, the video can no longer be viewed— unless you rent it *again*, of course.

Viewing Videos

To view a video, start by clicking the video's thumbnail on the category or search results page. This displays the video playback page, such as the one shown in Figure 37.7.

FIGURE 37.7

A typical Google Video playback page.

Most free videos let you view them directly from this page via the built-in video viewer. Use the transport controls under the video window to play, pause, fast forward, and rewind the video.

If you prefer to download the video to your hard drive for future viewing, click the Download button on the video playback page. This automatically downloads the video file to your hard disk; once downloaded, you can watch the video at your convenience.

If the video is available for purchase or Day Pass rental, you'll see buttons for Buy High Quality or Day-Pass High Quality. Click the appropriate button to make your purchase and download the video. (When a video is available for purchase or rental, the large video viewing window shows a preview of the video only.)

> **caution**
>
> Downloading isn't an option for all Google videos. Some video producers restrict viewing to online streaming only in an effort to combat piracy.

Downloading Videos from the iTunes Store

If you're the proud owner of an Apple iPod with video playback features (or just a iPod-less schmuck who wants to watch videos on his PC), you can find a lot of videos to download from Apple's iTunes Store. Just open the iTunes player and click the iTunes Store link in the Source pane. When the store's home page appears, click the Movies, TV Shows, or Music Videos link, depending on what type of video you want.

Purchasing Videos

iTunes offers a wide variety of material for purchase and download. Most TV shows go for $1.99 per episode, although you can also buy a "season pass" to view all episodes in a season for a discounted price. (Figure 37.8 shows some of the TV shows available for purchase.) Music videos typically go for $1.99 also; movies are priced from $9.99 to $14.99, depending on age and studio.

Purchasing a video is as simple as clicking the Buy button. Your credit card is charged, and the video is automatically downloaded to your computer. After the download is complete, it appears in your iTunes library, in either the Movies or TV Shows section. You can then view the item from within the iTunes player; just select the item in your library and click the Play button.

FIGURE 37.8

TV shows for download from the iTunes Store.

Transferring Videos to Your iPod

If you have a video iPod, you can transfer your downloaded videos and movies to your portable device via the iTunes software. Just check the items to transfer in the library window, connect your iPod, and let the transfer happen automatically. Remember, though, that video files are much larger than music files; you'll fill up your iPod's disk drive pretty quick if you load up a lot of long videos and movies!

THE ABSOLUTE MINIMUM

Here are the key points to remember from this chapter:

- Numerous websites offer videos for online viewing or downloading.

- Most major TV networks offer episodes of their top series for online viewing.

- Sites such as YouTube and Google Video let you view (and sometimes download) both commercial and amateur videos.

- Apple's iTunes Store sells many TV shows, music videos, and movies for download—and transfer to your video iPod.

38

MAKING YOUR OWN DIGITAL HOME MOVIES

If you have a camcorder and make your own home movies, you can use your computer system to make those movies a lot more appealing. With the right hardware and software, you can turn your PC into a video editing console—and make your home movies look a *lot* more professional.

And the neat thing is, you probably don't have to buy anything extra to do your video editing. If you're using Windows Vista or Windows XP and have one of the latest digital video recorders, all you have to do is hook up a few cables and start editing—because Windows includes its own powerful video editing program.

Configuring Your System for Video Editing

Preparing your PC for video editing is fairly simple. All you have to do is connect your camcorder or VCR to your PC system unit. How you do this depends on what type of camcorder or VCR you have.

If you have one of the latest digital video (DV) recorders that record on MiniDV tapes, DVDs, or hard disk, the connection is easy—assuming that your PC has a FireWire connection, that is. A FireWire connection (also called IEEE1394) is a fast connection that can handle the huge stream of digital data pouring from your digital video recorder into your PC. (Using any other type of connection, including USB 2.0, is not only slower for transferring video but might result in some degree of frame loss; in addition, not all video editing programs support USB transfer.)

If you have an older VHS, VHS-C, SVHS, 8mm, or Hi8 recorder, you need to convert the camcorder's analog video signal to digital format. You do this by installing an analog-to-digital video capture card in your PC, or using an outboard video capture device that connects to your PC via USB or FireWire. You'll plug your recorder into the jacks on the video capture card or device (typically using standard RCA connectors), and it will convert the analog signals from your recorder into the digital audio and video your computer understands.

> **tip**
>
> For best results, you should strive for a completely digital chain. Start with digital video shot on a digital camcorder, edit the video digitally with Windows Movie Maker software, and then output the completed movie to a DVD in WMV format.

Choosing a Video Editing Program

PC-based video editing software performs many of the same functions as the professional editing consoles you might find at your local television station. You can use video editing software to cut entire scenes from your movie, rearrange scenes, add fancy transitions between scenes, add titles (and subtitles), and even add your own music soundtrack. The results are amazing!

The most popular Windows-compatible video editing programs include

- Adobe Premiere Elements (www.adobe.com/products/premiereel/)
- Adobe Premiere Pro (www.adobe.com/products/premiere/)
- Pinnacle Studio (www.pinnaclesys.com)
- Ulead MediaStudio Pro (www.ulead.com/msp/)

Of more immediate interest is the fact that both Windows XP and Windows Vista include a full-featured video editing program—and it's free! The program is called

Windows Movie Maker (WMM), and although it's not as sophisticated as some of the other video editing programs, it should include all the features you need to do basic home video editing.

Working with Windows Movie Maker

Windows Movie Maker works by dividing your home movie into scene segments it calls *clips*. You can then rearrange and delete specific clips to edit the flow of your movie.

The basic WMM window is divided into four main parts, as shown in Figure 38.1.

WMM can display either the Tasks or Collections pane, but not both. Switch between them by using the Tasks and Collections buttons on the WMM toolbar.

FIGURE 38.1
Editing home movies with Windows Movie Maker.

Tasks pane   Contents pane   Monitor

Storyboard

Capturing Digital Video

Each movie you create with WMM is called a *project*. For most WMM projects, your main source material will be your original videotape(s). You use Windows Movie Maker to import the digital video file created by your digital camcorder.

The capture process works like this:

1. Connect your digital video camcorder to your PC's FireWire port and set the camera mode to play recorded video.

2. In Windows Movie Maker, select File, Import from Digital Video Camera. (Alternatively, you can click From Digital Video Camera in the Import section of the Tasks pane.) This launches the Video Capture Wizard.

3. When the Video Capture Device page appears, select your camcorder from the available devices.

4. When prompted, enter a filename for your captured video.

5. When the Video Setting page appears, select the desired recording quality you want to use for capturing the digital video and audio.

6. When the Capture Method page appears, select Capture the Entire Tape Automatically.

7. Click the Record button.

Your camcorder rewinds the videotape and then begins playback. WMM automatically records the playback from your input device. (Recording stops when you click the Stop button, or after two hours, whichever comes first.) The new clips you create will appear in the Collections area of the Movie Maker window.

> **tip**
>
> When you're capturing raw video into WMM, always use the highest possible quality level. For digital video, that's the DV AVI format.

Editing Your Video

You create your movie in the Storyboard area at the bottom of the Movie Maker window. You create a movie by dragging clips down into the Storyboard. You can insert clips in any order, and more than once if you want to. After the clips are in the Storyboard, you can drag them around in a different order. This is how you edit the flow of your movie.

When you get the basic flow of your movie in place, you can switch from Storyboard to Timeline view, shown in Figure 38.2. You switch views by clicking the Show Timeline/Show Storyboard button just above the Storyboard/Timeline. In the Timeline view, you see the timing of each segment, and can overlay background music and narration.

> **tip**
>
> As you work, you can preview your project-in-process with the Movie Maker Monitor. Just select one or more clips in the Storyboard/ Timeline, and then click the Play button on the Monitor.

FIGURE 38.2

Displaying your clips in Timeline view.

Working with Movie Maker's clips is fairly intuitive. Just drag things into place and move them around as you like, and you have 90% of it mastered. The major operations are described in Table 38.1.

Table 38.1   Windows Movie Maker Clip Operations

Operation	Instructions
Add a clip	Use your mouse to drag the new clip from the Contents pane into position in the Storyboard/Timeline.
Move a clip	Grab the clip with your mouse and drag it to the new position.
Remove a clip	Select the clip and select Edit, Delete. (Or just press the Del key on your keyboard.)
Trim a clip	Set the clip's start and end *trim points*; everything outside these two points will be trimmed.
Split a clip	Begin playing the clip in the monitor; when you reach the point where you want to make the split, click the Pause button, and then select Clip, Split.
Combine two or more clips	Select the clips (by holding down Ctrl while clicking each clip) and then select Clip, Combine.

Titles, Transitions, and Other Options

Windows Movie Maker also lets you add some neat bells and whistles to your video movies. For example, you can add

- Titles and credits (select Tools, Titles and Credits)
- Transitions between clips (select Tools, Transitions)
- Special effects, such as blurs, fades, film-aging, sepia tones, and double-speed and half-speed effects (select Tools, Effects)
- Background music (insert an audio clip the same way you insert a video clip)
- Narration (select Tools, Narrate Timeline)

Saving—And Watching—Your Movie

When you're finished editing, save your project by selecting File, Save Project. This does not save a movie file, however—it only saves the component parts of your project.

When your project is absolutely, positively finished, you actually make the movie. Select File, Save Movie to launch the Publish Movie Wizard. From here, you select where to save the movie file, the name for the movie file, and the quality of the saved file. When you finish the wizard, WMM creates your movie and saves it as either an AVI- or WMV-format file. (AVI is the preferred format if you'll be burning the movie to DVD.) Be patient—creating a movie can take some time!

Burning Your Movie to DVD

After you've created your final movie file, you probably want to share it with friends and family. There are a number of ways to do this.

You can always email the movie file as an attachment to an email message. The problem with this method is that movie files are large, which makes them difficult to send and download. You might not want to go this route.

An easier approach is to burn your movie to a DVD, which can then be played in any DVD player. All you need is a DVD burner drive in your PC and a DVD creation software program.

Choosing a DVD Creation Program

Chances are, if your PC came with a DVD burner, it also came with some DVD creation software preinstalled. If so, great! If not, you can check out some of the many third-party programs you can use to burn your own DVDs. Here are some of the most popular:

- **Easy Media Creator** (www.roxio.com)
- **Sonic MyDVD** (www.sonic.com)
- **Ulead MovieFactory** (www.ulead.com)

Burning a DVD with Windows DVD Maker

If your PC is running Windows Vista, you have a DVD creation program already installed. Windows DVD Maker is a new program that lets you quickly and easily create DVDs from the movies you make with Windows Movie Maker. Burning a DVD, complete with custom menus, is as easy as working your way through a wizard.

When you launch Windows DVD Maker, click the Choose Photos and Videos button. The next screen appears, as shown in Figure 38.3. Click the Add Items button to select which videos you want to include on your DVD. The videos you add now appear in the window; you can change the order of the videos by using your mouse to drag them up or down the list.

note

Windows DVD Maker is available only for Windows Vista. No Windows XP version is available.

FIGURE 38.3
Adding videos to your DVD list.

When you click the Next button, you can choose which types of menus you want for your DVD. As you can see in Figure 38.4, available menu styles are listed in the right pane; scroll through the list and click the style you want. You can also, if you want, click the Menu Text button to select different fonts and font sizes.

FIGURE 38.4
Choosing a menu style for your DVD.

These choices made, it's time to burn the DVD. Insert a blank DVD into your PC's DVD drive; then click the Burn button. Your selected videos and menus are now burned to DVD. Know, however, that the burning process can be lengthy; go get a pizza or something while you wait!

THE ABSOLUTE MINIMUM

Here are the key points to remember from this chapter:

- For the best results, stay all-digital throughout the entire video editing process; this means recording your original movie on a camcorder that records to MiniDV tape, DVD, or hard disk.

- Windows Movie Maker is a digital video editing program included with Windows that you can use to edit your home movies on your computer.

- In Windows Movie Maker, the bits and pieces of your project are called *clips*; you put together your movie by dragging clips into the Workspace area at the bottom of the Movie Maker window.

- Windows Movie Maker saves your movie in a WMV-format file; you can then use a DVD-burning program to copy the movie to DVD for playback.

- If you have Windows Vista, you can use the new Windows DVD Maker program to burn your movie to DVD.

Index

How can we make this index more useful? Email us at indexes@quepublishing.com

How can we make this index more useful? Email us at indexes@quepublishing.com